THE ILLUSTRATED BOOK OF
HERALDRY

THE ILLUSTRATED BOOK OF
HERALDRY

An international history of heraldry and its contemporary uses

STEPHEN SLATER

LORENZ BOOKS

THIS BOOK IS DEDICATED TO MA, THE DOGS, ALAN AND THE GANG OF FOUR

This edition is published by Lorenz Books, an imprint of Anness Publishing Ltd,
Blaby Road, Wigston, Leicestershire LE18 4SE; info@anness.com

www.lorenzbooks.com; www.annesspublishing.com

Anness Publishing has a new picture agency outlet for images for publishing,
promotions or advertising. Please visit our website www.practicalpictures.com
for more information.

Publisher: Joanna Lorenz
Managing Editor: Helen Sudell
Senior Editor: Joanne Rippin
Editor: Beverley Jollands
Picture research: Steve Slater and Veneta Bullen
Illustrators: Antony Duke, Marco Foppoli, Roland Symons,
and Alfred Znamierowski (for details see page 253)
Designer: Nigel Partridge
Production Controller: Wendy Lawson

© Anness Publishing Ltd 2013

A CIP catalogue record for this book is available from the British Library.

HALF TITLE: The arms of Josef Moise of Austria, granted in 1867.
FRONTISPIECE: The marriage of Isabeau of Bavaria and Charles VI of France
in a 15th-century manuscript.

PUBLISHER'S NOTE
Although the advice and information in this book are believed to be accurate and true
at the time of going to press, neither the authors nor the publisher can accept any
legal responsibility or liability for any errors or omissions that may have been made.

CONTENTS

INTRODUCTION

A product of the medieval battlefield and tournament, heraldry has been called both the "shorthand of history" and "the noble science". It is best defined as a hereditary system of colours and symbols, borne on the medieval war shield, for personal identification. The first part of this book traces the history of that system, looking at how and why it evolved, while the second part surveys the many different uses that have been found for it, by individuals and institutions all over the world.

No one knows exactly where and when heraldry was born, but its origins are usually attributed to an area of northern Europe around the Low Countries and northern France in the mid-12th century. To understand how it developed, we need to look at the structure of medieval society, and particularly at the armies of the period: how they were organized, how they fought, how they trained and what they wore.

Though new modes of fighting and fashions in armour meant that heraldry lost its original function on the battlefield, it has been adapted to serve the customs and art forms of successive ages, and continues to do so today. The second part of the book takes a sweeping look at the way heraldry has been used and applied throughout the world up to the present time. Diverse heraldic traditions are compared, through the way it is used by monarchs, politicians, the military, the police, corporations, educational and medical establishments, and finally by the individual.

Heraldry has long excited the imagination and can still inspire admiration, jealousy or derision. Its arcane language may make the subject seem difficult to grasp, yet the words it uses (which are explained in a comprehensive glossary at the end of the book) are both precise and evocative. Some see heraldry as a quaint pleasantry, others as a snobbish anachronism, but it is certainly a survivor, and still has the power to evoke a noble past.

▶ *A knight bearing heraldic arms receives his trophy from the Queen of the Tournament.*

THE HISTORY AND LANGUAGE OF HERALDRY

———

HERALDRY EMERGED AT A TIME WHEN FIGHTING MEN BECAME
UNRECOGNIZABLE – TO BOTH FRIEND AND ENEMY – INSIDE THEIR
SUITS OF ARMOUR. THE SOLUTION TO THE PROBLEM OF IDENTITY
LAY IN THE SHIELD, WHICH COULD BE DECORATED WITH A DESIGN
THAT WAS AS UNIQUE AS A FINGERPRINT AND VISIBLE FROM A
DISTANCE. AS ARMORIAL BEARINGS WERE HANDED DOWN FROM
ONE GENERATION TO THE NEXT, THEY CAME TO INDICATE
DESCENT AS WELL AS IDENTITY. FROM ITS FUNCTIONAL
BEGINNINGS, HERALDRY GREW INTO A SCIENCE OF HEREDITY,
WITH A SYSTEM OF LAWS TO REGULATE IT AND A UNIQUE
LANGUAGE THAT COULD MEET THE CHALLENGE OF
RECORDING IT ACCURATELY.

◄ *A jousting scene from a medieval tournament in
which a knight's lance is broken.*

▲ *An illustration from* The Genealogical History from Bruce to Edward I. *The shield in the centre shows an escarbuncle, a design that probably began as a shield boss.*

◄ *Duke William (middle) lifts his helmet at the Battle of Hastings to show his face.*

helmet worn by the European knight still allowed much of the wearer's face to be seen. In the mid-12th century the Anglo-Norman poet Robert Wace wrote that at Hastings the Normans "had made cognizances so that one Norman would recognize another", and the Norman French terms connoissances and recognitiones, both of which were used in the 12th century to describe armorial devices, testify to their roles as emblems of recognition. Yet there is an important fact to be remembered when reading Wace's comment – by his day, a century after Hastings, the well-dressed warrior had started to wear the great helm, which covered all of the face except for the eyes, making identification even more difficult than it would have been at the time of the Norman conquest of England.

The Genealogical History from Bruce to Edward I is a surviving manuscript from c1264-1300. It depicts medieval battle between knights who bear shields that are adorned with simple geometric patterns. One particular illustration (seen here) shows both riders and horses wearing "a coat of arms" as well as a knight banneret (top right), an oblong banner that ensured that even though a knight might not be seen, his presence on the field was evident.

▼ *Louis XII leaves for battle in 1502 in full war gear, as is his horse.*

running of the nation and if a treaty could be brought to fruition so much the better. Great battles such as Crécy (1346), Agincourt (1415) and Towton (1461) were the exception rather than the rule. Towton, where as many as 30,000 died, took place during the Wars of the Roses, but the actual campaigning that took place during the entire period of conflict, from the first battle of St Albans in 1461 to the death of Richard III at Bosworth in 1485, amounted to only a few weeks.

When it did happen, medieval fighting was a gruesome and bloody affair, with weapons designed for hand-to-hand combat. The longsword could sever entire limbs, and the warhammer could inflict crushing and fatal blows to the head. These

were the weapons of the knight and would have been too expensive for the ordinary foot soldier, who relied on weapons made by the local blacksmith, such as poleaxes, and billhooks. But these could pull a fully armed knight off his horse, or disembowel the horse to bring the knight down.

While armour gave the knight some protection, it had its disadvantages. An hour's fast fighting would be taxing for any man, but for a heavily armoured knight it could be lethal in itself. It should also be remembered that often more men died of disease while on the march between engagements than were killed in battle.

IDENTIFICATION IN BATTLE

With knights encased in armour, it is clear that armorial devices would have been exceptionally useful, both to their allies and their enemies. A scene in the Bayeux Tapestry records a moment when Duke William was forced to throw back his helmet, exposing his face for instant recognition, even though in 1066 the

CHIVALRY AND HERALDRY

Heraldry is so closely associated with that extraordinary medieval phenomenon, chivalry, that it is instructive to explore the interplay between the two, one being very much the plaything of the other. Literally, chivalry meant the lore of the horse soldier, or rather the man who could afford the horse, its trappings and the weapons of the mounted warrior, notably the lance: in other words, the knight. At its birth, heraldry was the province of the knights; it was through the loyalty of such men that wars could be fought and won.

THE CHIVALRIC CODE
The armoured knight and his force formed the backbone of the medieval European army. If disciplined, they could turn the tide of battle, but battles were sometimes won without the combat even starting: the sight of the armoured cavalry could be enough to cause their enemies to flee.

Without battles to keep them occupied, men in fighting mood could get bored and become a liability to the ruler, his people and the Church. Something was needed to curb the semi-legalized vandalism of marauding knights and it evolved in the form of the nebulous set of ethics now called the "code of chivalry", which gradually refined into a loose set of rules aimed at civilizing the high-born. It was a theme picked up by writers of the time, including Raymond Lull, Honoré Bonet and Christine de Pisan.

▲ *Medieval illustrations such as this used heraldry to depict the brotherhood of mounted knights in battle.*

Lull (*c*1232–*c*1315), an Aragonian of noble blood, was well versed in knightly deeds and wrote of love and the pursuit of it in the style of the troubadours of southern France. Amorous by nature, he often cheated on his wife, until he had a vision of Christ on the cross, which he interpreted to mean he was to change his life. His work thereafter was to convert the heathen to Christianity, through prayer, preaching and writing books, one of the most influential being his *Libre del Ordre de Cavayleria (Book of the Order of Chivalry)*, written in 1275. For centuries this was considered the standard textbook on the subject and was widely translated.

Christine de Pisan (*c*1364–*c*1430), a disciple of Honoré Bonet (*fl. c*1380), provided a fascinating insight into the workings of the medieval mind in her book of 1408–9, *Le Livre des Faits d'Armes et de Chevalerie (The Book of Feats of Arms and Chivalry)*, which deals with such varied themes as banning the use of poisoned arrows by Christians, and saving the souls of warriors. She was clearly acquainted with the latest trends in military thinking in the early 15th century, and tackled questions, such as "Should the Emperor make war on the Pope?" and "Can a madman be justly held prisoner?" Her answer – "No" – to the second question displays a level of humanity uncommon in her age.

▼ *Christine de Pisan presenting* The Book of Feats of Arms and Chivalry *to Queen Isabeau of France.*

◄ *Parade shield,
Flemish, 15th century.
Part of an attempt to
tame the warrior by
stressing the nature of
courtly love, here the
gallant knight tells his
lady "it is you or
death". Note the lance
rest top left.*

Drawing on such diverse sources as Roman military strategy and the love songs and martial epics of the German *Minnesinger* and French troubadours, Lull, de Pisan and others attracted the attention of the rulers of Europe, most of whom sought to make their courts centres of learning and chivalric enterprise. They also hoped that through such pursuits as courtly love, tournaments and orders of chivalry, they would pacify their unruly courtiers and weld them into a coherent force that saw loyalty to the overlord as a benefit rather than a hindrance.

In its simplest form the code required that its followers should honour their lord, defend the Church – including, when possible, taking up arms against the infidel – and protect the weak, the poor and all women. In reality, true followers of such noble aims were rare, and even those warriors who were held up by medieval writers and the Church as paragons of chivalry would today be looked upon in a very different light.

It says much of those times that one of the men who most epitomized the code of chivalry was not a Christian knight at all, but the infidel ruler Saladin (1137–93), Sultan of Egypt and Syria, who led the Muslim army against the Crusaders in Palestine. As for that most Christian monarch, Richard Coeur de Lion, his observation of the code was less punctilious: in 1191, over 2,500 prisoners in the captured garrison of Acre were put to the sword, for little reason other than Saladin had not observed the treaty between himself and Richard "to the word".

▲ *A scene from the Manesse Codex in which the victor receives his prize (a jewelled chaplet) from the Queen of the Tournament.*

LOVE AND HERALDRY

Heraldry had a great part to play in chivalric ideals. The winning of a good lady through love and brave quests was a popular theme, and books were liberally scattered with allegorical arms. Often medieval chroniclers used the castle as a symbol of a lady's virtue that was to be stormed and captured by the knight's love and passion.

The most delightful depictions of shields of arms appear in a unique survival from about 1300, the Manesse Codex, now in the University of Heidelberg. This collection of songs is illustrated with no less than 140 miniatures showing knightly troubadours – each identified by his shield – preparing for a tournament, sighing for love or wooing a mistress.

▲ *A depiction in ivory of knights assaulting the castle of love.*

MEDIEVAL MILITARY DRESS

Heraldry grew up during a period of radical changes in the dress of the military man and, as those changes took place, so did the nature of heraldry, or rather its application. In time, heraldry even came to be thought of as another weapon in the warrior's armoury – it could, and did, win or lose battles. So important to each other were the twin subjects of heraldry and armour, that not only did the terms "armory" and "armour" combine, but actual pieces of armour were often represented on shields, in crests and as heraldic badges.

CHAIN MAIL

In the late 12th century, when heraldry started to appear on the battlefield, the high-ranking military man was largely

▲ *The typical military dress of a medieval crusader c1250. The loose-fitting tunic was an ideal surface for the display of heraldry.*

▶ *A 15th-century chain mail shirt, a highly effective piece of protection.*

◀ *An illustration of the tomb effigy of William Longespée, showing the knightly gear that would render him anonymous but for his shield and tunic.*

encased in chain mail. Mail had been used by the Romans, who called it *macula*, meaning a net or mesh. Each link in medieval chain mail was forged of iron wire, the ends of which were hammered flat and riveted after the ring had been linked through four others. A chain mail shirt that has survived from the 15th century weighs around 9kg (20lb).

The later application of iron and steel plate tended to give better protection against the bruising blows of war hammer and sword, but chain mail was surprisingly good at keeping out ordinary arrows, and at the Battle of Arsouf in 1191, during the Third Crusade, Richard Coeur de Lion's men were said to have survived in spite of arrows sticking out of their mail like so many bird's feathers.

Long after mail had ceased to be the main form of body armour, it was still being used as flexible "in-filling" at points of the body where mobility was needed, such as behind the knees or under the arms, and plate armour could not be worn. Underneath the mail, a quilted undergarment called a "gambeson" was worn, which was padded with wadding: old rags, horsehair or bunches of dried grass – anything that would keep the wearer insulated, both from any extreme weather and the blows of an enemy.

PLATE ARMOUR

Gradually the knight laid off his chain mail in favour of iron or steel plate and, as the armourer found ways to provide more complex and composite armour, each piece acquired its own name. The chest and back were protected by the "cuirass". Legs were enclosed in "cuisses", elbows were protected by "couters" or "gard-de-bras" (the badge of Lord Fitzwalter), hands were enclosed in gauntlets or "mains-de-fer", the neck was guarded by an "aventail" (the badge of Lord Montague), and the shoulders sported plates known as "ailettes", bearing the arms of the wearer.

BADGES FROM ARMOUR

These are some of the pieces of armour that were taken up as badges by medieval knights.

▲ *A gard-de-bras, worn on the elbow.*   ▲ *A chamfron, worn by a knight's horse.*

▲ *An aventail, worn at the neck.*

▲ *The closed helmet.*   ▲ *A crampet, for the end of a scabbard.*

Iron and steel were not the only materials used for armour. "Plastics" (a general term for materials that could be moulded into shape) included "cuir-bouilli" (leather boiled in oil), bone and even cow-horn. The last, when heated, could be unravelled into translucent sheets and was sometimes also used as a cheap alternative to window glass, showing the ingenuity of the late medieval artisan. Leg guards, which were known as "greaves", shoulder-guards and even arm-guards could all be made of such materials. By the middle of the 14th century the linen surcoat had been largely superseded by the "jupon", a close-fitting quilted coat, usually decorated with the bearer's arms.

The great armour manufacturing areas of the 15th and 16th centuries were northern Italy – notably Milan – Nuremberg and the Low Countries. Military men living outside these areas who wanted the best had several options open to them. If they were very rich they might employ their own armourer. Failing this, they could purchase armour from travelling salesmen who visited the leading trading centres. The third option was to have a model made of their torso and limbs, in wax or wood, which could be sent to an armourer for measuring and fitting, and records in royal and noble archives bear testimony to this practice. A letter of 16 March 1520,

▼ *A tabarded knight at prayer depicted in glass, England, 1403.*

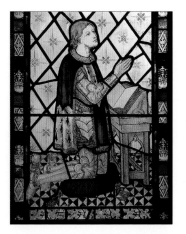

▲ *By the end of the 15th century, knights were discarding the heraldic surcoat in order to display their armour.*

from François I of France, asks that an "arming doublet" (an undergarment) belonging to Henry VIII of England be sent as a size guide for a new cuirass, which François wished to present to the English king.

By the end of the 15th century the well-dressed knight was encased almost entirely in steel plating, the brightness of which gave it the name of "alwyte" (all white). From the details of its lines and flutings,

◄ *The arms of Nuremberg used here as an armourer's mark in the 15th century.*

curves and edgings – just as today with the cut of a good suit – those in the know were able to tell where and even by whom the armour had been made. In addition, the manufacturer would have signed the plate with his punched maker's mark, which was sometimes heraldic. By the end of the 15th century the surcoat, tabard, or jupon, had become things of the past, for the armour itself was what was being shown off.

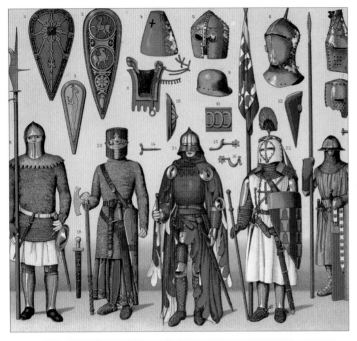

▲ *A depiction of the changes and adaptations in styles of armour and accoutrements from the 12th century to the 15th century.*

FIGHTING IN ARMOUR

Needless to say, armour, whether chain mail or steel plate, was not the most comfortable of coverings. In hot weather the knight could literally cook, while in winter he might freeze. Commanders often had to berate their men during battle for taking off vital pieces of armour, in an attempt to keep cool. Many a medieval treatise on warfare pleaded for caution among the knightly classes. It might be freezing cold, it might be unbearably hot (especially in Palestine), but on no account should you discard your armour: discomfort was far preferable to death.

Some measure of comfort would have been gained by the wearing of a doublet (a long-sleeved tunic reaching to the hips) and long hose, like tights. At points that needed to be flexible but also required protection, mail was attached to the material. The underside of the armour was lined with fine materials. As for the weight of armour, it is a fact that a full harness of

plate armour of about 1470 was no heavier – in fact it was sometimes lighter – than the full marching kit of a British infantryman of World War I. Furthermore, a fully armoured knight could mount his steed easily and without the aid of the crane seen in old films.

▶ *A tilt helmet, from the 15th/16th century, also known as the "frog face".*

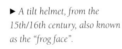

▲ *An English great helm, c1370.*

FASHIONS IN HELMETS

The head, being the most vulnerable part of the body to attack, had long been protected in war by some form of metal headgear. By the time the heraldic story started, the most popular form of helmet for the warrior in Britain and other European countries was a pointed conical iron helmet with a nose-guard, similar in form to those shown in the Bayeux Tapestry. This design allowed much of the bearer's face to be seen. Gradually the helmet lost its conical point and a flat plate of iron was riveted across the top of the head. More and more of the face became protected behind iron plating, and this style is known as the "pot helmet".

At this period, around 1200, most of the body was protected by chain mail, which would also have extended over the wearer's neck, hair and the sides of the face. It was made bearable by a cloth lining, which was probably padded. Over the mail head-covering a cloth cap would have been worn, also reinforced by padding. The helmet would have sat upon this "arming cap", which gave some degree of comfort to the wearer as well as acting as a shock absorber for any blows on the helmet. Further comfort was given by air holes cut in the side of the helmet.

Although some armorial devices made an appearance on the helmet as early as 1250, it was almost another century before the

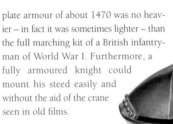

▲ *A barred tourney helm, 16th century.*

▲ Walter von Hohenklingen's tomb effigy. In death he chose to be depicted with all the accoutrements of his knightly rank, including tourney helm and shield of arms.

heraldic crest became popular. The pot helmet gradually evolved into the "great helm", made with a series of hammered plates usually rising to a gradual point.

A second, close-fitting helmet was made to fit under the great helm so that the knight now wore two layers of iron, and this in turn evolved separately, with or without a visor. This streamlined helmet, known as the "bascinet", was so popular with medieval knights that it was worn in various forms from around 1330 to 1550. It covered only the top of the head and the sides of the face, and chain mail was attached to its lower edges by cords. When the great helm, which tended to be relegated to the tournament, was worn over the bascinet each was cushioned from the other by a padded lining.

It was the great helm that became the main platform for the heraldic crest, which was usually made of lightweight materials such as hollow wood, paste board, stiffened cloth or leather stretched over a wooden or wire frame and filled with a combination of materials including tow, sawdust or even sponge. Both the bascinet and the great helm can be seen on the grave slab of Walter von Hohenklingen, in the Swiss National Museum, Zurich.

HORSE ARMOUR AND TRAPPINGS

The knight was a mounted warrior, and his horse was a valuable commodity that also needed its own protection. This led to the steed having its own "chamfron" or head-guard (the badge of the Earl of Shrewsbury) and "peytrel" or chest-plate. The horse could be dressed overall in the fashion of the day with a splendid "trapper" bearing the owner's arms. This was an embroidered cloth that reached down to the fetlocks, leaving only the horse's eyes, ears and nose uncovered. Its cost could be the equivalent of £20,000 ($30,000) today.

By the mid-14th century the combination of the skilled arts of the armourer and the embroiderer meant that Sir Geoffrey Luttrell could enter the lists dressed in a display of heraldic grandeur in which his personal arms appeared on no less than 17 separate displays.

HERALDRY BITES THE BULLET

Many surviving pieces of late harness show a proof mark: a bullet "bruise" in some inconspicuous place, by which the armourer had proved that the plate could withstand the shot of handguns. Firearms, increasingly used towards the end of the 15th century, are not respecters of rank or person, and were fired at a distance, which rendered heraldic identification superfluous. By 1500 the great age of heraldry on the battlefield was over. From then on it was used as an indicator of blood lines, marriage connections and degree (status).

▼ Sir Geoffrey Luttrell, preparing for tourney, from the Luttrell Psalter, 14th century. Sir Geoffrey's arms appear 17 times.

THE TOURNAMENT

running battles. The knights and their entourages fought violently with each other through town and village street at great risk of serious injury, not only to themselves but also to innocent locals, who were considered totally expendable.

Tournaments, "those games overseen by the devil", were railed against by religious men from the earliest days. As early as the 9th century, Pope Eugenius anathematized them, and a succession of popes attempted to ban tournaments, even going so far as excommunicating the participants. Their preachings usually had little or no effect. It is easy to see why the popes saw tournaments as the work of Satan, as some of Christendom's finest military leaders fell on the tourney field: men who, if they did have to fight their fellows to the death, the

War, which was never far from men's minds in the heyday of heraldry, needed training for. Archers had their practices at the butts, but military commanders pitted their skills against each other on the tourney field. Martial sports of some kind have surely existed from the earliest days of organized fighting. The Greeks and Romans made full use of military sparring matches and contests of strength and courage and so it was in the medieval period. This rough type of military "play" often so closely resembled real battle conditions that it often resulted in casualties – even deaths. If there was any difference between the tournament melée and the medieval battle, it was the involvement of judges, who attempted to bring some semblance of order to the motley business. Another difference was the weapons, which tended to be slightly less lethal than those used in warfare.

ORGANIZED MAYHEM

It is easy to imagine the medieval tournament as having all the atmosphere of a modern fair and sporting event combined. This may have been true when tournaments became formalized, but in the early days such events were more akin to

▲ *Tournament participants and audience at the lists, from a late 15th-century illustration of Froissart's* Chronicles.

▼ *A 16th-century tournament with broken lances littering the field. By this time the tournaments were more closely regulated.*

clerics felt should have aimed their aggression at the infidels in the Holy Land. Florent, Count of Hainault, and Philip, Count of Boulogne, were both killed on the tourney field in 1223, and as late as 1559 Henri II of France was mortally wounded during a joust, when his visor was pierced by the lance of Gabriele de Montmorency. Henri died in an age when the tournament was supposedly a formal and disciplined affair; certainly by the 16th century it had become somewhat more refined than the tournament that was held in 1240 at Nuys, near Cologne, when it is recorded that 60 knights and squires perished, trampled under horses' hooves, choked by dust in their armour, or simply succumbing to exhaustion.

TOURNAMENT EVENTS

The tournament was a series of contests reflecting the types of warfare enacted by the higher military ranks. The "melée" was the event that most closely aped the style of fighting that the combatants would probably encounter on a real battlefield. It more nearly resembled a mounted rugby scrum than any genteel sparring match. In the battle engagement, any number of mounted men slugged it out with swords, maces and other hand-held weapons.

Jousting was counted the most noble and prestigious sport to be enjoyed on the tourney field. In this, two mounted knights

▲ *A painting of a tournament in Siena in honour of Ferdinand I de' Medici, with the arms of participants and nobility displayed.*

▼ *The perils of jousting are shown clearly in this depiction of the death of King Henri II of France in 1559 at a tournament in honour of Philip II of Spain.*

bearing lances would run against each other in the "lists", an area enclosed by fences. In the early 15th century, to offset the increased danger of longer, heavier lances, a wooden barrier (the "tilt") was introduced to divide the course, with one man on either side of it.

Along the edge of the jousting field lay the spectators' enclosures and the tented encampments of the participants, all ablaze with heraldry. All the participants vied with each other in putting on the greatest display of splendour. They would be announced to the crowds by their heralds shouting out their names and titles, and often their arms would be shown to the crowds by men or boys dressed up as monsters, angels, ancient heroes or giants – surely a possible origin of the heraldic supporters of later days. With a blast of trumpets, the two knights would course towards each other, urging their horses to

▲ *The breaking of lances during the clash of contestants. Note the lance tips or coronels that were used for jousts à la plaisance.*

▼ *The extravagant splendour of the 16th-century tournament, this one held in Rome for the Vatican Court in 1565.*

build up the maximum speed possible in the area of the lists, which might be 200m (220 yards) or more. The clash of men and weapons, when it came, could be dramatic and, despite being mounted in a high-backed saddle, a knight could often be catapulted into the air by the force of his opponent's lance.

A joust would usually be *à la plaisance* ("of peace"), using lances with special blunted tips, called coronels. The lances were often made of hollow wood, so that they would shatter on impact. If, however, a grudge match, or joust *à outrance* ("to the end"), had been commanded, all was for real, with sharpened weapons. The competition carried on to the point where one man was either injured or killed.

The matches were closely monitored by the judge, who notched up tallies of broken lances, and at the end of the competition the winner might be awarded a prize. This could be anything from a ring, a gold chain, or a jewel, to a kiss from the "Queen of the Tournament", one of the ladies present who was chosen to reign over the proceedings. The ceremony of prize-giving could be both formal and glorious, with the prize handed over to the Queen of the day by a herald. The winner was ceremoniously brought forward and the prize presented by the Queen, with suitably gracious words of esteem.

▼ *The gorgeous apparel of a tourney knight and his horse was hugely expensive.*

THE COST OF TOURNEYING

The tournaments could make or break competitors. One of the complaints of the popes and other senior prelates against these events – beside the fact that they led to the maiming and death of many fine men – was that the heavy expense of participation led to the ruin of large numbers of poorer knights, who often pawned all their belongings, and even their estates, to finance their entry into the lists. But if a knight was prepared to take the risk, the rewards could set him on the road to greater things. And there was certainly money to be made at the tournament.

One such professional knight was William Marshal (1146–1219), who eventually served as adviser to no less than four English kings and was created Earl of

▲ *The effigy of William Marshal, of whom it was written "Behold all that remains of the best knight that ever lived."*

Pembroke. William was born into a good family, but the Marshal estates were devolved upon his older brothers. He was therefore expected to find his own way in the world, and did so in successful and dramatic fashion.

Apprenticed to William de Tancarville's household in Normandy, William Marshal was a quick learner in the ways of the medieval martial man. When, in a melée at a tournament in Maine, the young William gained the capture of three knights through his own prowess, he saw the way his life was to run. As in a real battle, it was ransom that could make or break a man's

▲ *Unsuitable for battle, the full regalia a knight wore for tournaments was for identification and to show his wealth and position.*

fortune. With the money and horses William won that day he was able to join the ever-growing number of knights who wandered round Europe from tourney to tourney, making good use of their fighting skills to amass wealth and increase their own prestige. These roving warriors attracted other such men to their side, and grew into a force of professional military men who came to form the backbone of many of medieval Europe's armies.

In 1167 he teamed up with a Flemish knight, Roger de Gaugi, agreeing to take part in as many tournaments as they could and divide the ransom spoils between them. William continued to take part in tournaments until 1183, and remained undefeated throughout 16 years of competition. Later, on his death bed, he recalled that he had taken over 500 knights prisoner during those years. Such was the life of the tournament roundsman.

THE FIELD OF CLOTH OF GOLD

Tournaments provided the major aristocracy and royalty of Europe with an arena in which they could show off their wealth and largesse. By the 15th century kings were keen to be the patrons of these gaudy and glorious shows. Marriages, coming of age, truces, treaties and alliances: all were seen as possible excuses for a tournament, the medieval equivalent of the ultimate party. The most incredible spectacle of this kind took place in 1520 and came to be known as the Field of Cloth of Gold.

It was a meeting at Guines in June 1520, between François I of France and Henry VIII of England, arranged to celebrate a peace between the two nations. For once, instead of fighting each other, each monarch attempted to outdo the other with a show of magnificence. Although other events were organized, the tournaments were the main excitements of the week. The participants were housed in two encampments, each with over 1,000 lavishly decorated tents. Between the two camps stood the Tree of Chivalry. This extraordinary structure bore the shields of the two monarchs, bound together by garlands of green silk. The tree's trunk was covered in cloth of gold and at its foot, in complete harmony, stood the heralds of both kingdoms.

▼ *A painting showing the famous tournament, The Field of Cloth of Gold, at the moment of the extravagant entry of Henry VIII of England, on 7 June 1520.*

THE ROMANTIC REVIVAL

Tournaments became few and far between in the first half of the 17th century, and seem to have died a natural death by the 1650s. There was a brief renaissance in the first half of the 19th century, when members of the European aristocracy, bowled over by the Romantic revival of medievalism, which included the historical romances of Sir Walter Scott, saw themselves as the proud and natural successors to Parsifal, the Swan Knight, and to Arthur and the Knights of the Round Table.

It was in Scott's own Scotland that the last great attempt at re-creating the medieval chivalric ideal was staged, to celebrate the coronation of the young Queen Victoria in 1837. The coronation was a toned-down affair, shorn of many of its more splendid trappings by a thrifty Whig government. This caused particular resent-ment in one young Scottish aristocrat, Archibald Montgomerie, 13th Earl of Eglinton. His stepfather had been one of those Tory gentlemen who considered themselves deprived of their rightful, if small, parts in the coronation ritual by Whig penny-pinching. As a lover of chivalry, Lord Eglinton decided to right the wrong done to him and his family. He could and would provide the chivalric splendour worthy of his race – he would revive the tournament.

The grand event was held at the Earl's estate at Eglinton, south of Glasgow. Lord Eglinton's enthusiasm fired many other noble souls into wanting to revive their family's fame – that is, until they realized the actual expense involved and the training and degree of expertise required for the event. So out of the original 150 entrants expected, only 13 knights actually turned out for the tournament. However, this in no way deterred the crowds that came to witness the fun. An estimated 100,000 people turned up but, as is so often the case, the British weather decided to stop play. The rain came down in buckets, turning the lists into a quagmire.

Although ridiculed by many at the time for its fanciful attempts at re-creating a golden age, which in reality never existed, what was truly amazing was that Lord Eglinton's attempts were probably as true to the 15th-century tourney scene as anything attempted since that period itself.

▲ *One of the contemporary illustrations of the Eglinton Tournament shows the procession of Lord Eglinton and other participants.*

▼ *The breaking of lances during the jousting at the Eglinton Tournament.*

BADGES AND LIVERIES

In medieval Britain, most of the populace would not have known the arms of even the greatest magnate, but they would quite probably have recognized the badge (also known as cognizance) – the distinguishing emblem – of the major nobility, as well as the liveries, or clothing, that were worn by their servants.

BADGES

The badge is a particularly British heraldic tradition but is also known in Italy, where nobility were represented by devices, known as *imprese* or "impresses". The badge became fashionable in England in the late 14th century. The emblem used could be a single charge taken from the arms of the owner or, as was often the case, it might be an entirely different object chosen at the will of the bearer. As such it was very personal, and in certain great families various members would possess their own badge, quite distinct from those of their relations. Some families made use of many different devices: Richard II of England's favourites were the white hart, and the seed pod of the broom plant, "broom cod" as it was called then. It is thought that a sprig of broom (in Latin *planta genista*) had given the name Plantagenet to his line.

Badges were particularly associated with the struggles for power between two royal houses, which later came to be known as the Wars of the Roses (1455–85). This

◄ A rare surviving pewter badge from the late 14th to early 15th century of the "broom cod" device of Richard II of England.

name was coined later from the supposed badges of the rival royal houses of York (the white rose) and Lancaster (the red rose). During this period of civil disorder, the retinues of the major nobility amounted to private armies, whose members would wear their master's badge and colours or "livery" to declare their allegiance. The sight of the badge could instil either comfort or fear in the minds of the peasantry, depending on which device they saw – it might belong to the troops of their own lord, or might be that of some mighty rival. Bands of armed men roving around the country, intent on mischief, were a phenomenon of the age. In this atmosphere,

◄ The badges and personal liveries of (top to bottom) King Edward III, Richard II and Henry IV from Writhe's Garter Book.

▼ A carving of the salamander, the badge of François I of France (1515–47).

▲ Worked into this chasuble are the combined badges of Henry VIII (the Tudor rose and portcullis), and Catherine of Aragon (the pomegranate), celebrating their marriage.

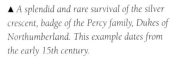

▲ A splendid and rare survival of the silver crescent, badge of the Percy family, Dukes of Northumberland. This example dates from the early 15th century.

wearing the badge of a particular lord gave some degree of immunity from prosecution in the local court, since the chances were that the magistrate was also in the pay of the same magnate.

THE BATTLE OF BARNET

The white mullet, or star, of the de Veres was partially responsible for one famous defeat during the Wars of the Roses. In 1471, Richard Neville, Earl of Warwick, the former friend and supporter of the Yorkist king Edward IV, was fighting against him, having now sided with his Lancastrian rival, Henry VI. The two armies met at Barnet. The royal troops wore the rising sun of York; Warwick's forces were wearing red tunics upon which was the white ragged staff. (The bear and the ragged staff of Lancaster were, initially,

▶ The tomb effigy of Sir Richard Herbert, who wears the famous Yorkist collar of suns and roses.

two separate badges, combined only in later centuries.)

On that day Warwick was joined by the troops of John de Vere, Earl of Oxford. At the height of the battle, which was fought in thick mist, de Vere's forces managed to drive the Yorkists backwards. After this success they attempted to rejoin the main Lancastrian force, and appeared out of the mist at some distance from their colleagues. Warwick's archers, mistaking the

star on Lord Oxford's badge for the Yorkist sunburst, believed they were being attacked by King Edward's men, and let loose a shower of arrows. Oxford's troops believed that their former comrades had turned traitor and what had lately seemed destined to be a Lancastrian victory soon turned into a shambolic defeat for them. Warwick was killed and King Edward was able to march on to Tewkesbury and complete the defeat of King Henry's cause.

LIVERY

Personal liveries could take the form of robes in a lord's colours (these did not necessarily have to be the same colours used in his arms), the wearing of his badge, or badges, and in some cases among the greater nobility, a collar. Such livery collars tended to differ slightly in the metal they were made of, depending on the rank of the wearer. The collar of interlocking "Ss" of the House of Lancaster was used by Henry IV, who granted the right to wear it to individuals as a mark of his favour, and it is still being worn in England to this day, notably by the heralds and kings of arms.

Various monarchs attempted to curb the powers of the rival nobles by passing statutes against the wearing of liveries and the maintenance of private armies. Richard II's statute of 1390 was prompted by these practices, and was aimed at those "…Who wore the badges of lords…so swollen with pride that no fear would deter them from committing extortion in their shires."

Other complainants at the time bemoaned those "Officers of great men that weareth the liveries, the which…robbeth and despoileth the poor", and "hats and liveries…by the granting of which a lord could induce his neighbours to maintain him in all his quarrels, whether reasonable or not." Richard II responded with an ordinance that aimed at inhibiting lords from "giving livery of company to anyone unless he is a family servant living in the household." Exceptions were made for some

▲ *A depiction in stained glass of a banner bearer for the Swiss city and canton of Berne, from the first half of the 16th century.*

▼ *Richard II portrayed in the* Wilton Diptych *of 1395, in which he wears his personal badges – a white hart and broom cods.*

▼ *The collar of an English herald – the Ss are a survival from the livery collar of the House of Lancaster.*

lords, but later monarchs continued to try to curb the power of the nobles by statutes of livery and maintenance.

As late as the reign of Henry VII, the king exercised such statutes (in 1495 and 1504) and could even apply them to his most trusted friends and admirers, as when he visited John de Vere at Castle Hedingham. Henry was led by his host to the castle through two lines of the earl's numerous servants, each wearing coats of their master's livery. The king berated his host for exceeding the limits laid down respecting the number of household retainers, saying "My lord, I have heard much of your hospitality, but I see it is greater than the speech…I may not endure to have my laws broken in my sight. My attorney must speak with you." A hefty fine was soon demanded.

▲ *The* impresa *of the Rusconi family – an ice crampon, a worthy device for a family based in the mountains of north Italy.*

▲ *One of the many badges, combining device and motto, used by the Visconti family, Dukes of Milan, in the 15th century.*

STATUTORY UNIFORMS

As well as the statutory attempts that were made to limit the wearing of liveries, laws were enacted throughout Europe to curb the populace's entitlement to wear certain furs, jewels or styles of dress. In numerous states, specific groups of people were made

▼ *An illustration from one of the books of ready-made* imprese *designs.*

to wear certain items of dress, or to have some sign to indicate their social status.

In 15th-century Germany the women in a layman's family had to wear a yellow veil. European Jews often had to wear a yellow patch – a theme taken up some five centuries later by the Nazis – and prostitutes were distinguished by a number of modes of dress, depending on their age and the country in which they lived. In the time of Charles V of France (1364–80), prostitutes had to wear on their arm a ribbon different to the colour of their dress.

IMPRESE

In northern Italy from the late 14th century onwards it was customary for the greater nobility to maintain *imprese*. These were badges that were usually accompanied by a personal motto or phrase. Families such as the Rusconis of Valtellina had just one *impresa*, an ice crampon. Ruling dynasties made use of many. The theme of the personal *impresa* on the

Italian model was later taken up by the jousting fraternities of France and England, who consulted poets and allegorical storywriters to achieve a suitable combination of badge and motto. Often, such an armorial marriage would exist for just one tournament or pageant, being discarded at will by the bearer. The noble warrior clearly had to have his wits about him if he wanted to achieve on each occasion a new and effective device, but help was at hand by way of books written by designers of these curiosities of conceit. The furnishing of a new *impresa* for every occasion was an expensive business, and it gradually diminished in popularity as the tournament declined in the 17th century.

MODERN BADGES

In England, the badge has been enjoying a comeback since 1906, when heralds started granting them again, together with the standard. It has been suggested that the marrying of badge and standard for modern-day armigers is illogical, because it presumes that they have a following in the medieval manner. On this basis, the standard and its "badge" should be granted only to institutions, such as schools and colleges. Nevertheless, the granting of a badge along with a new coat of arms to an individual had become commonplace at the English College of Arms by the end of the 20th century.

HERALDIC FLAGS

There is surely no more emotive symbol of belonging than a flag or standard. Such objects of attention are as old as history itself. Heraldry has appeared upon flags almost from its very start. There is a suggestion that heraldic designs make an early appearance in the Bayeux Tapestry, on the flags, pennons or guidons of the Flemish contingent in Duke William's army. On the opposing side, the "wyvern" or two-legged dragon of Wessex is held high by King Harold's standard-bearer. The lance pennons of Normans and Flemings at Hastings were obviously made of cloth, but it would seem that the standard of Wessex was carved in wood or metal.

▶ *A Renaissance interpretation of Roman standard bearers, which graphically illustrates the rousing effects of flags.*

▼ *Part of the medieval Powell Roll of Arms, c1345, showing designs for the banners of English high-ranking commanders.*

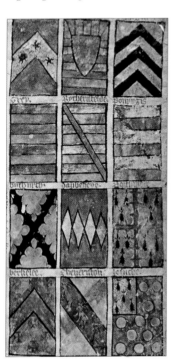

Whatever the materials, both armies made use of "flags" of some sort on that fateful day, and almost certainly they were meant as objects of veneration, both for individuals and for entire units.

KNIGHTS BANNERET

One type of flag, the banner, gave its name to a class of medieval military men, the knights banneret, or bannerets for short. These high-ranking commanders were able to bring a body of men to a battle under their own banner – a square or oblong flag bearing the knight's own arms. (In the 12th and 13th centuries the banner tended to have a width one-third of its length, whereas in later centuries it became square.) The banner was a most important indicator to the troops of their commander's presence on the field of battle. Held high above the banneret's head, the banner went wherever he did, and the two

▶ *A funeral banner* (Totenfahne) *of the Swiss Counts von Toggenburg c1436.*

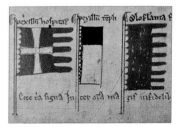

▲ *Banners of the Knights Hospitallers and Templar, and the Oriflamme of France.*

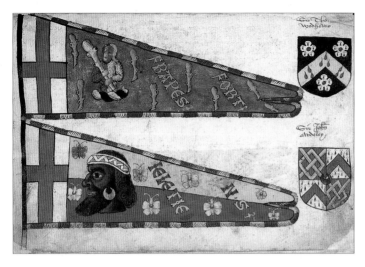

The most famous flag of this type was the Oriflamme of France, which was kept for centuries in the Abbey of Saint Denis (the burial place of the French royal family). Various suggestions have been made as to the exact appearance of the Oriflamme, but it would seem to have been made of red silk with golden trimmings, and hung from a staff of gilded wood or metal: hence its name, which means "golden flame". Some accounts say that the Oriflamme was last seen in use at Agincourt (1415), where its bearer, William Martel, Seigneur de Baqueville, lost his life defending it. Other chroniclers say it remained in the Abbey of Saint Denis until at least the 18th century, when it was described as being in a very unkempt state.

▲ *Standards of English nobility, from the first half of the 16th century – each with the cross of St George in hoist.*

were seldom separated, unless through the death of the banner-bearer.

The banneret could be so created on the battlefield as a reward for his bravery. Prior to that moment, he would probably have been a bachelor or "bas chevalier", a lower knight who bore as his rank a long pennon that had a triangular tail or tails, with his arms in a panel near the pole. Whoever was in overall command that day – a king, prince or other commander – would indicate his appreciation by taking the knight's pennon and cutting away the tails, thus making it into a banner.

The banneret had some special prerogatives. In France, he could place a banner-shaped weathervane above his castle, and could also choose his own *cri-de-guerre* or war cry. In the Low Countries, he had a circlet or coronet of rank in his crest.

PENNONS AND STANDARDS
Two other types of heraldic flag were popular with the knightly class. One was the pennon, a triangular flag that could bear either arms or a badge. The other was the standard, a long tapering flag, larger than the pennon, which could have a split or rounded end. Instead of the bearer's arms, the standard tended to show the badge or

device of the bearer. This could appear singly or several times, and was often accompanied by the motto or *cri-de-guerre*. The "hoist" of the standard (the area at the top of the flag near the pole) tended to bear the national device. The main background to the standard was made up of the livery colours of the bearer. While a knight bachelor was entitled to bear a standard but not a banner, a banneret was entitled to both.

THE GONFALONE
Flags are, of course, not the exclusive preserve of the nobility. The military places great importance on regimental colours, and in the Catholic Church the position of gonfalonier, or standard-bearer, of the Church, was one of the most prestigious offices the pope could bestow.

The office of gonfalonier takes its name from another type of flag popular among city states and other nations during the medieval period, the gonfalone. Such flags were often of huge size and bore many tails. They were carried hanging down from a cross beam, rather like the sail of a ship. Before a battle the gonfalone was blessed by the clergy and it was a great disgrace to lose it, for some were considered to have miraculous powers. Because of its size, a gonfalone was often borne on a cart, driven by a member of a particular family for whom the post was hereditary.

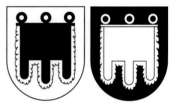

▲ *The characteristic shape of the gonfalone itself became a heraldic charge, perhaps adopted by families whose ancestors had been the hereditary bearers.*

▼ *A carroccio (flag cart) from the arms of the Grulli family, hereditary carroccio drivers to the City of Florence.*

HERALDS
AND THE LAW
OF ARMS

By the 15th century, heralds had become the acknowledged experts in everything associated with arms, and from that time the study and "noble science of arms" became known as heraldry. As with all matters of heraldry, the law of arms has varied widely depending on time and place, and medieval writers differed in their opinions concerning who should and should not bear arms. Some contested that only those of noble stock had such a right, while others suggested that anyone should be able to assume them. The matter continues to be debated among heraldists, though most governments now take little interest in it, apart from enshrining somewhere in law their people's right to adopt arms at will, and for those who have done so to protect their arms in the same manner as a surname.

◀ *A beautifully restored German* Totenschild,
*or death shield, for a member of the Jörg
family of Nördlingen.*

THE OFFICE OF THE HERALDS

Few countries today still retain any formal heraldic corporate body, but each nation retains its own distinct heraldic styles, laws and customs, reaching back through many centuries. The English College of Arms in London is today the most active, and the longest surviving, heraldic authority, having received its first charter of incorporation in 1484, during the brief reign of Richard III.

THE HOME OF THE COLLEGE OF ARMS

Richard III gave the officers of arms a house called Coldharbour in London, but his successor, Henry VII (1485–1509), promptly gave this building to his mother, Margaret Beaufort. It was not until 1558 that the heralds were once again given a permanent home, this time by Mary Tudor. Although the original building, called Derby House, was destroyed during the Great Fire of London in 1666, the College of Arms has had its home on the same site beside the Thames ever since. Set into the façade of the building are plaques bearing the heraldic devices of the Stanley family, Earls of Derby, who were the original owners of the house destroyed in the Great Fire. The heraldry includes the Stanley badge of an eagle's leg "erased a la quise" (torn away at the thigh).

PRINCIPAL OFFICERS OF ARMS

Since medieval times, officers of arms have been divided into three ranks: kings of arms, heralds and pursuivants. In England, the officer of state responsible for overall control of matters heraldic and ceremonial is the Earl Marshal of England, the Duke of Norfolk, in whose family the office is hereditary.

From at least 1300 (probably earlier) there seems to have been a territorial division of heraldic duties in England. North of the River Trent heraldic matters are controlled by Norroy (or "Northern") King of Arms. South of the Trent, the officer responsible for overseeing grants of arms and other such duties is Clarenceux King of Arms, who most probably takes his title from the private herald of the medieval Dukes of Clarence.

In 1415 William Bruges was the first officer appointed as "Garter King of Arms". Two years later he was given further precedence as the principal king of arms, a fact that was to rankle with the regional kings of arms who wished to lose none of their own powers. Among the duties of Garter is the overseeing of all patents of arms, heraldic matters concerning the Order of the Garter itself (the most senior order of knighthood in Britain, whence comes his title), and the introduction of new peers into the House of Lords.

THE MODERN ENGLISH HERALD

Like their late medieval forebears, heralds today are concerned on a daily basis with the granting of arms, both to individuals and to corporate bodies. They are also often consulted for their expertise in historical matters, from pedigrees to providing background material for television documentaries or films. More formally, they act as assistants and advisors to the Earl Marshal at great state occasions such

▶ *An English king of arms from early 1805, wearing his crown of office.*

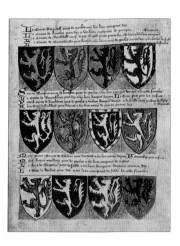

▲ *A page of an ordinary of arms – a list of charges used in heraldry – shows lions rampant and their combinations in family arms.*

as the coronation of the sovereign, or the state opening of Parliament. In addition to the officers employed on a full time, or "ordinary", basis, there are others who, through their own merit, are singled out by the Earl Marshal to be "extraordinary" pursuivants or heralds. They are honorary heralds who exercise ceremonial duties on an occasional basis. The extraordinary officers hold titles taken from the various peerages held by the Earl Marshal.

The English College of Arms is the largest heraldic authority and makes about 200 grants of arms each year. Other nations with heraldic authorities include Scotland, Ireland, South Africa and Canada.

THE ENGLISH HERALDS

Garter King of Arms The principal herald, whose title comes from his duties to the Order of the Garter.

Clarenceux The title probably originated with the herald of the Duke of Clarence, third son of Edward III; responsible for matters south of the River Trent.

Norroy and Ulster "Northern King", responsible for affairs north of the River Trent; his office was twinned with Ulster in 1943.

HERALDS:

All the heralds are named after possessions of the royal family, or, in the case of Somerset, the Beaufort family.

Chester   **Lancaster**   **Richmond**   **Somerset**   **Windsor**   **York**

PURSUIVANTS:

Bluemantle Named after the blue field of the arms of France.

Portcullis Named after the badge of the Tudors/Beauforts.

Rouge Croix Named after the red cross of St George.

Rouge Dragon Named after the supporters of the Tudor arms.

EXTRAORDINARIES:

Beaumont Pursuivant   **Matravers Pursuivant**   **Surrey Pursuivant**   **Howard Pursuivant**   **Wales Herald Extraordinary**

TABARDS AND INSIGNIA

At one time all heralds wore some form of official dress, but in most nations this custom came to an end after World War I. Now, only English and Scottish officers of arms maintain their ceremonial garb. On British state occasions, such as the coronation of a sovereign, the officers of arms will wear their full heraldic regalia of tabard and knee breeches, and carry their wands or staves of office, thereby continuing a tradition unbroken for seven centuries and more.

THE TABARD

In the 13th century, when the herald acted as his master's messenger or "envoy", he would probably have worn the latter's own tabard, or short surcoat, and this would most likely have been a cast-off garment that had lost its first bloom. The tabard of the time would have been constructed from several layers of cloth cut in the form of a thick letter "T". The front and back

▶ *Gentil Oiseau Pursuivant of the Holy Roman Empire, c1450, tabard athwart.*

▼ *Imperial heralds in the funeral procession of Spain's Charles V, 1558.*

◀ *The tabard of John Anstis the Elder, who was the English Garter King of Arms from 1718 to 1744.*

panels and both the sleeves were embroidered with the arms of the master. A pursuivant was singled out from officers of arms of higher rank by wearing his tabard "athwart": the shorter panels designed to fit over the arms were worn over the chest and back, with the longer panels over the arms. In England this practice was known from the 15th until the late 17th century, and it was customary for the tabard to be arranged in this way by the Earl Marshal when the pursuivant was admitted to the office. If the pursuivant was later promoted to the rank of herald, the tabard was turned around to its more normal position.

On certain occasions, heralds would wear the tabard of a lord other than their own, particularly during funerals of the major nobility, when they would wear tabards bearing the arms of the deceased. They might also have their tabards decorated with shields of other lords, knights and judges present at a tournament. This is splendidly illustrated in one of the great heraldic works of art, *Le Livre des Tournois* (The Book of Tourneys) by King René of Anjou (1409–80). He founded the Order of the Crescent in 1448 and, in between organizing countless tournaments, wrote the work in 1450 and helped to illustrate its pages.

From the 16th century onwards it would seem that officers of arms of different degrees – king of arms, herald and pursuivant – each wore a tabard made from materials commensurate with their rank; in France, each rank's garments were

▲ *Russian heralds at the forefront of the procession at the coronation of Nicholas II of Russia in 1896.*

distinguished by name. The practice is still maintained in England and Scotland, where kings of arms wear velvet, heralds have satin, and pursuivants silk damask tabards. Each tabard is heavy and the wearer has to be dressed by experts for ceremonial events.

A story is told of a recent state occasion when it was arranged that the English officers of arms should sit together in a row. As space was limited, they were packed together very tightly, with unfortunate results: the gold wires on the English royal lion and the harp of Ireland became knitted together, and after the ceremony the row of royal officers had to be prized apart.

◄ *King Edward VIII of England and his officers of arms in full regalia, at the State Opening of Parliament in 1936.*

CROWNS AND SCEPTRES

Kings of arms are known to have worn crowns from the 15th century, when they seem to have been set with little shields and lozenges. The English kings of arms today still include in their insignia crowns designed in the early 18th century bearing a standing circle of stylized leaves.

Officers of arms from various nations have long worn badges of office and carried sceptres or wands, which usually differ in detail according to rank. Garter King of Arms has a badge and sceptre for his office, both of which bear the arms of the Order of the Garter, while the sceptre also bears the royal arms.

In 1906 the English regional kings of arms, heralds and pursuivants were given black batons with gilt ends, each with the badge of their particular office attached at the head. These were replaced in 1953 with white ones based on earlier models, the heads of which were said to bear blue birds or martlets. The current rods still have a blue bird, which is similar to those birds in the arms of the College of Arms. The form carried by the officers ordinary also has a gold coronet at its head, while that of the officers extraordinary does not.

▼ *The neck badge of an English officer of arms, still in use today.*

▼ *The badge and sceptre of Garter Principal King of Arms.*

▼ *The old-style baton of Clarenceux King of Arms.*

THE RIGHT TO ARMS

Heraldic writers through the ages have concerned themselves over the exact nature of arms – who should bear them, when and why, and whether they indicate noble status. The feudal structure of medieval European society only served to help the heraldic cause – what was good for the local ruler was also good for his vassals. By the 14th century the users of heraldry included not only knights and their overlords, but also their ladies. Other sections of society, such as abbeys and their abbots, and towns and their burghers, were also keen to embrace the noble art.

THE SPREAD OF HERALDRY

The heady combination of colour and symbolism meant that heraldry was soon adopted and adapted to suit the requirements of the nobles of many European nations. On the fringes of Europe, in Russia, Lithuania, Poland and Hungary, the military elite saw the appeal of the new science. In Poland, where the noble tribe, or *ród*, was the essential unit of society, the old tribal symbols were adapted to fit the heraldic shield. Unlike the rest of Europe, one shield of arms was used by the entire tribe, and the distinguishing marks that identify family branches in other countries are virtually unknown in Polish heraldry. The Hungarian nobility went for family arms, and at least a third of these referred to the enduring battle against the Islamic "Turkish menace", which for centuries attempted to make inroads into the eastern borders of Christendom. Disembodied parts of dead Turks featured on many Hungarian shields.

Heraldry's pictorial nature made it an ideal medium for the decoration of houses, castles, cathedrals and town halls, on the grand or miniature scale. It could dignify the heading of an illuminated address, supply the design for a signet ring, or decorate

▲ *A Hungarian grant of arms from the early 16th century showing the age-old fight between the Hungarians and Turks.*

▶ *A page of a pedigree, with "tricked" arms of the Lambert family, from the herald's visitation notes of Wiltshire, 1565.*

▼ *A Flemish armorial pedigree, c1590, of the Despres family.*

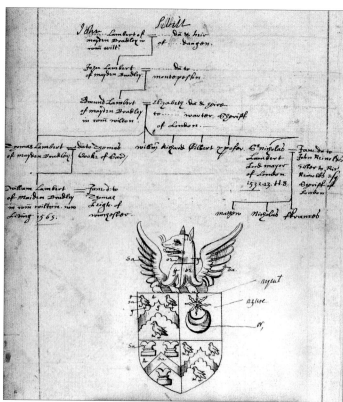

▲ *Christine de Pisan presents her famous and extensive works on chivalry to King Charles VI of France.*

the elaborate wedding arches erected by a loyal populace to welcome a princely bride and groom: all were excellent stages for the display of armorial bearings.

The desire to be identified by arms filtered down through the classes so that many a new-made man, with the power of money behind him, attempted to gain both shield and crest for himself and his heirs, and there were always purveyors of arms who were pleased to oblige with a suitable design: no matter that it was not lawfully gained, it looked good. To counteract the inroads that merchants and other self-made men were making into their prerogatives, the nobility looked to their pedigrees – their authentic arms provided proof of their noble descent and guaranteed their right to acceptance at court and to the ancient orders of chivalry.

THE REGULATION OF HERALDRY

In her book *Le Livre des Faits d'Armes et de Chevalerie*, Christine de Pisan describes a supposed discourse with her spiritual advisor, the Abbé Honoré Bonet, a famed writer on chivalry who had died many years before. Among the questions posed by Christine are, "If a man adopts arms already borne by another, may he retain them?" to which the answer is, "No". Another question is, "If a German knight entering the realm of France finds a Frenchman using the same arms, has the German a just cause for complaint?" Again the answer from Bonet is "No", as they are subjects of different countries and princes.

Which individuals and institutions are, or were, entitled to bear arms? The answer is not simple and depends very much on the age and the nation involved. In some countries, arms have been held only by the nobility. In France during the 17th century, however, even peasants were encouraged to bear a shield of arms, so that they could be taxed for it. In many countries, personal arms can now be adopted at will and may, as in Sweden, be lumped together legally with trademarks and afforded the same protection. Stronger protection tends to be given to civic and military heraldry.

England and Scotland have stringent and longstanding measures in place to protect arms, and during the reign of Henry VIII the English heralds were empowered by royal command to go into the shires and seek out false gentlemen who had assumed arms without due cause. These heraldic progresses were known as "visitations". In the Holy Roman Empire the right to grant arms was at times delegated to the *Hofpfalzgrafen* or "counts of the palace".

THE COURT OF CHIVALRY

In England and Wales the basis of the law of arms is that no one may bear and use them without lawful authority, and that arms are an inalienable right, inherited in accordance with the laws and usages of arms. If, in the view of an officer of arms, these laws are being infringed, the offended party has the right to take the case to the Court of Chivalry, which last sat in 1954 to hear a case brought by the Lord Mayor, aldermen and the citizens of Manchester against the Manchester Palace of Varieties Ltd. The plaintiffs had alleged that the defendants had made illegal use of the arms of the Corporation of Manchester on their company seal. The case was judged in favour of the plaintiffs.

The English Court of Chivalry has its origins in the Courts of the Constable and Marshal, and dates from the first half of the 14th century. As matters armorial were associated with the military class, the chief of the army sits in judgement.

▼ *The Court of Chivalry in session at the College of Arms, London, 1800.*

THE HERALDIC FUNERAL

People of wealth and station in society required a good send-off, commensurate with their rank. The art of "dying well" was much on the minds of the late medieval nobility of Europe, but in the main this meant shows of largesse to the poor and payments for masses to be sung to propel the soul heavenwards. However, just so that God and the angels would know exactly who they were dealing with, the trappings of rank were displayed prominently during the lying-in-state, at the funeral and at the place of burial.

By the 14th century it had become the practice at funerals of royalty and the nobility for a prominent display of heraldry to be included in the pageantry of the event, and these heraldic funerals became increasingly elaborate statements of the deceased's social status and wealth.

THE FUNERAL TRAPPINGS
During the procession the coffin would probably be covered by a pall bearing the arms of the deceased. For members of high nobility and royalty the bier might also be surmounted by a faithful representation of the dead person, dressed in robes of degree

▼ *The design of 1619 for the hearse of Anne of Denmark, Queen of James I.*

▲ *The "State Ship" of Charles V, Holy Roman Emperor, 1558. Part of the spectacle of the royal funeral in Renaissance Europe.*

and coronet. On either side of the bier would walk heralds bearing the elements of the deceased's heraldic achievement – his helm and crest, shield of arms, tabard, gauntlets, spurs and sword.

Central to the display in the church was the hearse, a large and often elaborate temporary structure made of wood, metal and cloth, built in the main body of the church. For higher ranks, the hearse was sometimes so elaborate it resembled the chapel in which the deceased would in due course be buried. The hearse had receptacles for burning tapers, in between which would be set the armorial bearings of the deceased, usually made of buckram.

Upon entering the church the coffin would be placed within the rails of the hearse, where the principal mourners would also take their places. The funeral of a high-ranking member of the nobility was attended not only by family members and other mourners, but even by the deceased's warhorse, decked out in the heraldic trappings of its master.

In Italy and Spain, well into the 20th century, the high-born would have lain "in state" at home before the funeral. The body lay either in a coffin or on a bed of state, dressed in court dress, with the bed itself covered with cloth of gold upon which

were embroidered the family arms. For the highest rank, household staff would hold mourning banners bearing arms. The hearse was also decorated by a number of

▼ *A show of knightly rank – the tomb of the Black Prince, in Canterbury Cathedral, England, displays his full knightly regalia.*

banners, standards, guidons and lesser flags, the exact number of which was regulated by degree. These and the rest of the achievement would in time be hung near to the burial place of the deceased, providing an awesome display of pomp.

THE HERALDS' ROLE

In Britain, the great age of the heraldic funeral was between 1500 and 1700. The marshalling of such events was largely the responsibility of the officers of arms, who jealously guarded their rights because of the fees due to them, which were known as "funeral droits". These were payable from the estate of the deceased and were considerable, the fee itself depending on the deceased's degree and the rank of the herald. The English heralds kept a keen eye on anyone – especially painters and engravers – who might encroach on their offices, and at times the various parties set to brawling with each other over their fees at the very door of the church, as the noble corpse was going to its final rest.

Every facet of the noble funeral was regulated by the heralds, from the number of mourners, their degree and the size of their trains, to the number, shape and size of the flags. The following letter to Garter Dethick, who held office from 1586–1606, gives some idea of the detail involved:

Good Mr Garter, I pray you, as your leisure doth best serve you, set down advisedly and exactly, in every particular itself, the number of mourners due to my calling, being a Viscountess of birth, with the number of waiting-women for myself, and the women mourners, which, with the chief mourner and her that shall bear the trayne, will be in number ten, beside waiting women, pages and gentlemen wishers. Then I pray you the number of chief mourners of Lords, Knights and gentlemen... Good Mr Garter, do it exactly; for I find forewarnings that bid me to provide a pick-axe etc. So with my most friendly commendation to you, I rest,

Your old Mistress and Friend,
Elizabeth Russel, Dowager.

▲ *The coffin of Christine, Duchess of Braunschweig-Bevern; the arms are those of her mother's family, Pfalz-Zweibrucken.*

The reply Mr Garter sent is very lengthy and includes the following details for the funeral procession:

That it include 4 Bannerolls [a type of heraldic banner showing "impalements" for family marriages], the Great Banner borne by a Knight or esquire, a preacher, a Garter King of Arms and 2 heralds. The Lady Chief Mourner was

▲ *The heraldic fittings on the coffin of the widowed Countess of Cholmondsley, 18th century, in Malpas Church, Cheshire, England.*

to have for her gown, mantle, traynes, hood and tippets, 11 yards of black cloth. Garter King of Arms was allowed liveries as a knight, 6 yards of cloth, the heralds 5 yards…

▼ *The heraldic achievements – the shield, sword, helmet, crest and so on – being carried by mourning attendants at the funeral of Charles VI of France, 1422.*

◀ The monument to Alice, Dowager Countess of Derby, d1636–7, thought to be a representation of a heraldic hearse.

THE ROTHES FUNERAL

The funeral of John, 1st and only Duke of Rothes, shows just what a heraldic funeral on the grand scale involved. The Duke had died on 27 July 1681, and his funeral took place almost a month later on 23 August. Having held the office of Lord High Chancellor of Scotland, he was afforded a full state funeral. It included every possible type of heraldic funeral trapping, as well as two complete regiments of artillery.

After the troops there followed the two conductors with crêpe in their hats and black staves over their shoulders, then two little "gumpheons" (gonfalones or square flags), one bearing a death's head with the words *Memento mori* ("Remember you must die"), the other bearing an hourglass with the words *Fugit hora* ("Hours fly"). Then there followed a line of poor men in mourning cloaks that bore the Duke's cipher and coronet. Next came a trumpeter, his banner charged with the ducal achievement, then a cavalier on horseback. Next was a banner of the ducal colours or liveries borne by a gentleman. He was followed by the Duke's servants.

There then followed the Pencil of Honour, a swallow-tailed flag bearing the entire achievement, then one with the paternal arms (Leslie), followed by the Standard of Honour (similar to the pencil but with a square end). The warhorse was led by two "lacquies", who were bareheaded. Two trumpeters followed, then the Bute and Carrick pursuivants of arms in mourning gowns and tabards. Another small group of heraldic flags then followed: the Great Gumpheon, another gumpheon bearing the arms of Abernethy with a "laurel wreath in mourning" and the Little Mourning Standard.

After a group of gentlemen in mourning gowns and hats, there followed another two pursuivants, Kintyre and Dingwall, after which came the spurs, gauntlets, the breastplate, targe (shield), helm and wreath, and sword. Two more retainers then led the deceased's packhorse, after which walked a goodly procession of officers and counsellors of Edinburgh, members of the judiciary and government and representatives of the peerage, followed by the last of the pursuivants, Unicorn and Ormonde. Two trumpeters then announced eight bearers with banners of kinship. On the paternal side (the right) were those of the Earl of Roxburgh, Hamilton of Evandale, the Earl of Perth and the Earl of Rothes; and on the left the descent through his mother from the Duke of Antragne, the Earl of Tullibardine, the Duke of Lennox and the Earl of Mar.

The mourning horse then followed, bearing a black trapper adorned with panels bearing the ducal arms. The last of the heraldic flags, the Great Mourning Banner, bore the ducal achievement and motto. Two more trumpeters announced six heralds: Islay, with the shield of Leslie; Albany, with that of Abernethy; Marchmont, with the crest, motto and wreath; Rothesay with the helm, coronet and mantling; Snowdon with the sword and Ross with the targe.

The Duke's servants and household officers followed, after which was led the Duke's horse for riding to Parliament covered with a richly embroidered saddlecloth. Next came a gentleman bearing the Duke's coronet (with cap), followed by two archbishops and then Lord Lyon (the principal Scottish officer of arms) in tabard and

▼ The funeral of Elizabeth I of England in 1603. The mourners carry banners of the Queen's ancestors.

The Chariott drawne by foure Horses vpon which charret stood the Coffin couered w.th purple Velvett and vpon that the representation. The Canopy borne by six Knights

mourning cloak carrying a diamond-shaped "hatchment" bearing the Duke's entire heraldic achievement.

More trappings of Parliament followed, including the Lord Chancellor's purse. Then followed the most extraordinary sight of the whole incredible spectacle: the coffin of the Duke itself, carried beneath a pall or mortcloth decorated with the arms of the Duke and his relations. These were interspersed with death's heads, ciphers and silver tears. Upon the cloth, which was borne along by close relations, was the Duke's coronet. The coffin was carried beneath a great canopy decorated like the pall, the poles of which were carried by noblemen's sons. Then followed the principal mourners and the mourning coach, the official procession being brought to a close by His Majesty's Guard.

The procession was said to have reached 8km (5 miles) in length. The entire affair cost about £30,000 ($42,000), the equivalent of some £3 ($4.2) million at today's prices, which was supposed to have been paid by the government, although in the end the family was left to pick up most of the enormous bill.

From the end of the 17th century, Protestant Britain saw a "noble rebellion" against the profligate cost of the grand heraldic funeral, which had become prohibitive even for the richest of families. Many of the traditions and the trappings that had been associated with such a funeral, such as armour for example, had themselves become long outdated and scarce, although up to that time there were still specialist manufacturers who carried on producing special "funeral armour".

▲ *The heraldic funeral par excellence – the coffin of the Duke of Rothes with a pall and canopy charged with his arms and teardrops. Note his coronet on the coffin.*

▼ *Just one small section of the Duke's funeral procession including his "cavalier" or champion and various types of mourning flags befitting a duke's degree.*

HATCHMENTS AND TRAPPINGS

From the medieval period until quite recently, the death of a member of the nobility was marked by a series of "memorials". While some were temporary, others were permanent, and were principally aimed at maintaining the status quo – the chief weapon in the armoury of status being heraldry.

TOMBS AND HERALDRY

On early memorials, whether in stone and brass, enamelled or carved, heraldry was limited to the bearer's own personal shield and crest. Soon, however, the place of burial was being used as a platform on which the nobility could show off not only the arms of their own family, but also those to whom they were united through marriage. By the Renaissance the grand monuments of the aristocracy displayed a series of shields for family marriages, often borne by fantastical figures such as angels. The children of the deceased were also often depicted on the tombs, kneeling with shields (for boys) and lozenges (for girls). The canopies and sides of the tombs, the dress of the effigies and even the most intricate of decoration might be used to support a display of heraldry. Death itself could be called upon to support the shield, or sometimes the shield of the deceased might be shown upside-down.

In Italy, gravestones often bear fully coloured arms of the deceased executed in *pietra dura*, an inlaying technique using a variety of coloured stones, but in most countries they tend to be carved in local stone and uncoloured. Whereas in Britain the flat stones set into the floors of many parish churches bear the arms of the deceased only, in Germany and the Low Countries they often bear a series of shields down the sides of the stone, those on the left for the father's side, those on the right for the mother's side.

CABINETS D'ARMES

During the Middle Ages, the trappings of knighthood were carried in the funeral procession and afterwards lay in the church near the grave of the deceased. In the Low Countries a new practice grew up in the 16th century, whereby the actual pieces of armour, sword, gauntlets, helm and tabard were replaced with painted reproductions, usually made of wood. These were grouped in a frame, together with the shields of the paternal and maternal grandparents. The background to the display was painted in mourning black. Such framed displays were called *cabinets d'armes*, or *cabinets d'honor*. It is thought that this practice led to the use of hatchments (a corruption of "achievement"), the

▲ *A good example of a* cabinet d'armes *for a member of the de Schietere family, of Bruges, who died in 1637.*

diamond-shaped mourning boards, many of which are still found hanging in parish churches in England today. The hatchment was hung outside the home of the deceased for a period of mourning, perhaps as much as a year and a day, indicating to visitors that a death had occurred in the family. The custom still persists in Britain, albeit rarely.

▲ *The hatchment for Prince Leopold, Duke of Albany, youngest son of Queen Victoria.*

▲ *A splendidly restored* Totenschild *for Bürgermeister Hans Jörg, portrait included.*

▲ *A Swedish heraldic mourning panel for Pér Brahe, d1680.*

DECIPHERING HATCHMENTS

From the background of the hatchment and the composition of the arms, it is possible to work out the sex and marital status of the deceased. For a single person (bachelor, spinster, widow or widower) the background is all black. Where no marriage has existed, a shield (for a man) or a lozenge (for a woman) bearing the patrimonial arms is shown. In the case of a bachelor the helm and crest also appear. As the diamond-shaped lozenge is thought a somewhat plain shape, it is sometimes accompanied by a decorative blue bow.

Things become more complicated when a marriage has been made. When one of the couple survives, the background of the hatchment is divided vertically black and white, with black – as the colour of mourning – behind the deceased's half of the arms and white behind the survivor's half. When a wife dies before her husband, her hatchment bears a shield with no crest (a bow often being substituted), and the right-hand half of the background is black. If the husband dies first the whole achievement is shown, with black behind the left half. If the hatchment is for a widower, an all-black background is shown with shield, crest and marital coat of arms. If it is for a widow, the marital coat appears on a lozenge. These are the simplest cases, and there are many hatchments whose composition taxes the onlooker and can prove hard to interpret: in the case of a man who has married several times, for instance, the arms of all his wives may appear, with separate backing for each marriage.

Although a family motto often appears on a man's hatchment, it is just as likely to be replaced by a Latin phrase relating to death and resurrection, such as *Resurgam* ("I shall rise again"), *In coelo quis* ("There is rest in heaven") or *Mors janua vitae* ("Death is the doorway to life").

While many English parish churches contain one or two hatchments to a lord of the manor, or previous vicar, some have splendid collections for a whole family: such as that of the Hulse family of Breamore, Hampshire, where the church displays a set of hatchments that date from the early 18th century to the 1990s.

HATCHMENT DESIGNS

Examples of designs on funeral hatchments, which declare the status and position of the deceased person. From top – left to right – these are hatchments for: 1) A married man, 2) a married woman (note the bow on the top), 3) a widowed man, 4) an unmarried man, 5) a widowed woman, 6) an unmarried woman, 7–10) a widowed man who has survived two wives.

THE COAT
OF ARMS

The phrase "coat of arms" is a variant of the more ancient term "coat armour", which describes one of heraldry's principal accoutrements, the surcoat or tabard, which was worn for much of the late medieval period over a warrior's armour. Coat of arms is therefore something of a misnomer, for while it originally meant an actual garment bearing armorial devices, it has now come to represent the entire panoply of the personal achievement of arms, including shield, helm, crest, mantling, motto and supporters – but without any sign of an actual coat. The style of the full achievement of arms has changed over the centuries, developing from simple representations to the florid artistic visions of the Rococo period and the absurdities of the 19th century, when a crest might not connect to its helmet, and mantling looked more like foliage than cloth. An important factor to remember when describing a coat of arms is that the shield is described from the bearer's position behind it. The heraldic right, called dexter, and the heraldic left, called sinister, are the opposite to the normal right and left.

◄ *The arms and proud motto of the Spanish family,*
Manrique de Lara.

THE COMPLETE ACHIEVEMENT

The heraldic achievement is a grand affair consisting of several component parts. The first is the arms themselves on the shield, surmounted by the helmet, the detail of which may change to denote the rank or degree of the armiger. On the helmet usually sits that other important heraldic accoutrement, the crest. Hanging from the top of the helmet is a loose piece of cloth known as the mantling. For the medieval knight this cloth once perhaps served to give some protection to the back of the helmet; in heraldry it is normally depicted in the main metal and colour of the arms.

The mantling is attached to the helmet by means of twists of cord known as the wreath or torse. As with the mantling, the twists tend to be in the principal tinctures of the arms. If a crest coronet or circlet is

▶ *A full achievement typical of those granted in modern times by the English College of Arms, in this case to the author.*

▼ *The same achievement as right, but this black and white depiction of it has been hatched – each colour is represented by a system of lines and dots.*

DON A NOBIS PACEM

LIVERIES

BADGE BANNER

CREST

MANTLING

CIRCLET (more often a wreath)

HELMET

SHIELD OF ARMS

dona nobis pacem

MOTTO

PAVILION OR MANTLE

CROWN OR CORONET

WREATH

CREST

BADGE BANNER

SUPPORTERS

SHIELD OF ARMS

COMPARTMENT

DECORATIONS

▲ The more elaborate full achievement of nobility, in this case the emperors of Germany, with crown and supporters.

achievement of any armiger. For those of higher rank the full achievement can be much grander, with the shield supported by men or beasts; if the holder has a title, such as count or duke, the coronet of rank will also appear. In Britain the coronet sits above the shield, between it and the helm. In other nations the coronet might appear on the helm.

If the armiger is a member of an order of knighthood, the circlet or collar of his order may encircle the shield. For titled members of the aristocracy, a robe or mantle might also appear as a backdrop to the arms. Sovereigns tend to replace the mantle with the pavilion – a domed cloth on which sits the crown.

Such an achievement is a complex and expensive composition to show in its entirety, so an armiger is more likely to denote ownership of property, whether on a book cover or a private jet, by using just the crest or the combination or crest and motto. Holders of a peerage might also place their coronet above the crest or simple shield of arms. Once arms have been granted they may be displayed at will.

borne this usually replaces the wreath (as in the author's arms shown left) although sometimes the two items do appear one on top of the other. In English heraldry a motto, if borne, appears below the shield; in Scotland, above it. If a badge is also borne by the armiger it might appear alongside the full achievement on a banner of the liveries, as seen here, but this is not common.

This combination – of shield of arms, helm, crest, mantling and wreath – is the

▶ The arms of Queen Elizabeth II: the shield is surmounted by the gold helmet of a sovereign.

THE SHIELD

Ever since its inception, heraldry has relied on the shield for the main display of armorial bearings. All other parts of the achievement – such as the crest, mantling, wreath and supporters – depend on the shield, and while there are many cases of a shield of arms being granted by itself, no one can be granted a crest unless the family has at some time previously been granted a shield of arms. Although armorial bearings are often found on different items such as banners and surcoats, it is the shield that is considered the armorial platform without equal.

EARLY SHIELDS

From the very beginnings of organized fighting, the shield was one of the principal means of protection, and was used to stop sword, axe or arrow. Once a weapon passed that first defence, the only things left to protect the soldier were his body armour and his own fighting skills.

The ancient Greeks used round shields, while the Romans preferred large rectangular shields with slightly rounded ends. Each nation's soldiers decorated their shields with various devices: these might be national, regimental or tribal in nature, but were not truly heraldic in that they

▶ *A rare medieval battle shield, an ideal platform for the heraldry that followed in the 13th and 14th centuries.*

were seldom personal, nor did they have any hereditary significance.

SHIELD CONSTRUCTION

At the start of the heraldic story in the second half of the 12th century, the shield was so long that it could cover almost half the bearer's body, and it was normally curved to fit around the torso. The shields used at the Battle of Hastings were kite-shaped and this style continued into the early 1200s, although by then the top edge of the shield was usually straight. Gradually, as the wearing of plate armour increased, the shield diminished in size until it was about a third of the height of the bearer.

Surviving medieval shields show that they were usually made of wooden sheets glued together in an early form of plywood. Several sheets of coarse-grained wood, such as beech or lime, were furrowed and bonded together using a very strong form of glue called "maroufle". Wood was a useful material in battle, as an opponent's sword would often lodge in it rather than glancing off, and this could

▼ *Round shields favoured by Greek warriors often showed devices that many centuries later appeared in heraldry.*

▼ *The seal of Count Conrad of Oettingen, c1229, shows heraldic charges almost certainly arising from the shield's construction.*

▼ *The English army at Hastings with long kite-shaped shields, the shape adapted to heraldic usage some 100 years later.*

▲ *Examples of heraldic devices that most probably arose from the construction of the medieval shield. Clockwise from top left, the shields are those of Valletort, Navarre, Mandeville and Holstein.*

give the shield-bearer a split-second advantage, which could make the difference between life and death. The shield was covered with leather (from horse, ass or buck), parchment or linen. The leather was first boiled in oil to make cuir-bouilli, another good defensive material. Often the exterior was also coated with gesso, or fine plaster, into which a decorative "diapered" pattern might be worked, resembling the designs woven into damask fabrics. Over the gesso surface the armorial bearings of the wearer were applied. These could either be painted flush with the surface, or moulded into slight relief.

SHIELD FITTINGS

The shield was given extra strength by nailing on metal studs, bands and other reinforcements, and some of these additions probably gave rise to heraldic charges themselves. Within this class of "structural" heraldry are examples such as the arms of the great Anglo-Norman family of Mandeville, whose "escarbuncle" (a wheel-like device in the centre of the shield) probably started off as a metal boss. The arms of Count Conrad II of Oettingen (c1229) show a "saltire" or diagonal cross, which probably originated as metal reinforcing bands, and those of Reginald de

Valletourt of Cornwall, from the time of King John, probably show not only the wooden slattings of the shield but the strengthening edge with its nails. It is also possible that the chain in the arms of Navarre started in similar fashion. Even the nettleleaf of Holstein was probably formed by a serrated metal border.

Various materials, from leather to padded cloth, were used for the inner side of the shield, and to these were fixed straps and padded cushions, the latter to allow extra comfort for the bearer and also to absorb the shock of sword and axe blows. Most medieval shields were also contoured to fit the body. Obviously the shield could not be held at all times; when not actually in use it was strung around the bearer's side by a leather strap known as a "guige".

All of this shows a sensible approach to the business of war as seen from the bearer's point of view. The medieval armourer was highly skilled and his shield, despite its size, was surprisingly light and well constructed, as was late medieval armour in general. The most important collection of surviving medieval shields is now in the University Museum of Marburg in Hesse, Germany. They originally lay in

▲ *The German and Italian knights in this 14th-century battle scene bear the flatiron or heater-shaped shield, which became the most common platform for heraldists.*

the Elizabethkirche in Marburg, having been placed there by members of the Teutonic Order, and it is from them that historians have learned much about the construction of the shield.

By the late 13th century the shield's size had diminished considerably, and it had taken the form of the "heater" shield, so-called because it was shaped like the base of a flatiron. The heater shield proved remarkably popular and it is this shape that in the main has served heraldry since the 14th century.

THE TOURNEY SHIELD

From the late 14th century a new form of shield appeared, specifically for use on the tourney field. It was in the shape of a rectangle with curved edges – usually with slightly concave sides and top and with a convex base. While the war shield retained its flatiron shape for centuries, for tournaments the shield became a much more decorated affair, with scalloped edges and

▶ *The simple heater shield of the late 13th century.*

▲ *As art forms changed to more elaborate and florid designs so too did the heraldic shield, although in this example the notch at the top for the lance does still survive.*

▲ *Knights taking part in a tournament of the 15th century bear concave shields specially designed for the tilt.*

flutings. The tourney shield often bore elaborate devices – sometimes they were partially heraldic, often not – which gave out bold messages of love and bravura, the former for the ladies sitting in the viewing galleries around the arena, the latter for any would-be challenger. For use in jousting,

the shield might also have a special notch cut out of the top corner to allow the lance to be "couched", or rested, more easily. By the late 15th century the armourer's expertise had advanced to such a degree that special rivets and bolts were often fitted on the body plates to take lance-rests and extra defences. There was at one time a tourney shield that could actually be fixed to the wearer's breastplate, and the lance rested at its corner.

THE SHIELD IN HERALDRY

Strictly, for the purposes of heraldry, the shield takes one of two forms. The first is the shield proper, which bears the arms of men, and the second is the lozenge, a diamond-shaped device used to display the arms of women. In fact, however, the shape of the heraldic shield varied considerably over the centuries and can reveal much about the period when it was used, and even the country of origin of the bearer. The tourney shield made its appearance in heraldry and, along with the heater shield, was often depicted as being tilted slightly to one side. There is nothing heraldically significant in this: along with

◀ *This monument to the Earl of Hereford from 1621 shows how the shield itself began to assume a non-martial appearance.*

▼ *With the Renaissance the mantling and helm became ever more intricate, as in this example from the mid-16th century.*

all the fancifully shaped shields that appeared on paper and in architecture, it simply reflected the artistic style of the period in which it was used.

FASHIONS IN HERALDIC ART

From the 12th to the 16th century, the shapes of heraldic shields followed the fashions of real shields used in battle, but after the Renaissance artistic licence made inroads into all manner of decorations –

including heraldry. Artists and engravers saw the shield, and the armorial accoutrements that surrounded it, as ideal objects for embellishment. The arms were placed in highly ornate frames, held up by cherubs and draped with garlands, until in many cases the actual arms appear as an afterthought in the decorative scheme. But the Renaissance treatment of heraldry was nothing compared with the Rococo style of the 18th century, when shields ceased to be anything of the sort, instead becoming swirling and curving creations resembling the inside of a seashell. The heraldic shield took on forms that a medieval knight would have gaped at – certainly the scroll-like edges and fantastical flutings would have caused more harm than good if he had borne such a shield on the battlefield, as the enemy's lance could have found plenty of handy points to

▼ *The climax of heraldic design was the fantastical Rococo period, when the arms became simply an excuse for the frame.*

▲ *The distinctive horse-head shield and the teardrop form are both shapes that are particularly favoured in Italy as a background for heraldry.*

affix to, rather than being deflected by the clean curves of the medieval shield.

The Rococo style had emerged from a great period of artistic and architectural triumph – the Baroque. No visitor to Rome can fail to be impressed at the sheer size of heraldic decoration lavished on the city by the popes of that period, each one seemingly wanting to outdo his predecessor by placing his own arms over gateways and triumphal arches, and on obelisks. The supreme example of heraldic ostentation must be the design of the church of Sant'Ivo alla Sapienza in Rome. Because Pope Urban VIII (1623–44) was a member of the Barberini family, the architect, Francesco Borromini, is said to have based his plan on the heraldic bees that appeared in the Barberini arms.

◄ *An 18th-century bookplate showing the elaborate heraldic style of the Rococo period.*

COMPLEXITY AND OBFUSCATION

At least the Rococo had some style about it, even if heraldry was corrupted to suit the contorted shapes of that style. What followed in the late 18th and 19th centuries can only be described as the heraldic doldrums. Shields became fat and unattractive, with tiny helmets perched above them bearing outsized crests and even more outsized wreaths, though each dropped well away from the top of the helmet upon which they were meant to sit. Perhaps the shields needed to be fat, given the complexity of designs they had to bear, which sometimes amounted to entire landscapes or complete historical accounts.

SHIELD SHAPES

These illustrations show how the heraldic shield developed from the traditional flatiron shape through the tourney shield with the notch, the complexities of the Renaissance and the Rococo, back to the simple designs of modern heraldry and the lozenge for a woman.

Late 12th, early 13th century

Late 13th, early 14th century

15th century

15th century

15th century

Mid-16th century

Late 17th century

Late 17th century

19th century

Lozenge for women

THE CREST

After the shield, the second most important constituent part of an achievement of arms is the crest. This is the three-dimensional object that adorns the top of the helmet. While many modern writers cite the shield on the tomb plate of Geoffrey, Count of Anjou as the first example of true heraldic arms, they often pass over the little lion that adorns the Count's cap. Possibly this is the forerunner of the heraldic crest, although helmets had long been "crested" with various devices, including the brush-like structures surmounting the helmets of Roman legionaries.

THE HELMET AND DISPLAY

The true "heraldic" crest would seem to have taken shape a century or so after the advent of armorial bearings. Manuscripts from the 13th century sometimes show heraldic charges painted on the sides of knights' helmets, and it has been suggested

▼ *The tomb-plate of Geoffrey, Count of Anjou, d1151. His conical cap bears a lion passant – was this in fact an early crest?*

that the paint and lacquer used probably acted as an early form of rustproofing. From the early 13th century the top of the helmet was often flattened out and heightened into a fanlike crest. These projections were ideal for the display of painted motifs, usually copied from the bearer's shield.

Even from this early period the crest would appear to have been associated with men of tournament rank – the higher nobility – and in later centuries in certain countries crests were forbidden to all except those entitled to enter the lists. Tournaments were the most costly of sports and the participants were expected to put on a really exciting display of colour and bravado. Some outstanding examples appear on the seals of German knights from the 13th and 14th centuries. They show crests in the manner of wind chimes or revolving plaques edged in peacock feathers, some of which would whistle and rotate as the bearer charged his opponent, like heraldic mobiles. Such a display – like the wings worn by Polish lancers in the 17th and 18th centuries (which also had whistles attached to them) – was probably intended to strike awe and even terror in the opponent, but also satisfied the vanity of the wearer.

In the 14th century a type of crest called the "panache" was popular, especially among English knights. It consisted of

▼ *These elaborate crests, taken from the personal seals of German knights in the late 14th century and early 15th century, show*

▲ *This crest from a helmet, c1350, is a rare survival of the buffalo horns so beloved by German medieval families.*

layers of feathers decorating the helmet, which rose to a peak, often following the contours of the bascinet – the domed helmet much in vogue at the time.

GERMAN CRESTS

From the 15th century crests became highly complex, and in Germany the craft of crestmaking was a profession of note.

German helmets were often surmounted by buffalo horns or pairs of wings (frequently decorated with charges

wind chimes and mobiles that would have been suitable for a dramatic grand entrance to the tourney field.

▲ *The arms of the Folkunga dynasty of Sweden; the buffalo horns on the helmet are adorned with little flags.*

taken from the shield of arms). It has been suggested that the curved shapes of such ornaments may have aided in the deflection of sword blows. The edges of these typically Germanic crests were further enhanced with little leaves or bells, but the most popular decoration of all was peacock's feathers, which featured on as many as half of all crests.

The spaces between the wings or horns afforded a platform for even greater elaboration: conical caps, towers and human figures were added to elicit the admiration of the tournament audience, and sometimes the crests of two families were combined to make a "crest of alliance". Often the human figures in medieval German crests were without arms, and their dress, or even their skin, forms the mantling of the helm – the material protecting its back and sides. In old German such limbless figures were called *Menschentumpf,* "men's torsos". Unlike German crests, those of the English and French

◄ *Menschentumpf (men's torsos) were popular crests in late medieval German heraldry.*

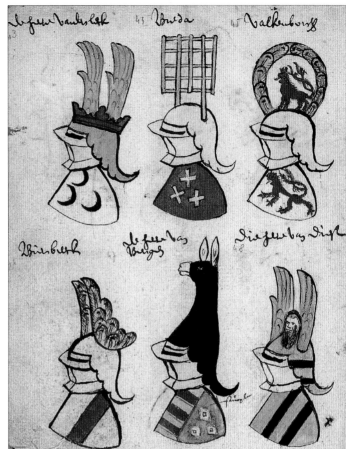

▲ *The Huldenberg Armorial, a Flemish heraldic armorial of the late 15th century, shows the wings and peacock feathers that were popular in North European heraldry.*

nobility tended to be separate from the mantling. Instead, the crest appeared to sit within a twisted cord of material known as the wreath or torse.

MULTIPLE CRESTS

In Britain, France, Italy and Spain, crests were seldom as complex as those found in Germany, and in those countries a family seldom used more than one crest, as opposed to German aristocracy and royalty, who often had as many as half a dozen or more crested helms above their shields, each crest tending to represent not so much a family as a fiefdom. In Britain, buffalo horn and peacock's feathers are almost unknown, and the heads of men or demi-creatures tend to be unaccompanied, unless by crest coronets. In Spanish

heraldry, crests were so rare that they are almost non-existent (only used by a few ancient noble families). Ostrich plumes are the usual adornment to the Spanish heraldic helmet.

Where an English family has assumed a second surname through marriage to a heraldic heiress, a second crest may be adopted. Occasionally, a second crest may be granted or assumed on some special occasion, usually by "augmentation" – an addition to the arms that in some way reflects the gratitude of the donor, who would usually be royal.

▲ *The arms of the Princes of Lippe, late 19th century. In German lands multiple crests were common within the arms of the higher nobility.*

GRUESOME REMINDERS

One of the most deadly creatures in all heraldry must surely be the viper in the crest (and on the shield of arms) of the Visconti family, the medieval rulers of Milan. The various stories of the viper's origin must have bought many a truculent Italian child to obedience. One tale tells of an enormous serpent that had terrorized the locality and had to be placated by regular offerings of fresh babies; it was finally vanquished by an early Visconti. Another story concerns Ottone Visconti, who is said to have killed a Saracen prince, Voluce, beneath the walls

of Jerusalem during the First Crusade. Ottone took Voluce's own crest – a ferocious dragon or serpent devouring a child – as his own. No family has enjoyed its heraldry as much as the Visconti, and a special place is afforded to the viper, which has been depicted in the fullest possible way through the centuries, and can be seen today throughout the world on the badge of Alfa-Romeo cars.

Human heads of various races recall past conflicts. Of these, the Saracen's head is the most common, reflecting the exploits of the Crusader knights. The Hazelriggs of Noseley in Leicestershire have as their crest a Scot's head, commemorating the family's part in the harrying of Scotland by Edward III (1327–77). Though they are not used as a crest, it is also worth mentioning the

three Englishmen's heads in the arms of the Welsh family of Bulkeley-Williams. Together with many other Welsh families, they claim descent from the 13th-century Welsh chieftain Edynfed Vychan. The heads commemorate an incident during a conflict between the English and the Welsh, when the chieftain surprised a band of soldiers from the household of Ranulph, Earl of Chester. In the action that followed, three of Ranulph's principal commanders were killed. The story goes that the Tudors, another family who claimed descent from Edynfed Vychan, also adopted the three heads as charges, but upon their arrival at the English court thought it prudent to turn the heads into three helmets.

The Hamond-Graeme baronets (extinct) of the Isle of Wight had – in addition to another – a rather gruesome crest: two erect arms issuing from clouds in the act of removing a human skull from a spike; above the skull a marquess's coronet between two palm branches. The whole composition is a prime example of a "paper crest", which could never actually have adorned a medieval helmet.

The story behind the crest refers to a member of the Graeme family, a follower of the Marquess of Montrose, who was

▼ *The infamous and highly ferocious viper of the Viscontis, devouring a child.*

executed in Edinburgh in 1650 after his attempt to avenge the death of Charles I. The Marquess's head was placed on the roof of the Tolbooth, the city prison, but his Graeme relative managed to retrieve it and hide it until it could be afforded a proper burial in the Montrose vault.

MANTLING AND WREATH

The crested helm was an elaborate affair that was further decorated with a large piece of cloth, secured to the top of the helmet by cords or other fastenings. In

▼ *The rather gruesome crest of the Hamond-Graeme family in which a skull is lifted from a spike in remembrance of an ancestor's 17th-century exploit.*

▲ *The early heraldry of the Scandinavian nobility closely followed the styles favoured in Germany, as here in the crests of the families of Thott (left) and Wrangel (right)*

of Sweden. The Wrangel crest shows the type of mantling that is reminiscent of its possible origin – a makeshift sunshade used by the Crusaders.

British heraldry this cloth helmet cover is called the mantling. Usually the mantling is bi-coloured – its upper surface bearing the principal colour in the arms and its underside the principal metal – although three or four colours may be employed, as is the case in Spanish and Portuguese heraldry.

In the earliest depiction of crests the cloth mantling was quite simply portrayed, hanging down as one complete piece of cloth covering much of the side of the helmet. Later, especially during the age of heraldic decadence in the 17th and 18th centuries, the mantling was slashed into many elaborate pieces, often resembling foliage rather than cloth. Families of ancient lineage tended to frown on such effete depiction and kept to the simple style of the 14th and 15th centuries.

◄ *An illustration from the Manesse Codex (c1300) in which a certain Herr Harwart fights a bear. The crest above the bear's head is of the early fan-plate type.*

The attachment of mantling and crest to the helm was often hidden by a wreath or torse of twisted cloth, usually in the same colours as the mantling. In Spanish and Portuguese heraldry, the mantling appears not to be connected to the helmet, but is portrayed rather like a backdrop to it. In the late medieval period it was not unknown for the mantling to serve as a setting for charges taken from the arms or family badge.

Various heraldic experts have suggested that both the mantling and the wreath may have originated during the age of the Crusades. Wearing any form of plate armour in the heat of the Middle Eastern sun cannot have been pleasant, and there are tales of knights actually cooking in their kit. It is possible that some degree of comfort may have been gained from adapting the local headdress and wearing it over the top of the helmet, and certainly the combination of simple mantling and wreath bears a strong similarity to traditional Arab headgear.

THE HELM AND CORONET

◀ *The helm show in King René's tournament book – here the crest of a knight who has offended a lady is struck down.*

to be in favour at the time. They were little used to indicate rank, and armorials show all degrees, from knights to monarchs, using the same type of helmet.

HELMETS AND RANK

From around 1500 the bearing of crowns and coronets on the helmets of those of royal rank became common, and at the same time the grilled "pageant helmet" was appearing, which had a number of ornamental bars across the face. During the Renaissance, the depiction of the grills, and even the metals of the helmet, became increasingly embellished according to rank. The helmet was soon to become yet another piece of "paper heraldry", with grandiose patterns, gold and silver edgings and specified numbers of bars depending on the rank of the bearer. The arms of the lesser nobility bore either the closed helm, which had a solid visor and fully covered the face, or the frog-faced tilt helm.

As early as the 12th century, the mounted warrior's helmet had become a platform for heraldic colour and charges, which were often painted on its side and may have helped to protect its surface.

▼ *Helmets of degree for French royals and nobles, in the second half of the 18th century.*

However, in terms of armorial bearings it was a long time before the helmet itself became a truly heraldic accessory – before the late 15th century it was included in the coat of arms simply as a support for the crest. The helmets depicted in early heraldic manuscripts and on monumental effigies followed whatever style happened

▼ *An Italian ornamental helmet with crest and wreath from around 1450–70, and other later additions.*

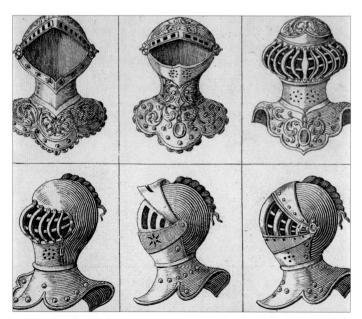

▲ *Heraldic crests were added to whatever style of helmet was popular at the time; here the crest of the Wittelsbach dukes of Bavaria surmounts a sallet helmet.*

▲ *The crowning of Queen Elizabeth II of Great Britain, in 1953, in Westminster Abbey. A coronation is the one occasion when all peers wear their coronets of rank.*

As with most heraldic accoutrements, it was France that led the fashion in the portrayal of helmets. French heralds not only drew up patterns for the helmets of different ranks – from the sovereign (all gold with visor open), down to new nobility (plain steel with three bars) – but also specified the position in which the helmet was to be depicted. Most faced right, or "dexter"; a helmet facing in the opposite direction ("sinister") indicated illegitimacy. Spain and Portugal followed suit with

▲ *A modern heraldic coronet, for a region of the Gabon – l'Ogooué-Ivindo.*

equally elaborate helmets, but in the Holy Roman Empire (centred on the German-speaking regions) no such contrived system of helmets developed. The German titled nobility used the grilled helmet but without any specific numbers of bars, while new nobility (down to the third generation) were supposed to use the closed helm. However, in the late 19th century, German and Scandinavian families of ancient lineage attempted to assert their superiority over the newly ennobled by setting their arms in the style of the 14th and 15th centuries, the helm being the great helm of that period.

The nobility of England knew only two styles of heraldic helmet. The barred helmet, in silver with gold bars, was given to the members of the peerage, or major nobility. Knights, baronets and gentlemen were given the plain steel closed helm, with the visor open for the first two degrees and closed for gentlemen.

CORONETS AND CROWNS

From the 14th century, crowns or jewelled circlets began to appear in the arms of many families, not only those of royal rank. At the same time, however, some documents of the age also show the arms

of rulers bearing crested helms without any distinguishing royal headgear. Crowns and coronets are common in heraldry, either above the shield or helm, or as charges.

Early heraldic coronets tended to be simplified versions of those worn by kings and princes. From a jewelled circlet rose a series of leaf-like embellishments, which in later centuries became formalized as fleurs de lis, strawberry leaves and other standard designs. The styles of coronets of rank among the aristocracy was set in the 16th and 17th centuries, although Europe's nobility had actually been wearing coronets for centuries.

The Renaissance brought with it an ever more formalized system of coronets, with tops constructed of specific numbers of leaves and pearls depending on the bearer's rank. In most cases these are heraldic conventions, and such designs were never actually worn. Southern European states took the heraldry of France as their model, while northern Europe looked to the Holy Roman Empire for styles and patterns.

The only nobility (as opposed to royalty) actually to wear their coronets were, and are, the British, where coronets are worn by peers on only one occasion – the coronation of the sovereign. At the moment of crowning the peers place their crowns on their heads. In recent times heraldic coronets have been designed for civic councils, not only in Europe but as far afield as Gabon in West Africa.

THE SUPPORTERS

Supporters, as their name suggests, are those heraldic accessories that support the shield of arms. They may be human figures, animals or mythical beasts, and very rarely they can also be inanimate objects. Supporters are by no means as common as the other components of a coat of arms, the shield, crest and helmet. They are mainly associated with the highest ranks of nobility and royalty. Various suggestions have been offered to explain the origins of heraldic supporters. One such

▲ *The seal of Gilles de Trazegnies, c1195, with its bear supporter.*

▼ *Angels supporting the arms of the Empire and Nuremberg, by Albrecht Dürer, 1521.*

▲ *An angel supporting a shield of arms on a medieval church roof, the possible origin of many a heraldic supporter.*

suggestion concerns the flights of angels that decorate many a medieval church roof. Often the angels hold symbols of saints or representations of the Passion, and some also support the shields of benefactors; perhaps the first supporters were echoing this device. Another explanation for the presence of supporters is as space fillers in the designs of medieval heraldic seals. In this context, supporters were a delightful conceit by which the seal engraver could avoid any large blank areas, which would not imprint well. An example of this is the seal of Gilles de Trazegnies, which shows his shield of arms suspended over the shoulders of a bear by its guige (the strap used to suspend the shield when not needed in battle). This seal has been dated to 1195, one of the earliest instances of a heraldic supporter. Almost half the seals of

▼ *The wildmen supporters of the Kingdom of Prussia, with traditional oak leaf nether garments and headgear.*

English barons found on a letter to the pope dating from 1300–1 have complex designs with Gothic-style archings and piercings. The spaces between these patterns and the shield are filled with dragons, lions or similar charges; often pairs of the creatures appear to be resting on the edge of the shield – very much like the supporters of a century or two later.

Supporters in the form of monsters – usually human figures of ferocious appearance, such as giants or wild men of the woods – could well have their origins in the fantastical displays put on during tournaments and pageants sponsored by noble participants. The knights would have their entrance announced by their servants, who would be dressed up for the occasion in the most fanciful of costumes.

HUMAN FIGURES

Since most members of the nobility of Europe like to trace their ancestry back to a warrior forebear, it is not surprising to find military figures supporting the shields of many titled families. Human supporters have been adapted to suit the period and the profession of the bearer, but possibly the most curious warrior supporters are two Augustinian friars, each bearing a sword, belonging to one of the princes of Monaco. They commemorate the legendary capture of Monaco in 1297 by

▼ *Francisco Grimaldi and his companion, both disguised as Augustinians, supporting the shield of the princes of Monaco.*

Francisco Grimaldi and his companions, who disguised themselves as Augustinians and thereby utterly surprised the garrison.

Soldiers often appear as supporters to commemorate a battle or campaign in which an ancestor proved himself. Such supporters are popular in British and Russian heraldry and Hungarian hussars support the shields of various Hungarian counts. Armoured knights were very popular in the 18th and early 19th centuries.

OTHER SUPPORTERS

In the Holy Roman Empire, some cities with rights of free trade and exemption from certain taxes bore their arms on the imperial *Doppeladler* (double-headed eagle). The families of high-ranking nobles – counts and princes of the Holy Roman Empire – also often bore their arms on the breast of this creature, surely one of the most impressive charges in the entire heraldic menagerie. Few English families were entitled to the use of the imperial eagle, associated as it was with a Catholic monarchy, but the Dukes of Marlborough and Earls Cowper (both princes of the Holy Roman Empire) and the Barons Arundell of Wardour made use of the right, with licence from the British monarch.

The grandest creature of all must be the *Quaternionenadler*, emblem of the Holy Roman Empire between the 15th century and 17th century. Here the double-headed eagle was fully displayed, with each pinion of its wings bearing a group of four shields representing the empire's lands.

▼ *The curious supporters of the counts de Grave – peacocks with human faces.*

▲ *The double-headed eagle of the Holy Roman Empire, 1587, the wings charged with groupings of shields.*

Curious marriages of monster and man also arise, surely none more exotic than the human-faced peacock supporters of the de Grave family in France.

Most supporters are borne in pairs, but this is by no means the rule. An early example of a single supporter is the goat-headed eagle of Count Gottfried of Ziegenhain (*Ziege* is the German word for goat) of the late 14th century. A branch of the Scottish family of Campbell has the unique distinction of placing its arms in front of a Scottish heraldic ship, the "lymphad". This was probably adapted from a similar vessel found in the arms of Lorne, which were also quartered by the Campbells.

Rarer than the single supporter are multiple supporters. Of these, the most curious example appears on the arms of the d'Albret family, former Constables of France. For this heraldic balancing act, the supporters are two lions, each wearing a helmet and supporting an eagle. A more modern example of multiple supporters was granted in 1981 to Air Chief Marshal Sir John Davis, Knight Grand Cross of the Order of the Bath. The supporters are two black eagles, but also, under the wing of one, a young eaglet appears, representing

▶ *The statue of a heraldic salmon supporting the arms of Greystock, made for Thomas, Lord Dacre (1467–1526).*

Sir John's former position as chief officer overseeing training of aircrews.

MODERN TRENDS

In England and Wales, supporters are currently granted only to peers of the realm, Knights of the Garter, Grand Cross, of the Orders of the Bath, St Michael and St George, the British Empire and the Royal Victoria Order. In Scotland supporters are granted to the Knights of the Thistle and holders of old feudal titles.

In recent years the British House of Lords

▲ *An unusual case of a single supporter, the heraldic ship of the Campbells of Craignish.*

▼ *A heraldic balancing act – the supporters of the d'Albrets.*

▼ *A mother eagle guards its fledgling – the allusive supporters (dexter) of the late Air Chief Marshal, Sir John Davis, GCB.*

▲ *A British bulldog supporter and an American bald eagle celebrate the marriage of an Englishman – Lord Hanson – to his American wife.*

has seen the exodus of most hereditary peers, who have been replaced by an increasing number of life peers. This wind of change has been reflected in the nature of the heraldic supporters granted to the "lifers", who often eschew traditional creatures such as lions, wyverns, dragons and griffins. In their place stand more personal figures such as family pets, for when life peers die so also do their supporters.

The crime writer, P. D. James, now Baroness James of Holland Park, has two tabby cats to support her lozenge of arms. Baroness Perry of Southwark, another fan of the feline species, also decided on two cats for her supporters – a tabby tom and a Persian female. The latter is depicted standing on a pile of books, as she is

not as big as the tabby. Dogs, too, have their day in the modern world of heraldry. Lord Cobbold chose for his supporters two golden labradors based on his own pets. Since Lord Cobbold is a hereditary peer, unusually his dog supporters will descend in the male line so long as the family continues.

▶ *A traditional choice of supporters – a lion and a stag – is depicted in the decadent Rococo style. The animals' general lack of interest means the shield isn't actually supported at all.*

▲ *The arms of Baroness Perry showing her domestic cat supporters.*

THE COMPARTMENT

Beneath the shield, placed as if to give supporters a foothold or resting place, is an object known as the compartment. Although instances of animal and human supporters lodged in parks or on mounds are known from the late medieval period, the compartment seems mainly to have been a product of the Renaissance, when heraldic artists expressed the artistic motivation of the age by showing the arms in

▼ *In the arms of the Old Town of Belgrade, the supporters stand on a battlemented compartment.*

elaborate frameworks, with the shield and supporters placed on splendid pedestals decorated with classical motifs, masks, foliate symbols and strapwork. Later artistic periods lent their styles to shield supporters and compartment alike.

By the 19th century the compartment had largely been reduced to a piece of metalwork looking rather like a bracket for an old gas lamp, with the heraldic supporters performing a rather precarious balancing act. Even more common was the use of the paper scroll as a platform, upon which stood horses, griffins, or even elephants.

Royal burghs of Scotland are entitled to stand their heraldic supporters on a special compartment that is formed of turretted and embattled masonry, often with the motto set in a plaque in the compartment, something copied in arms of the Old Town of Belgrade.

In recent years, the Canadian Heraldic Authority has included in many of its grants of arms to civic and regional authorities, compartments that reflect the geography, flora and even fish of the area. The supporters of the City of White Rock, for example, stand on a white rock charged with two forts, while the arms of the

▲ *Kangaroos support the shield of the Australian Northern Territory on a compartment of sand.*

Canadian Heraldic Authority itself rest on a compartment strewn with two maple leaves. The Authority's most curious innovation is its amalgamation of compartment and single supporter by placing a shield on a cathedra, or bishop's chair.

The English heralds have been granting compartments for some years, one of the most unusual being the arms granted to the Northern Territory of Australia in 1978. The grant of arms quotes the compartment as having a "grassy sandy mound", the shield of arms takes the brown colour of the local earth and bears the following charges: "Aboriginal rock paintings including a woman with styled internal anatomy".

▼ *The arms of Canada's cathedral churches shows an interesting combination of the single supporter and the compartment.*

I·HOLD·BEFORE·YOU·AN·OPEN·DOOR

MOTTOES AND INSCRIPTIONS

The coat of arms often includes a word or short sentence known as the motto. The position of the motto is somewhat nebulous compared to that of the shield of arms and crest. In England, where it appears below the shield, it is not even mentioned in a grant of arms and can be changed at will. Most mottoes are of relatively recent origin. In Scotland, however, the motto is considered a hereditary item much in the manner of the arms and crest, and is therefore mentioned in grants and matriculation of arms.

ANCIENT WAR CRIES

The motto probably has its origin in the *cri-de-guerre* or war cry of medieval warlords, used to rally their retinues and imbue in them a sense of loyal pride and bravura. In this league are the mottoes of the great Irish families of Butler and FitzGerald, who respectively rallied to their chiefs under the calls of *Butler a boo*, and *Crom a boo*. "A boo" was the Erse cry to victory, and Croom Castle a principal property of the FitzGeralds.

Scottish mottoes, which appear above the crest, are very much in the manner of the ancient war cry. Among the most famous are *Gang warily of the earls of Perth*,

▼ *The famous war cry of the Dukes of Leinster,* Crom a boo, *was later adopted as the motto on their arms.*

▲ *The simple* Through *motto of the Dukes of Hamilton, depicted above the crest, in typical Scottish fashion.*

and *Through* of Hamilton, and the less familiar but curious *Beware in time* of Lumsden of Innergelly, and *Enough in my hand* of Cunningham of Cunninghamhead, which is borne above the crest of a hand bearing the upper part of an anchor. Other branches of the Cunningham family bear *Over fork over* and their arms are charged with their famous "shakefork". This is said to commemorate one of the family who, while fleeing enemies, disguised himself as a farmworker forking hay. Mesmerized by the closeness of his foes, he nearly gave himself away until a companion whispered in his ear the words that now provide the family motto. Like many similar picturesque tales, they were almost certainly invented to give an ordinary heraldic charge a noble origin.

Among the abundant references to the bloody history of the Scots crown in the heraldry of that nation's noble families, are the crest and motto of Kirkpatrick. The

crest – a hand holding a bloody dagger – and the motto *I mak sikker* ("I make sure"), refer to the supposed outcome of a feud between Robert the Bruce and Red Comyn. Robert the Bruce managed to wound Comyn but the deed was finished by Bruce's follower, Kirkpatrick, who made the fatal thrust with his own dagger.

The motto of the Robertsons of Struan is *Virtutis gloria merces*, "Glory is the reward of valour." Like the crest – a hand grasping a crown – it refers to the capture in 1437 of the murderers of King James I by Robertson, the Chief of Clan Donnachaidh. An unconventional and unexplained feature of the arms is the figure of a naked man, chained and manacled, lying beneath the shield.

A curious happening is responsible for the motto *Prenez harleine tirez fort*, "Take aim and shoot strongly", borne to this day by the ancient family of Giffard of Chillington in Staffordshire, along with the two crests of a panther's head and an archer with a quiver of arrows and a drawn bow. They commemorate an event on the Giffard estate when Sir John Giffard was teaching his young son archery. A panther, a gift to Sir John, had escaped and was about to attack a woman and her baby. Sir John told his son to take aim with his bow and arrow. The lad did so, but with obvious trepidation, so Sir John whispered in his ear the words that became the family's motto. The boy did take aim, fired strongly, and according to legend, managed to kill the panther with a single shot.

▼ *The two crests of a bowman and panther belonging to the Giffards of Chillington.*

▲ A heraldic statement of the love borne between Sigismondo Malatesta, Lord of Rimini, and his lady, Isotta degli Atti.

▲ The proud motto of the Manrique de Lara family of Spain.

PIETY AND AFFIRMATION

Many mottoes urge both onlooker and bearer to espouse Christian values or even, as in that of the great French family of

▲ A statement of sovereignty – Vespasius Gonzaga, Duke of Sabbioneta, acclaims the freedom of his little state from the parent duchy of Mantua.

Montmorency – Dieu ayde au primer baron chrestien – to ask God to assist the family. Others affirm the nobility of the line, among them being Let Curzon hold what Curzon held of the Curzons of Kedleston in England (whose estate has remained in the family from the Norman Conquest until the present day), and the splendid Nos non venimos de reyes, que reyes vienen de nos of the great Castilian family of Manrique de Lara, which asserts "we do not come from kings, kings come from us".

INSCRIPTIONS ON THE SHIELD

Letters and words used as charges on the shield are not uncommon but tend to be frowned upon by many in the heraldic world as inauthentic. Nevertheless, letters and words are often used for the proudest reason, the "SPQR" (Senatus Populusque Romanus) of the Roman Empire being the most famous case. During the Renaissance, the rulers of northern Italy often combined their family arms with their ciphers, but the great mercenary general Sigismondo Malatesta went one better. He quartered his arms with his own initials and with those of his lover, Isotta degli Atti.

A lettered shield, worthy of remark, is that in the former arms of the island of Saaremaa in Estonia. In the first half of the

16th century the island's ruler, Bishop Johannes Kievel, was an admirer of Duke Friedrich III of Saxony, protector of Martin Luther. Consequently, he gave to Saaremaa a shield bearing the letters "DWGBE", the initial letters of Duke Friedrich's personal motto De wort Gottes blist ewig, "The word of God endureth forever".

▲ As a statement of loyalty, Bishop Johannes IV Kievel remembers the motto of Duke Friedrich III of Saxony, on the shield of the island of Saaremaa.

FEAR · KING

GOD · HONOUR · THE

THE LANGUAGE OF HERALDRY

Many people are baffled by the language used by heraldists in the English-speaking world. In many countries it relies heavily on Norman French, the language of William the Conqueror, which was spoken by the nobility in much of Europe during the period when heraldry was evolving. To take one example, "Vert three estoiles Or" would be the correct way to describe a green shield upon which were three gold stars with wavy rays, yet none of the descriptive words are English. In other nations, such as Germany, heraldic language is much nearer to modern-day usage.

The language of heraldry is known in the English-speaking world as "blazonry", from the old German word *blasen,* meaning to blow a horn. At a tournament, it was the duty of the medieval herald to call out the names, titles, genealogy and arms of the participating knights, accompanied by a flourish of trumpets, and the word thus also came to mean a public proclamation.

◄ *The unusual crest of the Davenport family of Capesthorne, England – showing an anonymous felon on his way to execution.*

COLOURS, METALS AND FUR

Heraldic language – no less vivid than the contrasting colours and bright metals of heraldry itself – paints a word picture of the luxurious accoutrements of medieval nobles. The terms suggest exotic and costly goods imported from the far corners of the known world, such as sable – the sleek, black fur of the marten, brought by merchants from far-off Muscovy – or gules, the rose-red dye produced in Persia and Turkey. The general term used to define all colours and textures on a shield of arms is equally picturesque and evocative: colours, metals and furs are together known as "tinctures", a word that at one time meant a dye or tint.

COLOURS AND METALS

To begin the "blazoning", or description in heraldic terms, of any shield of arms, it is necessary to deal with colour, since the very first word used in the description refers to the colour of the background or "field"

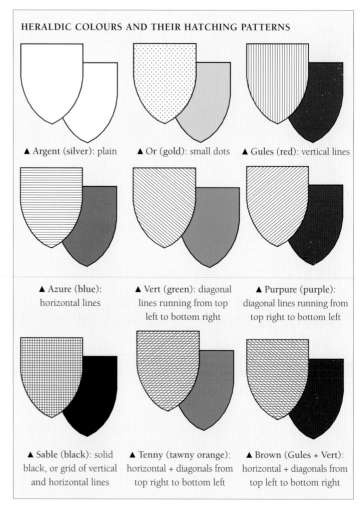

HERALDIC COLOURS AND THEIR HATCHING PATTERNS

▲ Argent (silver): plain

▲ Or (gold): small dots

▲ Gules (red): vertical lines

▲ Azure (blue): horizontal lines

▲ Vert (green): diagonal lines running from top left to bottom right

▲ Purpure (purple): diagonal lines running from top right to bottom left

▲ Sable (black): solid black, or grid of vertical and horizontal lines

▲ Tenny (tawny orange): horizontal + diagonals from top right to bottom left

▲ Brown (Gules + Vert): horizontal + diagonals from top left to bottom right

▲ *Two good examples of the reason behind the rule against colour on colour. From a distance identification would be very difficult.*

of the shield. There are five main colours in heraldry (although this differs slightly from nation to nation): red, blue, black, green and purple. Some mixed colours, known as stains, are also sometimes used. The two metals – gold and silver – are usually depicted as yellow and white. In British heraldry Norman French names are used for colours and metals, though gold and silver are also sometimes used in blazonry instead of "Or" and "Argent".

The colour green has intrigued heraldic writers for centuries. Some suggest that it was actually unknown in early heraldry, yet one of the earliest compilations of arms, illustrating the *Historia Anglorum* (written between 1250–59 by an English cleric, Matthew Paris) clearly shows the shield of one of chivalry's greatest names, William Marshal, with a field of gold and green.

THE RULE OF TINCTURES

An important heraldic principle governs the use of colours and metals: "Never place a colour on a colour or a metal on a metal". It is a very sensible rule, remembering that the original purpose of heraldry was quick and ready identification on the battlefield. Life could depend on it. A blue charge on a black field, for example, or gold on silver, would be difficult to distinguish in the melée of medieval warfare. However, as long as the charge lies partly on an opposite – such as a red lion on a field of gold and blue – this does not constitute a breaking of the rule.

The rule is not strictly observed in some countries, and Archbishop Bruno Heim in his book *Or and Argent* (1994) gives many examples of gold charges on a white field, the most famous being the arms of Jerusalem. Some heraldic writers have suggested, however, that the gold crosses on this shield were originally red, but that medieval painting methods and materials caused the red to oxidize, causing later heraldists to mistake the original colour.

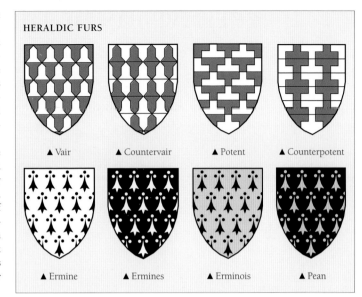

HERALDIC FURS

▲ Vair ▲ Countervair ▲ Potent ▲ Counterpotent

▲ Ermine ▲ Ermines ▲ Erminois ▲ Pean

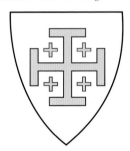

▲ *The arms of Jerusalem, possibly an exception to the rule against metal on metal, allowed because of the holiness of the city.*

FURS

In addition to the colours and metals, heraldry makes use of "furs" – patterns that suggest the costly furs worn by the medieval nobility. The two main furs are "ermine" and "vair", and each has several derivatives. Fur, just like a coloured field, can have any variety of charges placed upon it, and can take the place of either metal or colour.

Ermine is the highly prized winter fur of the common stoat. The animal's coat changes colour from chestnut brown to white except for the tip of its tail, which remains black. In heraldry, ermine is shown as a white field strewn with little black tail-tips, usually accompanied by

three black dots, which represent the fastenings by which the pelts were sewn into a robe. Ermine by itself constitutes the arms of the dukes of Brittany and makes a simple but splendid appearance in *The Book of Tourneys* of King René of Anjou.

Vair is indicated by a white and blue pattern said to represent the pelts of a species of squirrel, the blue-grey fur from its back arranged alternately with the paler fur from its underbelly. Vair was the arms of the Beauchamp family of Somerset, England and is often included in the quarterings of Henry VIII's wife, Jane Seymour.

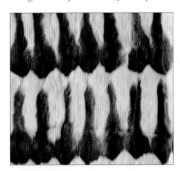

▲ *A real piece of vair, the fur made from the back and fronts of squirrel pelts sewn into a warm and handsome covering, from which the heraldic fur is derived.*

HATCHING AND TRICKING

It is, of course, not always possible to use colour in depictions of arms, and various methods of identifying heraldic colours in black and white have been used. The two most common are known as "hatching" and "tricking". Silvestro de Petra Sancta, a 17th-century Jesuit writer, devised the method of showing colours represented by lines and dots, which was later named hatching, and which has been universally used.

A simple description of a shield of arms can also be made by tricking: this involves a sketch of the arms being annotated with abbreviations for each colour, as in the example below. In this system azure becomes az, gules gu and so on.

▲ *An example of the tricking of a crest, where each colour is denoted by the letters of the heraldic tincture.*

THE DIVISION OF THE FIELD

The entire surface of the heraldic shield is known as the field, and its tincture is always described first in blazonry. It is said that the simplest arms are the best, and indeed there have been cases where an ancient family has borne for its arms a shield of just a single plain colour. The most famous example is probably the noble French family of d'Albret, which bore a shield simply Gules, while the English knight, Sir Thomas Holland (1320–60) abandoned his ancient family arms in favour of a plain shield Sable.

Of course, to allow for the numerous variations needed to ensure that every shield is unique, a more elaborate scheme is usually required. Any number of motifs, known as charges, may be placed on the field, from basic geometric shapes to representations of any object, animate or inanimate. Whether or not charges appear, the field may be divided into sections of different colours.

DESCRIBING THE DIVISIONS

When the shield is divided, or "parted", into various simple divisions or blocks, this is signalled by the words "party per", (divided by) or more simply "per", followed by the particular nature of the division, such as "party per chevron" (divided by a chevron) or "party per pale" (divided in half vertically). The descriptions of the

▼ *The field of the Fisher family of Lancashire is diapered with little fishes.*

▲ *The later version of the d'Albret family arms, the 2nd and 3rd quarters are the original arms – here hatched to represent gules – the 1st and 4th quarters were augmented by the King of France.*

divisions utilize the names given to the corresponding "ordinaries" – the fundamental geometric charges (see opposite). Where the shield is parted in an even number of small divisions the number of divisions is then specified, such as "bendy of six"; "paly of eight"; "barry of ten". Any parted field can bear another charge or charges of either a metal or a colour, without breaking the metal-on-metal, colour-on-colour rule.

In spite of their simplicity, it is quite possible for one of these basic divisions of the shield to comprise a family arms. For at least 650 years, the ancient English family of Waldegrave has used a shield that is simply Per pale Argent and Gules (a shield divided in half, one half silver, one half red). The Scottish dukes of Argyll, Chiefs of the Clan Campbell, bear Gyronny of eight Or and Sable; the Campbells of

London bear Gyronny of eight ermine and Gules, and the Swedish family of Natt och Dag ("night and day") derived its name from its simple shield Per fess Or and Azure (divided in two horizontally, one half blue for night and one half gold for day).

DIAPERING

Where a shield has a large expanse of field, the artist often adds textural interest with a faint overall pattern. This technique is called "diapering", and can lead to the most beautiful of heraldic art forms as long as the pattern is not mistaken for part of the heraldic design.

SHIELD DIVISIONS

The simplest way of creating arms that are distinct from any other, is to divide the surface of the shield into two parts by a line, one part a metal – gold or silver – the other a colour. Further variations can be made by subdividing the shield with more lines, and varying the edges of the lines in many ways. The option of adding furs to the variations makes the possibilities for new but simple geometric designs almost endless.

▲ (Party) per pale

▲ (Party) per fess

▲ (Party) per bend

▲ (Party) per bend sinister

▲ (Party) per chevron

▲ (Party) per saltire

▲ Tierced per pale

▲ Tierced per fess

▲ Quarterly

▲ Gyronny

▲ Barry (six)

▲ Bendy (six)

▲ Bendy sinister

▲ Paly

▲ Chevronny

▲ Chequy

▲ Lozengy

▲ Barry bendy

▲ Paly bendy

▲ Gyronny of twelve

▲ Pily

▲ Pily bendy

▲ Pily bendy sinister

THE HONOURABLE ORDINARIES

The most simple charges, or devices, found on the heraldic shield are geometric patterns called the ordinaries. These charges have long been considered to hold a special place in heraldry, hence the appellation "honourable". The ordinary normally occupies about one-third of the area of the shield, and can be borne alone or in conjunction with other charges. It can also itself bear further charges. In blazonry, the ordinary is always mentioned directly after the field.

Various theories about the origins of the ordinaries have been put forward, including the fanciful suggestion that the chevron, for example, is a charge suitable for the head of a family who gives shelter to other family members. An interesting but unexplained visual clue lies in a Roman mosaic representing the amphitheatre of Lyons in France (and now in the city's museum). The mosaic shows a wooden palisade around the arena that contains many of the ordinaries and subordinaries found in heraldry. Whether there is a link between a Roman geometrical conceit and heraldry, or if it is just a curious coincidence is still debated.

VARIATIONS ON THE ORDINARIES

Some of the ordinaries, such as the bands, can also be borne in smaller forms in pairs or more. These diminutive ordinaries have names that reflect their nature, so that chevrons give rise to chevronels, pales to pallets and two or more bends are described as bendlets. Any ordinary can be "voided" by having its centre removed to reveal the field or another tincture; it can also be "fimbriated", that is, edged with a narrow band of another tincture.

THE CROSS

The heraldic cross is formed by a combination of the "fess" (horizontal band) and the "pale" (vertical band). In its simple form it is set centrally on the shield, with each limb extending to one edge. The cross has bred more variants than any other

THE ORDINARIES

Although various writers quibble about the exact number of ordinaries, the following selection, with their diminutives behind them, is generally considered to be a complete list:

▲ The chief

▲ The pale and pallets

▲ Fess ▲ 2 bars ▲ A barrulet

▲ Bend ▲ 3 bendlets ▲ A riband

▲ Bend sinister ▲ 2 bendlets sinister

▲ Chevron ▲ 3 chevronels

▲ Saltire ▲ A fillet saltire

▲ Pall ▲ A fillet pall

▲ Cross ▲ A fillet cross

▲ Pile ▲ 3 piles in point

charge: some writers say there are over 30 variants, others over 50, while one 19th-century writer listed 450. Apart from the simple cross the most commonly met with are the "cross" patty (or "formy") where the four limbs are wide at their heads but narrow towards the central join, and the Maltese or eight-pointed cross, which is similar to the former except that the heads of the limbs are notched at their centres. If the bottom limb of the cross narrows to a point it is said to be "fitched". Crosses patty and "crosslet" can often be found with this variant, and are then described as a "cross patty fitchy" or "cross crosslet fitchy".

▶ A Flemish armorial c1560 showing ordinaries and divisions of the field.

VARIATIONS ON THE CROSS

▲ Cross potent:
T-shaped limbs,
resembling crutches.

▲ Cross patonce:
Concave, tapered
limbs, with each head
divided into three.

▲ Cross fleury or
flory: the accentuated
points end in the form
of a fleur de lis.

▲ Cross crosslet: The
heads of each limb are
themselves crossed.

▲ Cross bottony:
Straight limbs, each
headed with three
roundels or buttons.

▲ Formy (Patty)

▲ Maltese

▲ Moline

▲ Pommée

▲ Fleuretty

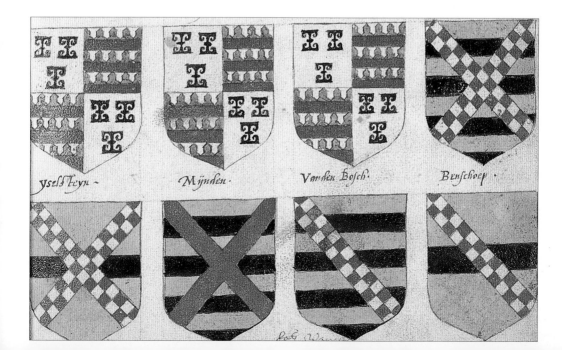

THE SUB-ORDINARIES

The lesser geometric charges are known as the "sub-ordinaries"; they can be borne singly or in groups according to their nature. The sub-ordinaries are deemed the less common of the geometric patterns found on shields of arms, but like many of the honourable ordinaries, most of them owe their origins to the construction of the medieval shield.

The most non-controversial sub-ordinaries are the "canton" (and its larger cousin, the "quarter"), the "bordure", the "inescutcheon", the "orle" and the "tressure". The last four are probably reminders of metal reinforcements that were part of the structure of the medieval shield. Other writers have also included further charges in the list of the sub-ordinaries, including the "lozenge" and its derivatives, the "rustre", "mascle", and "fusil", the "gyron", the "pairle", the "billet" and "flanches".

The bordure, or border, is simply that: a border around the edge of the shield. In Scottish heraldry the bordure is often used as a means of identifying junior branches of the family, the bordure bearing charges taken from the arms of the mother (see Difference Marks and Cadency). A similar practice is found in Spanish and Portuguese heraldry, where the bordure may even include small shields of arms of near relatives.

The inescutcheon is a small shield borne as a charge. It may be plain or may bear other charges and may be in any number, not just single. The arms of Burrell, Baron Gwydir, make use of this and another sub-ordinary, blazoned Vert on each of three escutcheons Argent a bordure engrailed Or, while the family of Hay, Earl of Erroll, High Constable of Scotland, are blazoned Argent three escutcheons Gules.

The orle appears as an inner border set between the middle and edge of the shield. French heraldists also call it a faux, or false, escutcheon, or inescutcheon voided.

The tressure is really little more than a narrow orle and often appears in pairs in Scottish heraldry where, garnished with fleurs de lis, it is usually associated with the royal arms of Scotland and other families allied to the Scottish monarchy through marriage.

The canton is a square or rectangle in the dexter chief corner of the shield, smaller than the less-common quarter. The canton often bears other charges and in the heraldry of some nations can be used to denote certain relationships.

Flanches are always borne in pairs, and are formed by arcs on each side of the shield extending from the upper corner to a point slightly to the side of the base.

The lozenge is a diamond-shaped charge that has several variants, the most common being the mascle – a lozenge with its centre removed to show the field. A rustre is a lozenge pierced with a circular opening, and a fusil is an elongated lozenge. A field patterned overall with lozenges is "lozengy"; with squares it is "chequy".

A billet is a small elongated rectangular

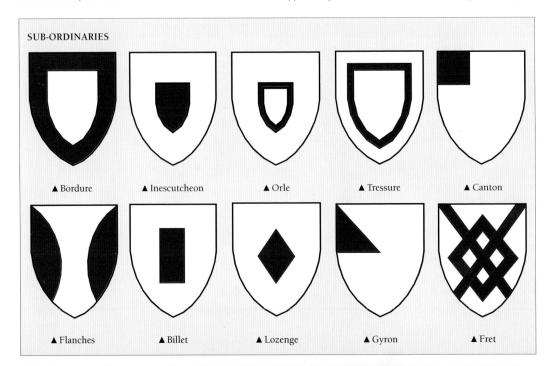

SUB-ORDINARIES

▲ Bordure ▲ Inescutcheon ▲ Orle ▲ Tressure ▲ Canton

▲ Flanches ▲ Billet ▲ Lozenge ▲ Gyron ▲ Fret

figure. Numerous billets are often strewn across the field, described as "billety".

The gyron is a triangular charge that seldom appears singly. Usually the shield is divided into a number of gyrons, arranged like the sails of a windmill, and the field is described as "gyronny of [the number of pieces]". The most famous example of a gyronny coat is that of the Scottish family of Campbell, who bear Gyronny of eight Or and Sable. Branches of the family often charge the gyrons with other charges or vary their edges and colours.

The "fret" is formed of interlaced bendlets and bendlets sinister. It can be encountered in the singular but is more often repeated to cover the whole field in an interlacing pattern, which resembles a garden trellis; this is then described as "fretty".

▲ *The nine billets, and fiddle, on the arms of the family of Winter of Bohlanden.*

OVERALL PATTERNS

Generally, if charges are repeated on a shield, their number tends to be less than ten, and is specified in the blazon. Furthermore, they are usually placed within the perimeter of the shield so that they appear in their entirety. Sometimes, however, small charges – which may be of any kind – are strewn in a plentiful degree all over the shield. This effect is described as "semy".

There are special terms for the strewing of certain charges. For example, a shield strewn with billets is billety and one strewn with fleur de lis is semy de lis. Any object, no matter how humble or curious, can be strewn across the shield – such as semy of coffee beans in the arms of the district of Haut Ogooué in Gabon.

ROUNDELS

Plain round charges called "roundels" are depicted in heraldic colours and metals. Whereas in most heraldics the roundel is

described simply in its true colour, English blazonry has a distinct name for each roundel. The "bezant", or gold roundel, is said to be named after the gold coin of Byzantium, while the "torteau", or red roundel, resembles a tartlet. A blue roundel is a "hurt", which may refer either to a bruise or to a hurtleberry (blueberry). Droplets are a variation of the roundel, and look something like tadpoles. They are known as "gouttés". Once again, in English heraldry Norman French is utilized: red droplets are goutté de sang – drops of blood – gold droplets are goutté d'or. A roundel bearing blue and white wavy bars is often used to denote water: this is termed the "fountain". It is seen in the arms of the Sykes family, since a "syke" is a spring or fountain.

The English family of Stourton makes use of fountains and a bend to tell the story of their ancient estate. Six springs rise at Stourhead, forming the source of the River Stour: three were originally inside the estate boundary, the other three outside. The Stourton arms, Sable a bend Or between six fountains, neatly describes the geography and history of the estate.

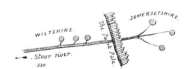

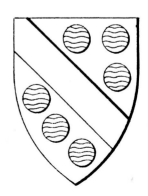

▲ *The six fountains and bend in the arms of the Stourton family reflect the position on the family property of six springs. A sketched map above explains the pattern.*

▲ *A novel use of semy – the chief in the shield of the Gabonaise region of Haut Ogooué is semy of coffee beans.*

LINES OF PARTITION

Heraldry is nothing if not inventive and over the centuries its regulators have come up with every possible method to ensure that each shield of arms can be unique. This is especially true of the many ways that a shield can be divided. To increase the number of possible variations, the edges of the divisions and the ordinaries, which are known as "lines of partition", can be drawn in many different styles.

Partition lines make the fullest use of the edges of the ordinaries and they are considered sufficiently distinctive for unrelated families to have a coat of arms that is identical in colour and ordinary, but with different edges. For example, a green cross with straight edges on a white shield may belong to a family unrelated to one whose white shield bears a green cross with wavy edges. In fact, lines are included in the blazon only if they are not straight.

Apart from the styles shown here, in recent years new lines of partition have been evolved by the heraldic artists of Scandinavia, South Africa and Canada.

COUNTERCHANGING

One of the most enjoyable stratagems in blazon is a partitioned shield that is counterchanged. Counterchanging is the

▲ Counterchanging in practice on the shield of a community in Greenland. The shield here is divided per fess.

COMMON LINES OF PARTITION

The following shields show a selection of the many ways in which the heraldic division can be varied.

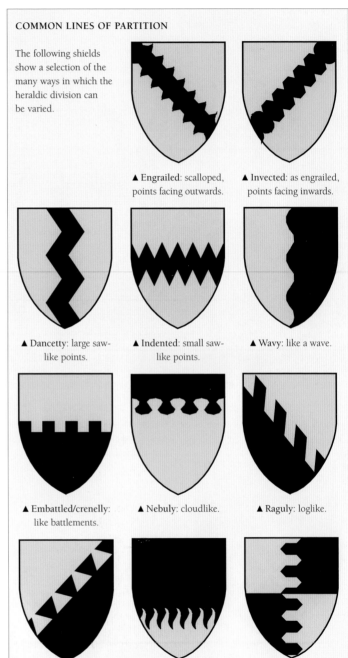

▲ Engrailed: scalloped, points facing outwards.

▲ Invected: as engrailed, points facing inwards.

▲ Dancetty: large saw-like points.

▲ Indented: small saw-like points.

▲ Wavy: like a wave.

▲ Embattled/crenelly: like battlements.

▲ Nebuly: cloudlike.

▲ Raguly: loglike.

▲ Dovetailed

▲ Rayonné: like flames.

▲ Urdy: serrated.

LINES OF PARTITION **81**

dividing of the shield in such a manner that it is part of a metal and part of a colour, and then by arranging the charges in such a manner that they be reciprocally of the same colour and metal. This sounds a complicated business, but counterchanging can in fact be one of the simplest and most effective ways of varying one very simple shield of arms from another.

The arms of the Anglo-Norman family of d'Abitot provide an example of how counterchanging can produce a striking design. The d'Abitot arms are Per pale Or and Gules three roundels counterchanged. They should be compared with the non-counterchanged alternatives, which are the arms of the Courtenay family (Or three torteaux) and its opposite, the arms of Dynham (Gules three bezants).

These three personal shields show how a certain configuration of charges can be changed through tincture. The families to which each shield belongs most probably bore no relation to each other, although changes of tincture were also sometimes employed for different members of the same family.

In the case of the Courtenay arms we can see how exact blazonry can be, the roundels each given its particular name, ie red roundels torteaux, and in the Dynham arms, gold roundels or bezants. Finally the d'Abitot arms combine these two designs but come up with something entirely different, by counterchanging both the field and the intersecting third roundel, resulting in a very distinctive shield.

EUROPEAN VARIANTS OF LINES OF PARTITION

Certain charges, divisions of the shield, partition lines and so on, are peculiar to a particular area or nation. In 1886, in his work entitled *Heraldry English and* *Foreign*, Robert Jenkins gave the following examples of variants and the names of some ordinaries that would seldom, if ever, be met with in English heraldry.

FAMILY ARMS

▲ Van Zirn ▲ D'Arpo ▲ Fromberg ▲ Von Tale

▲ Kauffungen ▲ Gleisenthal ▲ Lindeck ▲ Kunige

FRENCH VARIANTS OF ORDINARIES

▲ Chevron Failli ▲ Chevron Ployé ▲ Chevron Enlassé ▲ Bande Anchée

---

▲ *The shield of the Courtenay family: Or three torteaux.*

▲ *The Dynham shield – a reversed version of the Courtenay shield: Gules three bezants.*

▲ *Finally the shield of the d'Abitots: Per pale Or and Gules three roundels counterchanged.*

BLAZONRY

The term blazonry refers to the special and distinct language that is used in the description of heraldry. Many a casual visitor to the world of heraldry can be baffled and put off by the nature of blazonry, but in fact it is a very user-friendly language, so exact in its phraseology that, once learnt, it enables one heraldist to impart to another an accurate and full description of any coat of arms through a concise verbal picture. Blazonry is a precise language, which it needs to be, for the nature of heraldry itself depends on the uniqueness of each coat of arms.

DESCRIBING A SHIELD

Any charge can be married to any other in any number of ways to make up a shield of arms. Often, the more ancient the arms, the simpler the design. It is in fact possible to have a shield of arms bearing no charges at all. The d'Albret arms were originally simply Gules (a plain red shield) though in 1389 they were "augmented" with the arms of France, becoming Quarterly one and four Azure three fleurs de lis Or two and three Gules (the shield was divided into four, quarters one and four were blue with three gold fleur de lis in each, quarters two and three remained the original red colour).

We have seen some of the fundamental charges employed in heraldry. Let us now see how they are "blazoned". The blazon needs to include all the details of tincture and number that an artist would need in order to reproduce the shield accurately. It always follows a set pattern:

1 The field, including any divisions
2 The ordinary
3 The principal charges on the field, followed by any lesser charges
4 Any charges on the ordinary
5 Any sub-ordinaries
6 Any charges on the sub-ordinaries

A further refinement of the language of blazonry is the means of describing the exact position on the shield any charge might take. The names of these parts and points of the shield are explained in the box.

THE PARTS AND POINTS OF THE SHIELD

For the purposes of accurate description, the heraldic shield is divided into different areas.

The dexter (right-hand) and sinister (left-hand) sides of the shield are always described from the point of view of the bearer of the shield, a throwback to the days when shields were actually carried. So from the reader's viewpoint, right is left and left is right. Most heraldic charges, particularly animate ones, are drawn so they are facing dexter, as it is considered the more "worthy" side. So from the point of the viewer, rather than a bearer, any lions, for example, on the shield, would usually face the left-hand side of the shield.

A B C: chief (top part of the shield), sub-divided into:
A: dexter chief point
B: middle chief point
C: sinister chief point
D: honour point
E: fess or heart point
F: nombril or navel point
G H I: base, sub-divided into:
G: dexter base point
H: middle base point
I: sinister base point

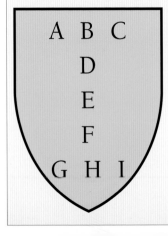

Here are three examples of how blazonry describes a shield. The first example is the arms of the family of Winneberg: Gules a bend Argent indented between six crosses couped Or.

1 The field is described first: Gules – a plain red background.

2 The next most important feature is the ordinary, in this case a bend Argent, noting any partition line, here indented.

3 Any lesser charges follow: between six crosses couped Or.

The arms of the town of Gerville, Seine-Maritime, France, is described as: Argent on a bend Azure between two Phrygian caps Gules three mullets of six points Or.

The more complex arms of the Johnson family, Suffolk, are described as: Sable on a fess between two double manacles Argent three pheons Gules on a chief Or a demi lion between two lozenges Azure.

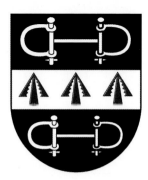

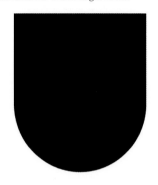

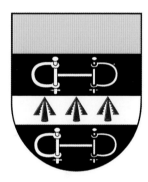

4 The charges, and their colour, on the ordinary are then described: three pheons [arrowheads] Gules.

1 The field is silver, the ordinary: on a bend Azure. ("On" anticipates point 3 below. As the lines of partition are straight they are not mentioned.)

1 The field: Sable.

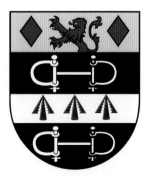

5 If a chief is borne in addition to another ordinary, as here, it is mentioned next: on a chief Or.

2 The lesser charges on the field: between two Phrygian caps Gules.

2 The ordinary: on a fess.

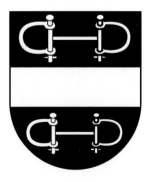

3 If any charges are borne on the ordinary, these are mentioned next: three mullets [stars] of six points Or.

3 The lesser charges on the field: between two double manacles Argent. (As both fess and manacles are silver, the colour is mentioned only once.)

6 Any charges that appear on the chief now follow: a demi lion (the head and top half of a lion) between two lozenges Azure.

HERALDIC BEASTS

Although the earliest heraldry consisted mainly of simple geometric patterns – for easy identification at a distance – beasts, birds and monsters had begun to figure as emblems on shields and flags long before the birth of heraldry itself. We know that in ancient Greece the Athenians took an owl as their city's symbol. In ancient Egypt many of the gods were depicted partly or wholly in the forms of animals that lived alongside human beings, such as the jackal, cobra and hawk. The Bible records the instruction, "Every man of the children of Israel shall pitch by his own standard, with the ensign of their father's house" (Numbers 2:2), and of the 12 tribes of Israel no less than half took an animal as their symbol.

THE LION

Lions were in evidence at the very birth of heraldry – perhaps they were even the very first charge. When knighted in 1127 by his father-in-law, King Henry I of England, Geoffrey, Count of Anjou was given a shield bearing fanciful golden lions. The lion, believed to be the king of beasts, was

▼ The lion, king of beasts: a page from a Dutch ordinary of 1570 shows family arms charged with the lion rampant.

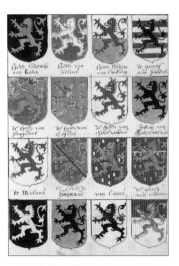

naturally a favourite symbol among the fighting men of medieval Europe, and was one of the more exotic beasts of the medieval heraldic menageries.

All postures or inclinations of an armorial charge are termed "attitudes", and this is especially relevant to creatures. Not surprisingly the lion is afforded the greatest number of attitudes – some writers have given it as many as 60 different positions. Besides its attitude, a lion or any other creature may also be distinguished by attributes. For example, a lion "passant" (attitude) may also be "langued" (tongued) in a tincture other than the normal red, and "armed" with teeth and claws.

Heraldry is an exact science. It needs to be if the individuality of a shield of arms is to be preserved, therefore attributes and attitudes are important. It could be that one family's blue shield bears a gold lion "rampant", another's a gold lion "rampant guardant" (looking at the viewer), while a third has a gold lion "rampant reguardant" (looking backwards): there is enough difference in the position of the head to give three distinct arms. Adding a forked tail ("queue fourchée") to the lions provides three more distinct arms.

OTHER BEASTS

Obviously many an early bearer of a lion chose the creature to reflect his own ferocity and bravery. The same may be said of those who chose bears, wolves and other carnivorous animals. Strength could be suggested by other creatures. The noble Moravian family of Pernstein bore on a white shield a black auroch's head "couped affronty" (with no neck visible, facing the viewer). According to a family legend the founding father of the Pernsteins was a charcoal burner of extraordinary strength called Vénava. He managed to catch a wild auroch and led it to the court of the king at Brno, where he cut off the poor beast's head with a single blow of his axe. The king was so impressed that he gave Vénava great estates and the right to commemorate his feat on his shield of arms.

▲ This 1823 Bavarian grant of arms, to Baron Peter Kreusser, includes a variety of beasts from the heraldic menagerie.

LIONS OR LEOPARDS

In 1235 the German emperor Frederick II presented Henry III of England with three leopards as a living shield of arms. Was this a reflection of the English arms at that time? If so, are the creatures in the English arms meant to be leopards? Confusion arises from the interpretation of heraldic terms describing the attitude of the lion. In English heraldry, the creature most often shown rearing up on one hind foot and boxing with its front paws is a lion "rampant", whereas if it is walking sedately across the shield it is a lion passant. In the arms of England the three lions are "passant guardant", walking and looking at the viewer. In French heraldry, the lion is always assumed to be rampant, while the creature that appears passant guardant is always a leopard. Furthermore, in French heraldry a rearing lion, looking at the viewer (in English "rampant guardant"), is called a lion léopardé, and a lion passant is a léopard lionné!

MOST COMMON ATTITUDES OF THE LION

▲ *Statant*

▲ *Combatant*

▲ *Rampant*

▲ *Rampant guardant*

▲ *Couchant*

▲ *Passant*

▲ *Salient*

▲ *Rampant double-queued*

▲ *Rampant reguardant*

▲ *Rampant queue fourchée*

▲ *Sejant*

▲ *Cowed*

▲ *A taste of the local flora and fauna from the Baltic States: left: Polvamaa, Estonia; middle: Balozi, Latvia; right: Auce, Latvia.*

Like many heraldic stories, it is impossible to know whether the auroch appeared on the Pernstein shield before or after the legend arose, but it is carved on the family's former castle at Pardubice.

While many men of warlike disposition would not have minded being represented by a bull, there must be few that would have chosen to bear its castrated equivalent, the ox. However, if Nicholas Upton, the 15th-century English heraldic writer, is to be believed, he was instrumental in the granting of a shield charged with three oxheads to a gentleman who had had the misfortune to have been maimed in the testicles by the thrust of a spear.

Another creature that Upton might have thought equally suitable for this client

would have been the beaver, whose scent glands, located near its rear, were sought after for various medicinal cures. Upton, along with other medieval writers, believed that these glands were in fact the beaver's testicles and that, when it realized that men were after them, it sensibly chose to sacrifice them by castrating itself with its teeth. Beavers, once common in much of Northern Europe, are now found only in the forests of Scandinavia and the Baltic States, and they appear in the arms of the Estonian district of Polvamaa.

Heraldry gives symbolic protection to all creatures, great and small, and whereas warriors might choose martial beasts such as lions, bears and wolves, country communities

▼ *A marvellous depiction carved in stone of the porcupine badge of King Louis XII of France, 1498–1515, Chateau de Blois.*

▲ *The elephant in the arms of the Counts of Helfenstein, an unusual animal charge, chosen as a delightful pun on the family's name.*

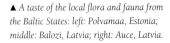

often prefer to commemorate gentler creatures. In Latvia, the rivers and forests yield up their wildlife to local heraldry. The arms of Auce – a black crayfish on a red field – enjoyably break the colour-on-colour rule. In the arms of Balozi a frog sits below a chief charged with water-lily leaves, while squirrels in the arms of Baldone and hedgehogs in those of Vilaka recall the creatures found in many gardens.

◄ *The arms of the Pernstein family of Moravia bear the popular bull's head as both a charge and a crest.*

▲ *Vénava kills his auroch in a relief carving at the family seat, the Castle of Pardubice.*

▲ *The camel on the arms of the city of Petropavlovsk, in the old Russian Empire, at the cross-roads where East met West.*

EXOTIC BEASTS

Of the more unusual animals, elephants were relatively well known to medieval heraldists (Henry III of England was given one for his menagerie by Louis IX of France in 1254). The elephant was used as a symbol of strength and dependability, and as such it was chosen for the arms of the city of Coventry in England. A particularly enjoyable example appears in the Zurich armorial roll (1335–45) for the von

▼ *A tigress looks in the mirror at itself (third quarter) in the arms of the English family of Sibell. While she was beguiled by her own image her cubs were left unprotected.*

Helfenstein family of Swabia, chosen for its punning value with the family name.

Other exotic beasts in the heraldic menagerie include that of the eastern territories and cities of the old Russian Empire (such as Petropavlovsk) who favoured the camel in their civic heraldry, and when Sir Titus Salt, Baronet, of Saltaire, Yorkshire was granted arms, he chose as a crest the alpaca, from whose fine wool he had made his fortune.

ANIMAL PARTS

It is not only whole creatures that are used in heraldry; various parts of their anatomy make their way on to shields. Wolves' teeth famously appear on the Kinsky arms of Bohemia, while others include the bones of fish, and various types of amputations. The bits of animals that are all quite commonly used in heraldry include heads that are either "erased" (torn off at the neck) or "couped" (clean cut), various horns and antlers, and even the paws ("gambs") of bears and lions, which can also be either erased or couped.

DOMESTIC ANIMALS

Cats, dogs and horses are all corralled into heraldry, as are the unfortunate victims of the hunt: boar, deer, hares and rabbits. The stag hunt was for centuries the exclusive

▼ *The wolf's teeth on the shield of the Czech Count Kinsky, seen here on a beautifully crafted embellishment on a wrought-iron gate. The teeth themselves are very stylized.*

sport of the nobility, so it is no wonder that, after lions, deer probably appear most commonly upon shields and are therefore afforded the next largest group of personal attitudes. The English Cottington family enjoy two hinds in their arms "counter-tripping", which have the rather comical appearance of a Push-me-Pull-you.

Greyhounds are popular in Italian heraldry, while in British heraldry the talbot, a large and powerful ancient hunting hound, is often found. However, man's best friend comes no truer than the dog on the crest of a Mr Phillips of Cavendish Square, London, who early in the 19th century was swimming in the sea off Portsmouth when he got into a strong current and was in danger of being drowned. A perceptive Newfoundland hound saw his predicament, leapt into the water and dragged him to safety. When Mr Phillips found that his canine saviour was a stray, he took the brave dog home and gave him every kind attention that he deserved. Furthermore, the Phillips family recorded this happy outcome in a new heraldic crest and motto, the full blazon being: Upon a mount Vert in front of a Newfoundland dog sejant, reguardant proper an escutcheon thereon, in base waves of the sea, and floating therein a naked man, the sinister arm erected all proper. The motto is *Auspice Deo extuli mari*, "God being my leader, I brought him out of the sea".

▼ *Mr Phillips' faithful friend, the dog who saved his life and became his crest.*

HUMAN FIGURES

Human beings – and parts of them – appear often in heraldry, mainly reflecting enemies of the medieval period. The human figure is usually shown fully clothed or, if nearer to nature, is girded around the loins with an extremely uncomfortable "vestment of leaves" described by one English heraldic writer as "vegetable knickers". However, a naked man in all his glory appears in the arms of the Scots baronets Dalyell of the Binns and a breast of sorts, distilling milk, appears in the arms of the English family of Dodge.

Hungarian heraldry affords many instances of the human being in action, whether it be of the bloody kind – slitting the throat of an unfortunate deer or shooting a Turkish soldier – or gentler pursuits such as playing the organ, or reaping corn.

KINGS AND QUEENS

Naturally, the appearance of kings and queens in heraldry is counted to be the highest of all honours. In most cases the monarch commemorated tends to be anonymous, but the Castilian family of de Avila has in its arms an imprisoned king in chains, representing King François I of France, taken prisoner by Don Diego de Avila in 1528 during the Battle of Pavia. The Savoyard family of Amoreto also keeps a Moorish king chained to the chevron in its arms.

The Weldons, Baronets of Rahenderry in Ireland, have the bust of the Virgin Queen, Elizabeth I of England, as their crest. Family records say only that it was given as a mark of distinction by the Queen herself for some great service done to her by a Weldon.

VICTIMS AND VILLAINS

The Spanish family of Miranda commemorates a famous legend on its shield of arms. It bears the busts of five virgins, rescued from rape and murder by Alvar Fernandez de Miranda, while on pilgrimage to Santiago de Compostella. The arms of the city of Lichfield in England record a less favourable fate than that of Alvar's virgins: on old seals of the city council the shield bears "on a landscape proper several martyrs in divers manners massacred."

The English family of Davenport of Capesthorne Hall in Cheshire has what is thought to be a unique crest of a felon's head within the noose from which he is about to be hanged. It refers to the power of life and death, "without delay and without appeal", which the Davenports exercised over vast areas of forest land in north-east England.

HEARTS AND OTHER ORGANS

Human hearts often make their appearance on shields of arms, one forming the central charge in the arms of the Scots family of Douglas. Sir James Douglas was a close companion of King Robert the Bruce of Scotland (1306–29); at the end of his life the king, who had long wished to take part in a Crusade, gained Sir James's promise

▲ *The wildmen in the arms of the Wood family, traditionally girded with oak leaves.*

▼ *The all too realistic nature of Hungarian arms borne out here in a grant of 1636.*

▼ *King François I of France stands in chains on the shield of the de Avila family.*

▼ *The virgins saved from a "fate worse than death" by a member of the Miranda family.*

▲ *The crest of the Davenport family of Capesthorne – showing an anonymous felon on his way to execution.*

that he would carry the King's embalmed heart to Jerusalem and bury it in the Holy Sephulchre. When the King died in 1329, that is just what Sir James set off to do, but was killed in battle on his journey. Some say he threw King Robert's heart into the fight before following it to certain death. The Douglas family added a red heart to their arms, which was later crowned.

The north Italian family of Colleoni bore three pairs of testicles on their shield. In

▼ *The three pairs of testicles of the Colleoni family, adorning the ceiling of their castle of Malpaga, near Bergamo, north Italy.*

the virile and thoroughly human Middle Ages this was no disgrace, but the dubious gentility of the late 19th century led these vital charges to be described in some ordinaries as three upside-down hearts.

Female genitalia appear on the shield of the medieval Italian family of Conati, but perhaps the most bizarre example of heraldic "vivacity" can be seen on the shield of a Hungarian gentleman, István Várallyay, who in 1599 was granted arms of male sexual organs beneath an arm grasping a mallet. As many Hungarian family arms vividly portray the severed parts of dead Turks, this shield could be taken to represent some particularly unpleasant fate befalling yet another Turkish soldier captured in battle. In truth, however, these particular parts are those of a stallion – Várallyay was a farrier and gelder in the Hungarian army and, being proud of his swiftness and expertise in castrating horses, wished the fact to be recorded in heraldry.

The Indian state of Wankaner has in its arms a representation of the Hindu adoration of the god Shiva, through the veneration of the male phallic symbol of the *lingam*. The arms show Shiva's *trishul*, or trident, wrapped around with snakes, and the round-ended raised stone sculpture that represents the *lingam*, or generative force.

ARMS AND LEGS

Parts of the human body feature regularly in heraldry. The most common are arms or legs. The arms of the Isle of Man are Gules three legs conjoined in fess point in armour proper. They were borne by the ancient kings of Man, and appear as a quartering in the arms of Montagu, Stanley and Murray, all later Lords of Man. The legs probably derive from a Norse symbol for luck introduced by Man's Viking invaders.

A curious human appendage is the wooden leg of the Swede, Per Larsson, who when fighting during the Thirty Years War had his leg amputated. On his eventual ennoblement he took the name Stöltenhielm (*stolt* means "stilt") and a wooden stilt was a main feature in the arms he adopted.

▲ *István Várallyay's shield, with the curious charges that actually celebrate the bearer's profession of farrier and gelder of horses.*

▲ *The arms of the Indian state of Wankaner bring the Hindu worship of Shiva to heraldry.*

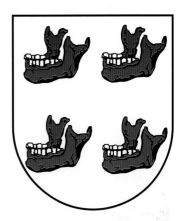

▲ *The highly literal arms of the Portuguese family of Queixada, whose name means simply "jawbone".*

FOWL, FISH AND PLANTS

After animals, the second most popular heraldic charge is birds – most usually the eagle but also less exalted species. Fish of various kinds also sometimes appear, and flowers, trees and even vegetables have also played their part in the heraldic story. Of flowers, the rose and the lily are most commonly met with, and each has a stylized form – the five-petalled heraldic rose and the fleur de lis.

▲ *The stork in its vigilance on the arms of the Hungarian family of Ballint of Técső. If it slept the stone would fall and waken it.*

▼ *The heraldic aviary in the coat of arms of the Barons Arundel shows the imperial eagle behind the shield, the owl as a supporter, and six hirondells (swallows) on the shield.*

HERALDIC BIRDS

If the lion is the king of beasts, the eagle, for medieval heraldic writers, was the queen of birds. From Roman times it was associated with empires, and black eagles were said to be the bravest of all. Both the Byzantine and Holy Roman emperors considered it personal to them.

Many other birds, real, fanciful or fantastic, inhabit the heraldic menagerie, particularly the martlet or *merletten*. The martlet, a swift-like creature, has no feet when depicted in heraldry (and the *merletten* has neither feet nor beak), because it was believed by medieval writers never to land. Such birds were spoken of by Crusaders who had seen them in the Holy Land. The martlet was often given as a heraldic charge to younger sons of the English nobility, as a reminder to "trust to the wings of virtue and merit, and not to their legs, having no land of their own to put their feet on."

The pelican also displays a mixture of fact and fancy. In heraldry it is often depicted using its beak to wound itself in the breast ("vulning"), using the blood it sheds to feed its young. Such a symbol of self-sacrifice is therefore often found in religious arms.

CREATURES OF THE WATER

The dolphin, the most commonly occurring sea creature in heraldry, is classed as a fish by heraldic writers, as is the whale, although both are, of course, mammals. All

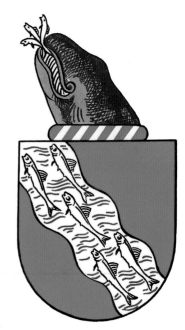

kinds of fish have appeared as various heraldic charges, but size and ferocity seems to have been foremost in the minds of the medieval heralds. Not surprisingly, therefore, numerous arms can be found bearing the pike, such as the Portuguese family of Lucio, and the Czech town of Dolni Breszov.

▲ *The ferocious and all too realistic pike devouring a smaller fish in the arms of the Czech town of Dolni Breszov.*

FLOWERS

Heraldic writers have credited the rose with many properties. It is seen as an emblem of secrecy, being good, soft, and sweet-smelling, but surrounded by evil, signified by its thorns. In medieval England the rose was a popular symbol within the royal family, reaching its zenith during the reigns of the Tudor monarchs. The white rose was a favourite badge of the royal house of York. The red rose of the rival house of Lancaster has a less certain provenance, but it is certain that Henry Tudor (later Henry VII) took it to be the Lancastrian symbol when he united it with the white rose after his marriage to Elizabeth of York in 1486.

The double Tudor rose was a favourite device of Henry VII's son, Henry VIII, and on his marriage to Catherine of Aragon he combined it with the Queen's badge, the pomegranate of Granada. An abundance of roses and pomegranates erupted throughout England, until the eventual divorce of the unhappy couple led to the defacing of any such badge in public places and churches. This must have left Herr Arnold

▼ The fleur de lis of the French kings from their crypt in the abbey of St Denis. The shield is encircled by the Order of the Holy Ghost (St Esprit).

▲ Left: the rose and pomegranate charge on the arms of Herr Arnold Bilson – a design he might later have regretted after the divorce of Henry VIII and Catherine of Aragon. Right: The potato flowers of the French town of Ploudaniel.

Bilson, presumably a German merchant in England, in an awkward situation: he had been granted arms charged with a Tudor rose and pomegranate "dimidiated" (halved).

The fleur de lis, the heraldic lily, was associated with the royal house of France long before the advent of heraldry. It is possible that the fleur de lis is a heraldic representation of the flag iris, though one of the many legends surrounding the symbol is that it evolved not from flowers but from three toads, supposedly the arms of Pharamond, King of the Franks in the first half of the 5th century.

As part of the French royal insignia, the fleur de lis can be traced back to the reign of Robert II, "the Pious" (996–1031), son of Hugh Capet. The royal coat of arms, of a blue shield strewn with golden fleurs de lis (semy de lis), made its first appearance during the reign of Louis VIII (1223–6). It is supposed that the number of lilies was reduced to three during the reign of Charles V (1364–80) in honour of the Holy Trinity, although his successor, Charles VI (1380–1422) is known to have used both semy de lis and three fleurs de lis on different occasions.

In modern heraldry, the semy variant is called "France ancient", the three fleurs de lis "France modern". It is possible that the change was an attempt by the French monarchs to distance their arms from their old enemies the English kings, who, starting with Edward III (1327–77) had asserted their claim to the throne of France by quartering the French arms (France ancient) with the lion of England. If such

a ploy was indeed attempted, it did not work, for Henry V of England (1413–22) changed the French quarters in his arms to France modern.

HERALDIC PLANTS

As for other plant life in heraldry, it can lead from the exotic – as with the palm trees in the arms of Maintirano, Malagasy Republic – to the humble, including the potato flower of Ploudaniel, Finistere, France, and the thorn bush (Spina) of the Italian family of Malaspina.

The broom plant, or planta genista is the emblem of humility, and became the badge adopted by the royal house of Plantagenet. Wheatsheaves, or "garbs", according to Guillaume, were the symbol of plenty and could signify the "harvest of one's hopes". Fruits also symbolized plenty.

The clover leaf, or "trefoil" frequently appears, not least as the shamrock, the plant symbol of Ireland. If a narrow tapering stem is shown projecting from it (or from any other leaf or flower), it is said to be "slipped". Heraldic variants of the trefoil have different numbers of leaves: the quatrefoil (four leaves), cinquefoil (five leaves) and the octofoil (eight leaves), which in England is the mark given to the ninth son.

▼ The arms of the Italian Princes di Massa, which includes the thorn tree of the arms of the Malaspina family.

MONSTERS AND FABULOUS BEASTS

People like to be thrilled by the unknown or strange, so it is not surprising to find in medieval armorials many examples of mythological creatures such as griffins, dragons, centaurs, unicorns and mermaids. Such monsters may have been the product of pure imagination, but it is more likely that they were the result of the need to exaggerate – most medieval heraldists and their patrons having heard at second-, third-, or even fourth-hand of the strange and wonderful creatures discovered in the far-off Indies or Americas.

▶ *The arms granted to Josef Moise in 1867 during the reign of Emperor Franz Josef of Austria includes a fire-breathing panther.*

▼ *The vibrancy and imagination of medieval heraldry is shown here in the wyvern crest of Sir John Grey de Ruthin.*

We have seen how medieval heraldry treated the relatively familiar lion, putting it into positions that would probably cause the real beast to fall over backwards. The panther was depicted equally fantastically, usually spouting flames from nostrils, mouth and even ears. Medieval bestiaries were the fuel for further heraldic fancies. These works, often wonderfully illustrated, told of cockatrices, bonacons and wyverns: fabulous creatures best encountered only in books and manuscripts. So ferocious were they that often they could turn people to stone on sight, or kill with their breath. Most medieval folk believed these creatures really did exist, and for someone who considered even the next village to be foreign territory, monsters provided just one more reason not to venture far from their own doorsteps.

THE DRAGON

Said to be the greatest of all serpents, the dragon had a scaly body and wings (usually depicted as bat-like). Its head was often horned and tufted, its tail thorny and pointed. It is quite possible that it had its origins in the unearthed fossils of prehistoric beasts. The sheer size of the skeletons that would have been found from time to time throughout the known world, would have been enough to overawe the finder, and real dragons are still alive and well on the island of Komodo off Indonesia, tales of which must have passed between traders many centuries ago.

Dragons lived in caves or deep in the earth's core, where fire was their constant companion; no wonder then that dragons themselves could breathe fire. In British heraldry the dragon is shown with four legs, but this is a late development, for

▲ *A centaur with a bow aiming skywards, an apt charge to appear on a badge for a German Army anti-aircraft unit.*

▲ *The wyvern, a heraldic beast used in England who in earlier times may well have been a dragon.*

▲ *The heraldic griffin, often seen as the guardian of treasure.*

▲ *The bonacon here seems gentle, but its unique defensive technique was all too awesome and far from benign.*

before the 15th century it was usually shown as having just two. In English heraldry the two-legged dragon tends to be called a wyvern or a basilisk, though in the rest of Europe the matter is not so distinct.

THE GRIFFIN

The heraldic monster with the forepart of an eagle and the hindquarters of a lion is called a griffin, or gryphon. Although not quite as popular as the dragon in heraldry, it nevertheless captured the imagination of many noble minds, for the griffin was the guardian of gold and hidden treasure, and was therefore a creature to be met on many a medieval quest.

▲ *The unicorn on the arms of the Polish noble tribe of Boncza – one of the few mythical beasts in Polish heraldry.*

In British heraldry a so-called male griffin is shown without wings, its body covered in tufts of formidable spikes, which are usually of a different colour to the rest of its body. Confusingly, the ordinary griffin is also normally depicted as having male sexual organs: just what a female griffin should look like is not made clear by heraldic writers. In English heraldry the griffin when in the rampant position is described as being "segreant".

THE UNICORN

Many a medieval prince kept a so-called unicorn's horn in his collection of curios, though in reality this was likely to be the tusk of a narwhal. The subject of many noble fantasies and legends, the unicorn is considered by many to be the most beautiful creature in the heraldic menagerie. In effect it is part horse, part heraldic antelope, with a large twisting horn or tusk issuing from its forehead. It is also depicted as having a lion's tail and a little tuft of hairs under its chin. So pure a creature is the unicorn that it is often entirely white, apart from its horn, tufts, mane and hooves, which are gold. When regally collared and chained, unicorns are the supporters beloved of the Scots monarchs.

In medieval romances, tales were told of how the usually untameable unicorn would befriend a gentle damsel of noble birth whom it sensed to be a virgin. When the noble creature had found such a lady it would lay its head in her lap and go to sleep. It was only at such a moment that hunters could steal in and capture or kill this wonderful prey.

The purity of both the unicorn and virgin was made much of by medieval writers, who compared the two symbols to Christ and the Virgin Mary. Because of this sacred connection some heraldic authors of the medieval period considered that the unicorn should not be sullied by placing its image on shield or crest. However, by the 16th century it had become a popular charge in heraldry all over Europe, appearing on shields as far apart as Poland, where it is borne by the Herb (clan or tribe) of Boncza, and in Italy by the Bardi family of Florence.

▲ *An exotic flavour is given to the ancient theme of the mermaid in the arms of Mouila in the Gabon, where a sirene was said to haunt the local river luring men to her lair.*

OTHER BEASTS

Like the salamander, depicted as a lizard surrounded by flames, the phoenix often appears in the arms of towns and cities that have been rebuilt after destruction in war. Classical writers asserted that only one phoenix existed at a time, and lived for 500 years. Knowing its end to be near, it made a nest that the sun's rays ignited, frying the poor bird. Out of the embers came its successor.

A creature peculiar to English heraldry is the bonacon. Somewhat like a bull with blunted horns that were turned inwards, the bonacon was said to defend itself by emitting burning excreta which could cover an enormous area.

MARINE MONSTERS

The mermaid was busy luring sailors to various fates, happy or decidedly nasty, from earliest times. Said to be half woman, half fish, she probably arose from sailors' sightings of the dugong or sea-cow.

The sirene seems to be a curious cousin of the mermaid with two tails. A version is found in the arms designed in the late 20th century for the commune of Mouila in the Gabon. Said to appear from time to time to claim a local man for her husband, the sirene displays two splendid scarlet tails. The white sister of Mouila's sirene appears in the arms of several European families, including the Amari of Sicily.

INANIMATE CHARGES

Heraldry has always made full and free use of every kind of object, and coats of arms reflect life's events from the cradle to the grave. The arms of the French town of St Germain-en-Laye include a very grand baby's cradle that also bears the date – 5 September 1638 – on which the future Louis XIV was born. At the other extreme, the last resting place of one of the earliest humans, found during mining activities in northern Rhodesia (now Zimbabwe), is suggested by a skull in the arms of Broken Hill, granted in 1954. A complete skeleton in a somewhat reflective pose in the civic arms of Londonderry, Northern Ireland, recalls the unhappy fate of a local nobleman, Walter de Burgo, who was starved to death in a dungeon on the orders of one of his own family members.

CLOTHING AND ACCESSORIES

All kinds of dress can be met with, from the mundane (the breeches in the arms of the family of Van Abbenbroek from Zeeland) to the curious (a French wife's hood, the heraldic badge of the English 16th-century nobleman Lord Ferrers). As early as the 14th century, fashion was appearing on the nobleman's shield. The lady's sleeve or "maunch", which had a pendulous pocket to house the owner's prayer book or missal, was a popular charge in English and French heraldry throughout the late medieval period.

A medieval lady might well also have treasured a necklace of Baltic amber, such

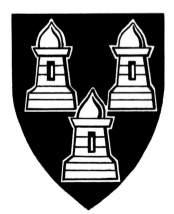

▲ *From the cradle – Louis XIV of France's birth is remembered in the arms of the town of St Germain-en-Laye.*

▲ *To the grave – a rather bored skeleton of Walter de Burgo in the arms of the city of Londonderry, Northern Ireland.*

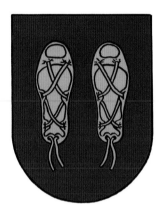

▲ *A pair of sandals is the charge for the Spanish family of Abarca.*

▲ *The buildings of the gentry – three of the cotes that they kept their doves in, the punning arms of the English family of Sapcote.*

▲ *The way we earn our bread – the sewing machine in the arms of Clydebank, Scotland, home of Singer sewing machines.*

▲ *The inventor, proud of his works – the corrugated boiler flue that made a fortune for Samson Fox of Harrogate.*

as the one found in the arms of the Lithuanian coastal resort of Palanga, where lumps of the fossilized resin are often washed up on the beaches.

BUILDINGS AND WORK

Fortresses and bridges appear on shields, as do homes, from the stone building in the arms of the town of Frontenhausen, Bavaria, to the Inuit igloo that forms the crest of the Territory of Nunuvut, Canada. Even the turrets of Indian homes, or *gonkhs*, find their way on to the arms of Halvad Dhrangadhra in Gujarat. A church features in the punning arms of the Asturian family of Iglesia.

The workplace, whether it be the coal mine of the community of Bütten (in the arms of Landkreis Peine, Westphalia) or a

▲ *The food we eat – the sugar loaves of Waghausel, Landkreis Karlsruhe, Germany, appearing here in the trademark of the sugar refinery of that town.*

▲ *The warrior chef. The cheese grater and noodle flattener crest of the Master of the Kitchens to the Holy Roman Emperor.*

sewing machine made in a factory at Burgh of Clydebank, Scotland shows that heraldry can reflect the lifestyle of the worker just as well as that of a medieval knight. Whether the corrugated boiler flue of Samson Fox of Harrogate, England or the section of bracing in the arms of the Bossom baronets (also English) constitute good heraldic charges, is open to dispute.

Both knight and motorway magnate need to eat, and the kitchen has often figured in heraldic imagination, sometimes turning the most mundane objects into comical or bizarre charges. Even the proverbial kitchen sink probably features on a shield somewhere – certainly the table does. Charges taken from the kitchen include the sugar loaf of Waghausel, Landkreis Karlsruhe, Germany; the standing dishes in the punning arms of the English family of Standish; a trivet (Trivet of Cornwall); and a kettle hanger for the town of Zwijndrecht in the Netherlands. So important was the medieval kitchen in the running of a noble or royal household that the Master of the Kitchens to the Holy Roman Emperor was afforded his own very distinctive crest – a cheese grater and a noodle flattener.

TRANSPORT

In the last two centuries the railway has cut its way across the heraldic shields of towns from Swindon in England to Kaisiadorys in Lithuania. The former has a conventional locomotive of the late 19th century (there was much correspondence between the town council and the College of Arms in London over the exact make of the locomotive), while in the arms of the latter, four stylized silver steeds, streaming steam and smoke, pass back and forth across a black shield to represent the two major railways running through the town.

Cars also found their way on to the proud shields of factory towns such as Koprovince in the Czech Republic, the home of the first Czech car, the President, which rolled off the production line in 1897. Air travel was to make its mark on shields from the early 20th century onwards, a startling example being found in the arms of the commune of Sandweiler

▲ *The four rather dashing stylized iron horses of Kaisiadorys, Lithuania.*

▼ *The President car on the arms of Koprovince in the Czech Republic.*

▲ *A jet lands on the runway of the airport at Sandweiler, Luxemburg. Traditional heraldic ordinaries with a modern flavour.*

▲ *The arms of the aviator, Mary, Duchess of Bedford, drawn up and insisted upon by her husband, in spite of the heralds' disapproval.*

in Luxemburg. Sandweiler is home to Luxemburg's international airport, so a passenger jet lands on an intersection of runways in the arms.

One aircraft that had rather a bumpy journey through the heraldic skies, made its maiden flight in the unofficial arms of Mary, wife of the 11th Duke of Bedford. The Duchess was a well-known lady aviator in the 1930s and her husband wished the College of Arms to record the fact in a

grant of arms to his wife, but the heralds would not sanction the design, which the Duke had himself helped to create, including the Duchess's favourite plane, the Spider. This seems not to have bothered His Grace one jot: he claimed that his family, the Russells, had long ago used arms not granted by any herald, and what was done in the past was good enough for his dear wife in her own time.

Even the parachute has been used as a heraldic charge, most notably in the arms of Ste Mére-Eglise in Normandy, commemorating the day in 1944 when the paratroopers of the US Army's 101st Airborne Division landed in and around the town's church – one man even found himself draped across the church tower, an event memorably depicted in the film *The Longest Day*.

SPORTS AND GAMES

Heraldry can also catalogue the lighter side of life, such as the tennis-playing youths in the arms of the Tosetti family of Massiola, northern Italy. In Britain where the weather is not so propitious for outdoor sports, board games find their way on to the heraldic shield, as in the arms of

the Pegrez family with its backgammon boards, and the arms of the Matthias family of Lamphey in Pembrokeshire: Gules on each of three dice in perspective Argent 11 ogresses six in front three on the sinister two on top.

▲ *A tennis match in the arms of the north Italian family of Tosetti, in which, for reasons unknown, the players are not wearing any clothes.*

▼ *Three backgammon boards appear in the arms of the English family of Pegrez.*

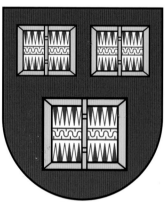

◄ *The arms for the French village of Ste Mére Eglise in Normandy, commemorates the landing of American paratroopers at the church, during the liberation of the region from Germany in 1944.*

▲ A skiing warrior in the arms of the town of Lillehammer, Norway.

▲ Arms of Sir George Edwards – blue skies and Concordes for a life in aviation.

▲ The town of Spa in Belgium, famous for its waters, has the old spa as its arms.

▲ The local coal mine in the arms of Bülten in Landkreis Peine, Germany.

▲ Oerlese and ...

▲ ... Rietze, towns in Germany that maintain a heraldic link with local farming.

▲ The sails of the ships in the arms of the Scottish Royal Burgh of Elie and Earlsferry are charged with the arms of local lords.

▲ The ship, star and crescent in the arms of the Danish port of Nörresundby were originally on a seal and adapted to a shield.

▲ A detailed depiction of an oared 18th-century sailing ship for the Crimean port of Kostroma.

PUNNING HERALDRY

The richness of heraldic imagery and imagination is nowhere more apparent than in those arms that have been devised as a play on the bearer's name. Punning or, as it is known in Britain, "canting" heraldry, can account for almost half the designs of some nations' heraldry.

Although the great majority of arms dating from the early days of heraldry were of a simple geometric nature, the heraldic imagination at work in the arms of León and Castile (which have always featured a lion and a castle) is a good example of the simplicity of the practice.

A PLAY ON WORDS

The motto of the Scudamores is *Scuto amore divinis* ("The shield of divine love"): the shield bears a gold field with a red cross patty fitchy. The Montagus (or Montacutes) bear three fusils (elongated lozenges) conjoined in fess, the tops of which are supposed to suggest the tops of mountains or *mons acutus*. The prize for the most tortuous wordplay must probably go to the arms of the powerful Mortimer family, whose arms include blue and gold bars with a white escutcheon over all. The blue represents the skies of

▶ *The simplicity of punning or canting – the quartered arms of Castile and León, Toledo Cathedral, 16th century.*

▲ *The three bear's paws of Trebarefoote.*

▲ *The three hands of Tremayne.*

▲ *The Scudamore shield of divine love.*

▲ *The family arms of Rotenhuet (red hat) of Silesia.*

▲ *The arms of the Rosensparre (rose chevron) family of Denmark.*

▲ *The family arms of Swinhufvud (swine head) of Sweden.*

the Holy Land, the gold its sands, while the escutcheon is said to represent the Dead Sea or *mortuo maris*.

In Cornwall, the local placenames offer plenty of opportunities for good puns on the number three through their common prefix "Tre". Trebarefoote has Sable a chevron between three bear's gambs (feet) erect and erased Or, and Tremayne has Gules three dexter arms conjoined at the shoulders and flexed in triangle Or, fists clenched Argent.

One of the most delightful examples has survived through the skill and imagination of the late medieval English stonemason who, asked to fashion the crest of a member of the Mordaunt family for a tomb in Northamptonshire, produced a grinning Moor showing all his teeth – literally "Moor's dents". A modern-day equivalent is the former Aeroplane and Armaments

▼ *The Moor shows off his splendid set of teeth in the Mordaunt crest.*

Experimental Establishment based at Boscombe Down in England. The English heralds came up with the local bird, a bustard, standing in a coombe (valley) on a down. That left the "Bos" which was provided by pinning the poor bustard's wing with the boss from a horse's bridle.

A EUROPEAN TRADITION

Medieval wordplay ranges from the commonplace to the curious. The Zurich armorial roll, held in the Swiss National Museum, supplies many splendid examples of punning German arms from the early 14th century. The Rand family arms are Sable a turnip Proper leaved Vert (*Rande* is German for "turnip"). The von Helfensteins of Swabia have Gules on a quadruple mount Or, an elephant statant Argent and as the Old German word for "beggar" is *betler*, the Betler family arms are Argent a beggar habited in Sable, his

shoes Or, on his shoulder a knapsack of the field, suspended by a cord Gules, a pilgrim's staff in his sinister hand, and in his dexter a begging bowl, both of the last.

Scandinavian heraldry has a long history of punning, and has made excellent use of the device. The medieval period produced the simple arms of the Swedish noble families of Sparre – Azure a chevron Or (*sparre* is a roof span, or chevron) – and Swinhufvud: Azure a boar's head couped Or (*swinhuf* meaning swine's head).

Probably the most innovative of modern punning heraldry emerged in Finland in the latter half of the 20th century. A good example is the arms of the municipality of Aanekoski, which translates from the local dialect as "sounding river" (*ääni* means "voice" and *koski*, "rapids"): Sable on a bend wavy Argent three horns stringed Gules.

▲ *The bustard stands in his coombe.*

▲ *The sounding rapids of Aanekoski, Finland.*

MESSAGES AND
DECLARATIONS

It might seem that once the design of a shield had been settled it would
never change. On the medieval battlefield or tourney ground this would
have been true, but heraldry is a great adaptor and certain traits have crept
in over the centuries that would not have been used by a 13th-century
knight. Above all, heraldry was the plaything of the European aristocracy,
and arms could be a useful way of accentuating their owner's place in that
closely knit class. Coronets of rank started to appear in the 15th century,
and special marks of favour granted by a grateful monarch could be thrust
in the faces of rivals by displaying them in a coat of arms. Relationships to
other families through marriage could be indicated by placing the two sets
of arms together. In England if a wife had no brothers she was deemed a
heraldic heiress, her children having equal right to have her father's and
mother's arms on heraldic quarters, and as other generations married
heiresses, so the original arms could be pushed into one corner of the
shield by other symbols.

◀ *The arms of the Princes Bagration of Russia, with
the princely mantle and crown.*

AUGMENTATION OF ARMS

Rulers have always availed themselves of orders and decorations to reward those who have served their country, but there is another way for a grateful ruler to thank the patriot or the peacemaker – by the augmentation of armorial bearings. Augmentations are additions to arms that in some way reflect the gratitude of the donor. They are added either by "honour"– when the grantee has performed deeds of merit – or by "grace", whereby the sovereign grants part of his or her arms to a relative. It cannot be said that Henry VIII did much for his wives, but he did give augmentations of grace to the families of three of them.

The augmentation is often a charge from the donor's own arms, or a new coat in the form of a quartering. In the latter case (in British heraldry) the new quarter of augmentation takes first place, with the old arms moving into the second quarter. Crests and supporters may also be given as augmentation. In Britain, an augmentation takes the form of a new grant from either the College of Arms (England and Wales) or Lord Lyon (Scotland), which tends to include a special citation mentioning the reason for the augmentation.

▼ Colonel Carlos' royal companion in the branches of an oak tree is commemorated in the family arms.

▲ Dr Lake bravely rides on in the crest of augmentation, while his 16 wounds are on the 1st quarter to the family arms.

AUGMENTATIONS OF CHARLES II

The reason for the granting of augmentations of honour is neatly summed up in the words of the English King Charles II who, after the Civil War, issued a warrant to Sir Edward Walker, Garter King of Arms, to grant "unto any person of eminent quality, fidelity and extraordinary merit that shall desire it, such augmentation of any of our Royal Badges to be added unto his Armes, as you shall judge most proper to testify the same".

Among the augmentations that Sir Edward granted, several referred to Charles II's escape after the defeat of the Royalist forces at Worcester in 1651, in which he was aided by loyal friends, Early in his escape, the King and his companion Colonel Careless evaded their pursuers by hiding in an oak tree at Boscobel House. This episode was remembered in augmentations to Colonel William Carlos (as his name was now) and the Penderel brothers, tenants of Boscobel. Both families received a full grant of arms which included an oak tree surmounted of a fess charged with three crowns.

Among other extraordinary episodes of the King's flight was riding pillion on the bay horse of Mistress Jane Lane, disguised

as a tenant's son. Not only were the Lanes granted a canton of the royal arms of England, they were also later granted a crest of augmentation: Out of a wreath Or and Azure a demi horse Strawberrie colour, bridled Sable, bitted and garnished Or, supporting an imperial crown Gold.

During the English Civil War an augmentation was granted to Dr Edward Lake for his valour at the Battle of Edgehill in 1642 when he was wounded no less than 16 times, one of which rendered his left arm useless. He was then said to have taken his horse's reins in his teeth, an action that is recorded in the crest of augmentation. All 16 wounds are also remembered in the coat of augmentation, which took the first quarter of his arms. This shows a dexter arm in armour grasping a sword, from which flies a flag of St George. The cross is charged with a lion

▲ The arms of Abensberg, Bavaria, (left), later augmented with swords (right) for the town's help in the Napoleonic wars.

▼ Drake's ship does its balancing act upon the globe of his extravagant arms.

▲ *The arms of concession to Christopher Columbus; the original family arms are in the base of the shield.*

passant guardant from the royal arms, and in each quarter of the flag are four red escutcheons, one for each wound.

VOYAGES OF EXPLORATION

The late medieval period saw the monarchs of Europe vie with each other in gaining for themselves the wealth of the wider world. They were aided by professional sailors who put their lives and ships at risk in return for a small part of the riches and prestige they might present to their sovereign, but all too often these great voyagers received shabby compensation for their efforts. They could, however, receive heraldic recognition. The shield borne by the descendants of Christopher Columbus contains four separate quarters as augmentations, the original family arms being relegated, almost as an afterthought, to a point in the base of the shield. A crest of the royal orb, a rare distinction in Spanish heraldry, was also given together with the motto:

A *Castillion y Leon, nuevo munda, dio Colon*, "To Castile and León, the new world was given by Colón".

Another explorer, Vasco da Gama, of Portugal, received the ancient shield of arms of Portugal as an augmentation: Argent five escutcheons in cross Azure each charged with five plates. He was also given the crest of a demi man dressed "a l'Indienne" holding a shield of the augmented arms and a branch of cinnamon, all evoking his epic voyage to India and the Spice Islands.

The English adventurer, Sir Francis Drake, was said to have been using the arms of another Devon family of the same name, whose head complained to Elizabeth I, calling the famous explorer an upstart. The Queen retorted that she would give Sir Francis arms which would far outshine those of his namesake. Those arms, Sable a fess wavy between two estoiles irradiated Argent, neatly sum up his voyages between the North and South Poles. The crest is a case of paper heraldry and could never be used on any helmet. Various depictions show a ship on top of a globe being guided by a hand from clouds, holding a golden cord; above the clouds a scroll with the motto *Auxilio divino* ("By divine aid"). The blazon of the crest also includes "in the ship a dragon Gules regarding the hand".

FRENCH AUGMENTATIONS

The French monarchs were not usually forthcoming with granting any augmentations, but they could not avoid acknowledging the part played by Joan of Arc in the eventual eviction of the English. In 1429, Charles VII granted to Joan's family a simple but splendid shield

▲ *Vasco da Gama's voyages to the Spice Islands are remembered in his crest of concession (augmentation).*

▲ *A diplomatic alliance remembered heraldically – the viper of the Viscontis is augmented by the fleur de lis of France.*

of a blue field charged with an erect sword supporting the French crown and two fleurs de lis in fess. These arms recall an account by the chronicler, Holinshed, that Joan wielded a sword "With five floure delices graven on both sides", and although there is no evidence to suggest Joan used the arms, they were used by the descendants of her brothers, upon whom Charles VII conferred the name Du Lys.

Both the Viscontis of Milan and the Medicis of Florence could be said to have been awarded augmentations "of grace" by French monarchs. In 1395 Charles VI

▼ *The arms of Joan of Arc's brothers' descendants, her sword upholding the crown.*

▲ *Heraldry in 3D: the arms of the Medicis with the topmost roundel charged with the fleur de lis of France.*

conceded by special diploma to Gian Galeazzo Visconti the right to quarter the arms of France (ancient) within a double border the external Gules the internal Argent. The Medici arms are thought to include a pun on their name, the red roundels in the shield possibly being pills (*palle*) handed out by doctors (*medici*). In 1465 Louis XI granted the Medicis the right to replace the top roundel with a blue one charged with three gold fleurs de lis.

RALLYING TO ARMS

The arms of many Polish families evolved on the battlefield, and they offer some unusual examples of augmentation. In 1386 the neighbouring states of Poland and Lithuania were joined through the marriage of the daughter of the last Polish king of the Piast dynasty to Grand Duke Jagiello of Lithuania. The Polish arms (a white eagle on a red field) were afterwards quartered with Lithuania's charging knight.

Under the Jagiellon dynasty, if a man was raised to nobility through valour, it became the custom to give him a shield charged with an arm in armour holding a sword. This coat was known as the "Pogonia". Later Polish kings – notably those of the Vasa dynasty – would grant foreigners, such as ambassadors, who had offered good service to the state, part of the Polish eagle as an augmentation. (Venetian ambassadors to London also managed to obtain augmentations to their arms, and several examples are extant which bear in their design the lion passant guardant Or of the English sovereign.)

The arms of Moravia, Azure an eagle displayed chequy Argent and Gules, have long been considered one of the most beautiful in medieval heraldry. When the Moravians came to the aid of the Holy Roman Emperor Frederick III (1440–93) he granted them the right to change the white chequers of the eagle to gold. In 1848, the year of revolution, Moravians supporting the Czech independence movement pledged support to the ancient eagle with white and red chequers, while German-speaking Moravians used the augmented gold and red chequered bird as their symbol.

Many Russian noble arms include the ciphers of sovereigns and charges taken from the arms of the Romanov emperors, but surely the most augmented arms of all must be those of Count Alexander Suvorov-Rymniksky, commander of the Russian Armies, whose brilliant strategies helped to bring about the eventual defeat of Napoleon. As commander-in-chief of the Russo-Austrian Army during the Second Coalition, he drove the French out of northern Italy in 1799 and was created Prince Italiysky. He had also previously defeated a Turkish force on the banks of the River Rymnik in Turkey in 1789. The augmentations to his arms included a "rendering of the map of Italy", an escutcheon bearing the name of Emperor Paul I, and two lightning bolts issuing from thunderclouds striking a crescent reversed above a river in bend inscribed *R Rymnik*. His services to the Russian nation were commemorated not only by an imperial decoration, but also by the Soviet Union.

▲ *The proud eagle of Moravia sports its distinctive golden chequers.*

► *Count Torelli's arms are augmented not only with the Visconti viper but also with his master's personal* impresta *and* motto.

The German emperors made full and free use of the Prussian eagle (often as supporters) in augmentations to those who had assisted in their rise to imperial power in the 19th century. Alexander von Schleinitz, Prussian Foreign Minister, received supporters to his arms of two Prussian eagles charged on the breast with the arms of Hohenzollern. Otto, Prince Bismarck, who brought about German unification, was granted a Prussian (black) and a Brandenburg (red) eagle as supporters: they supported two armorial bearings, those of Alsace and Lorraine, the territories regained from France in 1870–1.

LATER AUGMENTATIONS

In the late 18th and early 19th centuries heraldry in most countries was in a state of decay, or rather decadence. The augmentations granted to the military and

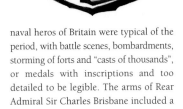

naval heros of Britain were typical of the period, with battle scenes, bombardments, storming of forts and "casts of thousands", or medals with inscriptions and too detailed to be legible. The arms of Rear Admiral Sir Charles Brisbane included a

chief "thereon on waves of the sea a ship of war under sail between two forts, the guns firing and on the battlements the Dutch flag all proper". Colonel James Stevenson-Barnes had a canton charged with his gold cross and the Portuguese Order of the Tower and Sword; his arms also included a chief bearing a curtain of fortification and the name *St Sebastian*.

Medals and decorations remained in vogue as augmentations to arms well into the 20th century. On 2 May 1918 the Finnish city of Vaasa was informed that: "To commemorate the time when Vaasa as the temporary capital was the heart of the liberation of Finland [from Russia], the Senate have decided to give the City the right to add the Cross of Liberty to its coat of arms." Another Finnish city, Mikkeli, housed the headquarters of Marshal Mannerheim's army, and on 21 December 1944 the medal of the Cross of Liberty was suspended from its shield. This was the second augmentation given to Mikkeli, in 1942 it was granted a pair of crossed marshal's batons.

▼ *One of three shield designs supplied by the heraldic artist to the Vaasa authorities for consideration. Here the augmentation is simply placed on the heraldic charge.*

▼ *Another suggestion put before the committee made the augmentation of the cross more prominent.*

▼ *In this suggestion the charge becomes secondary as the augmentation takes pride of place with the star of the order.*

ABATEMENTS AND DEGRADATIONS

Augmentations were marks of honour, given in the main to the strong and heroic, those who had rendered great service to their sovereign and their nation. But military men can also go astray. They may contravene the code of chivalry, or even betray their own country. What then should become of such traitors, debauchees, boasters and other miscreants? For the treacherous knight, his class had a most terrible ceremony – "the degradation from knighthood".

KNIGHTS AND KNAVES

John Selden, in his work *Titles of Honour* (1614), describes the case of Sir Andrew de Harclay, Earl of Carlisle, who in the 16th year of the reign of Edward II (1307–27) was condemned as a traitor,

▲ *The reversed royal arms of Portugal on the shield of Castello-Rodrigo, a rare case of an abatement put into practice.*

having secretly treated with the Scots against the King's favourite, Hugh Le Despenser. Edward was told of Harclay's doings and ordered the Earl's immediate apprehension. Harclay was seized at Carlisle and brought against a court of his peers. The Earl was found guilty, and sentence was pronounced against him that the sword (which he had received from the King "to defend his Lord" and with which he had been made Earl) should be taken from him, and his gilt spurs hacked from his heels by a "knave", after which the Earl's sword was to be broken over his head. The Earl was divested of his tabard, his hood, his coat and his "girdle". When this was done Sir Anthony Lucy (one of the judges) said to the Earl "Andrew, now art thou no knight but thou art a knave."

Selden also quotes the case of Sir Ralfe Grey, a Knight of the Bath who was

◀ *The defaced arms of Henry Courtenay, Marquess of Exeter, attainted and executed in 1539 after falling foul of King Henry VIII.*

▼ *The arms of Plommenfelt, a Swedish nobleman. His arms were erased after he was declared "dead" in punishment for slandering the Swedish king.*

degraded from knighthood. The Constable of England, being empowered to sit in judgement, said to the accused, "The King has ordained that thou should have had thy spurs stricken off by the hard heels, by the hand of the Master Cooke… and here thou mayest see, the Kings of Armes, and Heralds and thine own proper coat of armes which they should teare off thy bodie, and so shouldst thou as well be degraded of the Worship, Noblenesse and Armes, as of thy Order of Knighthood."

The Constable had with him another coat of arms, reversed (upside-down) as a sign of dishonour, which should have been worn by Sir Ralfe on his way to the place of execution, but it seems that he was spared this further token of degradation as the King remembered the good service done by the former knight's grandfather to the King's "Most Noble Predecessors".

In the case of knights of certain orders, the Garter included, further punishment could be expected. In addition to the measures taken during the service of degradation, their trappings of knighthood – targe, helm and crest – were to be torn down from their place in the chapel of the order, and literally kicked out into a nearby ditch; the knight's shield was also broken in pieces. In the Catholic Church a similar ceremony of defrocking was ordained as the most serious penalty reserved for clergy who had broken ecclesiastical laws.

CIVIC BETRAYALS

The 17th-century heraldist John Guillim cited the case of Sir Aimery of Pavia, a Lombard, an unworthy Captain of Calais in the time of Edward III (1327–77), who sold the town to the enemy for 20,000 crowns. Guillim described Sir Aimery's arms as "Light blue, four mullets yellow, two in fess, as many in the chief, reversed (upside-down)".

In Portugal, the town of Castello-Rodrigo was made to bear a shield charged with the arms of Portugal reversed, because the townsfolk had closed the gates on a rival claimant to the Portuguese throne who subsequently proved victorious. This is one of the very few cases of an abatement put into practice.

MARKS OF ABATEMENT

Various English books on heraldry include certain marks of dishonour that have been termed "abatements". They employ charges and stains – the lesser and rare colours tenny (tawny or orange) and sanguine (blood red) – borne together in a fashion otherwise uncommon in heraldry. The sixth edition of John Guillim's monumental work *A Display of Heraldry* (1724), "improved" by Sir George Mackenzie, listed the abatements. They are illustrated below. Most of these abatements were probably the doodlings of some herald in the Tudor period. The English herald J. P. Brooke-Little, in his foreword to his revision of Boutell's *Heraldry* (1970), asserted that "there is no such thing as a mark of dishonour in English heraldry." Nor does such a system exist anywhere else.

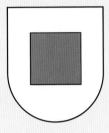

▲ A delf tenny: he who revokes his own challenge.

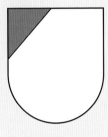

▲ Argent a point dexter parted tenny: a boaster of martial acts.

▲ Or a point in point sanguine: effeminacy.

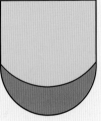

▲ Or a point champaine tenny: one who kills a prisoner after surrender.

▲ Argent a gore sinister tenny: a coward to his enemy.

▲ Or a plain point sanguine: a liar.

◀ A combination of two marks of abatement: Argent a gusset sinister sanguine: he who is "devoted too much to the smock", or womanizing, and Argent a gusset dexter sanguine: a man too fond of drink. If guilty of both, the man should bear both gussets, as here.

▲ The shield reversed: a traitor, also denotes death.

FANTASTICAL ARMS

Heraldry has long been seen as an accoutrement of the high-born, both present and past. From the 15th to the 17th centuries, heraldic writers increasingly sought to bestow arms on those of high rank in history and legend. Rulers, saints, biblical characters and legendary figures both good and bad, were assumed to have borne arms, as their like did in more recent times. No matter that documentary evidence was at the least scant, the heraldic writers felt that it was their duty to invent retrospective arms for those who were thought to be worthy of them.

HOLY ARMS

The holy Trinity – God the Father, Son and Holy Ghost – was represented in the "Arms of the Faith", the three joined in one upon the shield. The symbols of the Passion can often be found on a series of shields displayed in parish churches throughout Europe. The three kings, or wise men, who

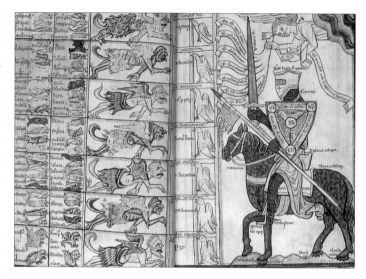

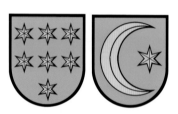

▲ ▼ *Attributed arms for the three wise men: Casper, top left, Balthasar, top right, and Melchior, bottom.*

visited the Christ child also had arms attributed to them by medieval heraldists. As for Satan, the Prince of Darkness, he also held a rank of sorts and was therefore afforded arms in medieval manuscripts: a shield with frogs and a fess accompanied him as he dragged the souls of fallen knights from the field down into hell.

In India, the arms of various Hindu gods, in particular Hanuman the monkey god, appear in the arms of several states.

▼ *The charge attributed to Hector, champion of Troy, and one of the Nine Worthies thought to deserve posthumous arms.*

▲ *A Christian knight, his shield charged with the attributed arms of the holy Trinity, rides out to fight vice and heresy, shown here in the form of devils, in a 13th-century illuminated manuscript.*

THE NINE WORTHIES

Many allegorical tales of the medieval period concerned the Nine Worthies of the World, a group composed of those who were believed to have been the greatest warriors of history. Their characters were especially appealing to the writers of the early Renaissance, who attempted to recreate their heroic feats.

Three of the Worthies were outstanding commanders of the classical world: Hector of Troy, Julius Caesar and Alexander the Great; three were biblical heroes of the Old Testament, Joshua, Judas Maccabeus and David; and three were European Christian warriors, King Arthur of the Britons, King Charlemagne of France, and Godfrey de Bouillon, the leader of the First Crusade. The Worthies of this splendid band were notable rulers and generals, men to be feared and followed, and would therefore surely all have merited arms. Consequently, armorial bearings were devised for all nine. The arms given to the Worthies by heraldic

▲ *Four Saxon kings who lived long before heraldry was established, are depicted with attributed arms in the quarters of the stained glass shield at Capesthorne Hall, Cheshire, England.*

▼ *The arms of the princes Bagration of Russia, whose ancestral claims are declared with King David's harp, and the sling he used to slay Goliath.*

writers of the 16th and 17th centuries reflected the attributes and character generally attributed to each man. Ferocity, bravura, steadfastness and mercy naturally featured strongly. Many of their arms therefore bear lions in various attitudes, and creatures such as wyverns, dragons and double-headed eagles. The Jewish heroes bore symbols usually associated with the Tribes of Israel.

OTHER ATTRIBUTED ARMS

Some families still extant today make use of arms attributed to supposed early ancestors of theirs. The English family of Temple quarters in its arms Or an eagle displayed Sable attributed to Leofric, Earl of Mercia, who was the husband of the more famous Lady Godiva. However, this claim to fame in family history is mundane compared to that of the Russian Princes Bagration, who claim descent from King David of the Jews,

◀ *A spirited depiction in Celtic style of arms attributed to King Arthur by the Cornish artist Dennis Ivall.*

and bear in their arms his harp, and the sling and stone with which he slew Goliath. Other Russian princely families bear in their arms the figure of the Archangel Gabriel, from whom they claim descent.

Men such as King David, Julius Caesar or Leofric, Earl of Mercia, all obviously lived long before heraldry was invented. The shields they were given posthumously are therefore called "attributed arms". Some of the most famous arms are those attributed to King Arthur and his Knights of the Round Table, and these have been extensively used in artistic depictions of the Arthurian legends from medieval times up to the pre-Raphaelites.

King Arthur has at least three separate shields of arms attributed to him, including Azure three crowns in pale Or, and Vert a cross Argent in the first quarter a figure of the Virgin holding the Christ Child Or. Arthur's first knight and champion, Sir Lancelot du Lac was given Argent three bendlets Gules, and Sir Perceval bore a shield Purpure semy of plain crosslets Or.

ALLIANCES

The joy of heraldry is that it can, by colours and symbols, make an instant visual statement in the most splendid manner, and over the centuries its supporters adapted it to suit their own needs. By the late 15th century, its purpose on the battlefield was in the main lost (due to the discourteous nature of gunfire and to the pride of the wearer in his splendid new "alwyte" armour), but heraldry found other uses. As far back as the 13th century, arms were being married to others to symbolize family ties through marriage, and that was not all they could express. Individuals of knightly rank could, and indeed did, make use of their arms to express ties of friendship and devotion, passion or duty.

EXPRESSIONS OF UNITY

In times gone by, kings would set their arms alongside those of other rulers to assert that they were part of an international élite without equal, and according to medieval thought it was a position they maintained when they were elevated to heaven, where a special "celestial palace" was reserved for the souls of deceased royalty. At the other end of the heraldic

▶ *The unity of marriage: again heraldry is utilized in a 15th-century manuscript which shows Isabeau of Bavaria arriving in Paris for her marriage to Charles VI of France, with their impaled arms much in evidence.*

hierarchy, the local landowner could also choose to decorate his castle or manor house with the arms of his equals in the locality. A charming example can still be seen at the former home of the Fairfax family at Gilling Castle in Yorkshire, England. The castle's Great Chamber was decorated in the Elizabethan period with a frieze of

▲ *As these crusading knights gather for their voyage to the holy land their arms are proudly displayed on shields and banners.*

painted trees, from which hang the shields of all the landowning families that governed the local administrative districts, or "wapentakes".

▲ *Another use of heraldry was to extol the merits of feudalism. In the Armorial General, 14th century, the arms of the King of England are followed by those of his vassals.*

Elsewhere the comradeship in arms of various knights was recorded less formally. Graffiti is by no means a product of the modern age: witness the crudely etched shields, crests and signatures scratched into the stone and plaster of the Sanctuary of the Nativity in Bethlehem some seven centuries ago by Crusaders, who were probably part of a contingent of knights from Flanders.

▲ *Alliances of brotherhood were an important function of heraldry in the 13th century, a fact borne witness to by the graffiti such as this crest left behind by crusading knights in the Church of the Nativity in Bethlehem.*

▶ *Three versions of the Brackenhaupt (hound's head) crest.*
1 Crest of Lentold von Regensburg.
2 The differenced crest of Oettingen.
3 The crest later adopted by Hohenzollern of Brandenberg.

CREST PARTNERSHIP

On 10 April 1317 Burgrave Friedrich IV of Nuremberg, a member of the Hohenzollern family, purchased a new crest for his arms from Lentold von Regensburg. Burgrave Friedrich paid 36 marks for the privilege, an enormous sum in those days. The crest in question was a golden *Brackenhaupt*, a hound's head with red ears. At the same time, Lentold von Regensburg reserved the right of certain of his relations to use the same crest during their lifetime. In September of the same year, the Burgrave exacted from Lentold another document in which the latter confirmed that, "I give full power and right to the Burgrave to use the crest as if I were present myself, in case others should contest his right to use it."

Prior to the purchase, the Burgrave had entered into a *Helmgerossenschaft* (crest partnership) with the Counts of Oettingen, the crest in this case being a *Schirmbrett* (wooden panel) ornamented with peacock feathers, typical of German crests of the period. This crest partnership had existed between the two families principally because of a marriage alliance, but had lapsed by the time that the Burgrave purchased the second crest from Lentold von Regensburg. However, the Oettingens attempted to cling to their interest in a possible succession to the estates of the Burgrave and promptly adopted the *Brackenhaupt*, much to the annoyance of the Hohenzollerns.

A lengthy heraldic dispute now ensued, which was resolved in 1381 when a panel of noble and royal arbitrators decided that the Oettingens could continue to use the gold hound's head, but would have to difference its red ears with a white saltire from the Oettingen shield of arms. Furthermore, it was decreed by the heraldic judges, the "saltire must be at least a finger's breadth and this clearly visible". The Oettingens have honoured this ruling to the present day.

GIFTS OF FRIENDSHIP

On some occasions, German knights purchased the arms of others. In 1368 Hans Traganer, sold his arms and crest to Pilgrim von Wolfsthal, vowing that he and his offspring, would from that moment forever cease to use their arms.

Arms and crests were not only sold but also handed over as gifts. In 1286, Duke Otto of Austria bestowed upon Count William of Julich his crest – a crown with peacock feathers – as a mark of friendship. In 1350, at the Holy Sepulchre in Jerusalem, Matthew de Roya bestowed upon the knight Hartmann von Cronenberg, his crest of a boar's head. Heraldry was symbolically important in medieval society in many different ways.

▼ *Alliances through marriage are recorded through a heraldic pedigree of the English family of Hesketh, 1594.*

THE ARMS OF WOMEN

From the evidence of seals, it would seem that between the 13th and 15th centuries it became customary for European noblewomen to use the arms of their fathers and husbands on shields alone, without a crest. The seals themselves were often of an oval shape, similar to those of ecclesiastical institutions and clerics. As with the seals of armigerous men, those of armigerous women also often show the bearer herself, sometimes holding a shield in each hand. Some medieval monuments also show women bearing shields.

STATUS IN THE FAMILY

Although heraldry by its nature related to the individual, it quickly became the ideal medium to denote noble alliances, none more so than marriage. By the 15th century a complex system of marks and marrying of arms could show the viewer the exact status of the per-

son or persons whose arms they were studying. Sons, daughters, wives and widows were all able to denote their place in the family unit. Furthermore, the family could show its alliance with other families of noble status through the heraldic pedigree. In Britain, this was particularly true during the Tudor and Stuart periods, when the old nobility was increasingly on the defensive against merchants and other "newly made men" who were keen to acquire the trappings of gentility, including of course, family arms.

The clues to marital alliances, so important to the nobility of Europe, and the symbols of marital status and placing in the family unit, are complex and evolved over centuries. These are ongoing, with new rulings being enacted in recent years by the heraldic authorities of Canada and England on the rights of daughters and married women.

▲ *Joan, Countess of Surry's seal, c1347, perhaps the origin of the lozenge shape that was later chosen to display a woman's arms.*

THE LOZENGE

A shield, being an article of warfare, was traditionally associated with men, and as such it was not considered appropriate for women. From the late medieval period, a diamond-shaped device – the lozenge – came into use for the armigerous lady

▼ *In the formative period of heraldry, 1150–1300, it is not uncommon to find women depicted with shields of their family arms, as here on this Welsh lady's tomb in the Priory Church, Abergavenny.*

◄ *The armorial garments of this medieval English lady were probably never worn but used simply as an illustrative device to proclaim her noble status on funerary memorials and manuscripts.*

▼ *Three generations of English women. From left: a widow with impaled arms, not an heiress, her daughter, a widow heiress, her granddaughter, a spinster, quartering her father and mother's arms.*

▲ *A depiction of the arms of Queen Juliana of the Netherlands before her succession as HRH Princess of Oranje-Nassau, Duchess of Mecklenberg.*

although, like so much in heraldry, just when the diamond was first used in this way is not clear. A remarkable English seal has survived from around 1347 for Joan, daughter of Henrie Count de Barre, widow of John de Warrenne, Earl of Surrey. Included in the seal's complex design are five tiny lozenges, the central lozenge bears the arms of Warenne, the lozenges in the flanks, of de Barre, and those above and below the arms of England – Countess Joan's mother was Eleanor, daughter of King Edward I of England. The seal is also diapered with castles and lions rampant for the countess's grandmother, Eleanor of Castile, first wife of King Henry.

By the 15th century the diamond or lozenge had become the normal platform for the display of the single woman's arms in Britain, France and the Low Countries, and so it continues to this day, the somewhat harsh shape being softened at times into the oval. However, whereas the oval has sometimes been used by men, the lozenge seems an entirely female device.

The unmarried woman simply uses her father's arms on the lozenge or oval, sometimes accompanied by a blue bow and

ribbon, a symbol of maidenhood. (A heraldic writer in the 1800s suggested that unmarried spinsters in danger of remaining so should unite in an "order of the lozenge" and advertize for partners.)

While a bachelor is entitled to the family arms on a shield surmounted by helm, crest and motto, in most heraldic traditions a woman, married or not, cannot bear a crest. In Germany an unmarried daughter

can bear the shield of her father's arms surmounted by a wreath or torse. In Scotland, a woman who is a clan chief is entitled to bear the crest above a lozenge or oval.

▼ *The lozenge is rather a hard shape and attempts were made to "feminize" it, as in this 18th-century display of the arms of the Duchess of Kendal, mistress of King George I of England.*

IMPALEMENT AND MARRIAGE

When marriage was depicted on seals and monuments in the early days of heraldry, it tended to be by way of complete shields of arms for the families of both the husband and the wife, shown separately. In the late 13th century a process started by which two separate arms were placed side by side on a shield. At first, in order to fit both arms on to a single shield, each was simply chopped in half, or "dimidiated", in a somewhat unfortunate way. This curious marriage of two separate arms did not persist for long, and by the end of the 14th century the practice of showing the full set of charges for both coats on one shield had become the norm. In heraldic terms, the wife is called "femme" and her husband "baron", which in this context does not indicate rank.

DIMIDIATION

An example of the earlier practice of dimidiation can be seen in the arms used by Margaret of France after her marriage in 1299 to Edward I of England. Before marriage, the Queen as a daughter of France would simply have borne the ancient arms of France. Queen Margaret's seal shows her shield divided in half vertically, with the lion of England for her husband on the dexter half, and the lilies of France on the sinister side. As both

▲ Dimidiation threw up some curious creatures, such as in the arms of the English port of Great Yarmouth. Here the royal lions of England have their hind parts replaced with herrings.

charges are cut in half by the dividing line, the front half of the English lion is married to the fleur de lis of France.

Not only marital coats suffered from dimidiation. The arms of some cities and towns (the English Cinq Ports being the most famous examples) also showed heraldic alliances in such a fashion, and dimidiation could result in some fascinating combinations. It is slightly modified in the arms of the Czech town of Zlonice.

▲ The dimidiated arms of Margaret of France after her marriage to King Edward I of England in 1299.

◄ In the arms of the town of Zlonice in the Czech Republic, the eagle's head transcends the impalement line.

▲ In much of Europe, when two arms are shown for husband and wife, the charges are turned to face each other; in heraldic terminology they are "respectant".

Here the sinister half of a black eagle is dimidiated with a coat per fess but, while most of the eagle is sliced through, its head is left intact and allowed to enter the dexter half of the shield.

IMPALEMENT

The word "impalement" sounds like some medieval form of torture (just as the "bend sinister" of the bastard seems to imply some hideous heraldic secret), but the term is simply used to denote a side-by-side alliance of two coats on a shield. It was the practice for which dimidiation paved the way, the difference being that impalement shows the charges of the two coats in their entirety. The only exception is made for some bordures or charges said to be "in orle", or following the edge of the shield. These are still cut off by the vertical division of the two coats. The placing of two or more separate coats of arms on a single shield is called "marshalling".

Marital impalement is particularly observed in British heraldry, yet even here there are differences in practice. In England it is used when the wife has brothers who will carry on her own family arms, so that she is not classed as a heraldic heiress. In such a case the children born to the marriage inherit only the arms of the father. In Scotland, however, impalement is used in

▲ This hatchment for a Dutch widow has her arms upon an oval-shaped shield as opposed to a lozenge.

▲ In the impaled arms of a French princess. The lozenge is within the cordelière.

▼ The arms of a Dutch widow impaled with those of her husband and surrounded by shields recording marital alliances.

▲ A page from a Flemish pedigree and armorial of 1590, with the husband's achievement (centre) turned towards his wife's lozenge.

both cases, whether the wife is a heraldic heiress or not. In France and the Low Countries no distinction is made.

In much of Europe a marital coat is denoted not so much by impalement as by two separate shields set "accolee", or side by side. Often these are tilted to touch each other at one corner, and the charges of each shield are turned towards each other, instead of facing to the left as is the more normal position. Should a bend be included in the design of the husband's arms this too is turned, giving it the appearance of a bend sinister. In Germany the shields of both husband and wife are surmounted by helm and crest; a display of two complete achievements is there known as an *Allianzwappen* or *Ehewappen*.

WIVES AND WIDOWS

In a recent ruling, the English kings of arms ordained that a married woman may bear her paternal arms, even if her hus-band is not armigerous, on a shield or ban-ner differenced by a small escutcheon of a contrasting tincture in the corner or else-where on the shield, in a manner most suitable to the design.

Furthermore, the ruling states that even if the wife comes from an armigerous fam-ily she may bear her husband's arms alone, the shield charged with a small lozenge. Widows revert to the lozenge but with the impaled arms of husband and wife. In Europe it has often been the practice for the widow's lozenge to be placed within a "cordelière" (knotted cord). In England a divorced woman may revert to a lozenge of her family's arms, her divorced status shown by the differencing of a small mas-cle in some suitable place on the lozenge.

HEIRESSES AND SIMPLE QUARTERING

From the late medieval period onwards, pedigrees and other family papers and memorials show the contents of shields being marshalled in an ever more complex way, through a heraldic stratagem known as "quartering". This was a method used throughout European heraldry, principally to display alliances made through marriage, and it indicates how

▼ *Many a church interior shows the pomp and piety of the local nobility through memorials that are bright with heraldry. This English couple have their family arms above their heads while the husband's family, the Newdegates, celebrate a previous marriage with quartered shields at the head and base of the memorial.*

estates or fiefdoms were established and built up through such alliances.

As with other aspects of heraldry, quartering differed in various minor ways between nations, and it is important to remember this when viewing a quartered shield. Mistakes can be made when reading the messages that are declared, unless the rules of the nation in which the arms evolved are also taken into account.

ESCUTCHEON OF PRETENCE

In England, a heraldic quartering occurs after a marriage with a heraldic heiress – a woman who has no brothers, so that her family lacks a direct male heir. In such a case, the husband, instead of placing his wife's arms beside his on the marital shield (as an impalement), places them upon a small shield in the centre of his own arms. This small shield is called an "escutcheon of pretence", the husband in this case "pretending" to be the male head of his wife's family. Any children born to such a marriage are entitled to bear not only their father's arms, but also those of their mother (on a shield for a son, or a lozenge for a daughter), as quartering.

HOW QUARTERING WORKS

In the simplest case, where just one heraldic heiress has married into the family, the shield or lozenge is divided in four quarters. The patrimonial arms appear in the top left and bottom right hand quarters (numbered 1 and 4) and the arms of the heiress are placed in the top right and bottom left hand quarters (2 and 3).

The next heraldic heiress who marries into the family again takes her family arms to her husband, who places them in the centre of the already quartered arms, as another escutcheon of pretence. In the next generation, these arms appear as a new third quarter (bottom left) of the quartered arms. The shield should always have an equal number of quarterings (although this was not so in past times), and until a third heiress enters the scheme, the patrimonial arms are repeated in the fourth quarter

▲ *In England the widow who is also a heraldic heiress reverts to the lozenge of her husband's arms with an escutcheon of pretence – here we see the arms of Nelson with a quartered escutcheon.*

(bottom right).This is all well and good until a fourth heiress is married.

Supposedly there can only be four quarters which have all now been used up, but heraldry can be pragmatic and the term "quarter" is used for any number of separate arms on one shield. It is possible for a newly armigerous man, without any quarterings to his family arms, to marry the heiress of an ancient family with many quarterings. The children of such a marriage will bear not only their father's arms, but also all the quarters of their mother's arms. Therefore in just two generations a shield can go from simple to complex.

NATIONAL VARIATIONS

Elsewhere, the adding of quarterings and the nature of what in England would be thought of as an escutcheon of pretence, have their own system and meaning. In Scotland the escutcheon is reserved for an important fiefdom, usually one associated with a title held by the holder of a peerage, while in Germany the escutcheon is normally reserved for the family arms and the quarterings are kept for the arms associated with various fiefdoms and families that brought territory to the estate now held by the family.

In Britain more than one crest can be borne by a family, usually when two or more surnames are used in a hyphenated form. Noble German families usually place a crested helm above the shield for each quartering, and some families of courtly or princely rank may display as many as 20 crests above the shield. In Scandinavia as

▼ *The escutcheon of pretence for an heiress is clearly displayed in the centre of her husband's shield.*

a family was advanced to a higher degree the arms tended to be augmented with the addition of quarterings – the escutcheon being kept for the original family arms.

In England and Wales, marriage to a non-armigerous wife was simply indicated by a blank impalement or escutcheon. It seems an absurdity, but some authorities thought it necessary to show the exact heraldic status of the husband. The pedigree books of the House of Lords for peers of the realm record many such heraldic curiosities. No similar practices seem to be employed outside England and Wales.

◄ *The arms of the Counts von Creutz in the House of Nobility, Helsinki. The background quarters were added as the family passed up the ranks of the nobility.*

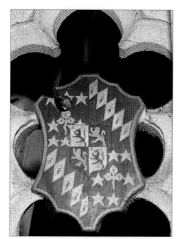

▲ *In Germany and Austria the escutcheon is usually reserved for the original arms.*

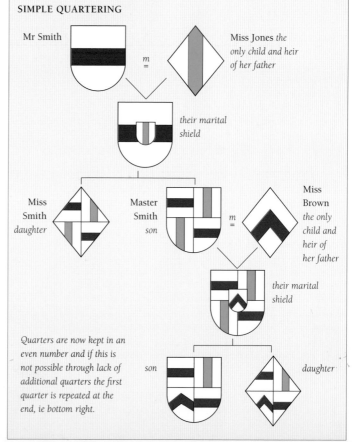

SIMPLE QUARTERING

Mr Smith   *m =*   Miss Jones *the only child and heir of her father*

their marital shield

Miss Smith *daughter*   Master Smith *son*   *m =*   Miss Brown *the only child and heir of her father*

their marital shield

son   *daughter*

Quarters are now kept in an even number and if this is not possible through lack of additional quarters the first quarter is repeated at the end, ie bottom right.

COMPLEX QUARTERINGS

In Britain, families of ancient lineage may have shields bearing many heraldic quarterings, sometimes running into hundreds. Heraldists divide into two schools of thought about multiple quarterings. There are those who despise such a shield, believing it to be a vulgar show of pretension. Others see it as a welcome chance for a piece of heraldic detective work – working back through the various quarterings with the help of pedigrees. A many-quartered shield can lead the viewer into all kinds of adventures when trying to decipher it: they may make their own family connection, or turn up stories of murder, mayhem, heroes and heroines. It can be fun to make a map locating all the families illustrated on just one shield, though in some cases the map will have to be very large.

REPEATED QUARTERS

Should an heiress whose family has amassed its own heraldic quarterings marry into the family, these are in turn placed in their own chronological order. The English scheme provides the viewer with no clue as to which heiress brought in which quarters, but Scottish heraldry provides the clue by keeping such a set of quarters together in an impartable group or "grand quarter".

In Britain, should an armiger have no sons but several daughters, each is classed as a co-heiress, and all are equally entitled to transmit their father's arms to any children they may have in marriage. Looking closely at the grand quarterings of the Dukes of Buckingham and Chandos, it is possible to see that some individual quarters are actually identical with others dotted around the shield, because they represent marriages to the descendants of co-heiresses, and since at any time the English aristocracy represents less than one per cent of the nation's population, marriage within that group is bound to throw up such heraldic curiosities.

The great Anglo-Norman family of de Clare terminated with the three daughters and co-heiresses of Gilbert de Clare, Earl

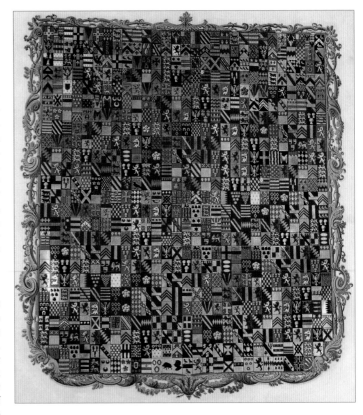

▲ Possibly the most impressive collection of quartering ever used for an English family, these are the 719 quarters of the Dukes of Buckingham and Chandos.

of Hereford and Gloucester (their brother, Gilbert, having been killed in 1313). These grand ladies were able to transmit the arms of de Clare, Or three chevronels Gules, to their children, who also married into great families. It was therefore possible for a family such as the Grenvilles to marry into other families of rank and antiquity, each of whom represented an heiress of the de Clares.

PEDIGREES

In continental Europe it was at certain times necessary for noble families to prove their ancestry by showing descent from 16 great-great-grandparents, all of whom were expected to be armigerous. Such an armorial pedigree is called "Proof of Seize-quartiers". Not only was such a proof desirable for those wishing to attend a

royal court or trying to enter one of the various orders of chivalry, but also for those attempting to become officers in certain military regiments.

A lesser pedigree was also often used in continental Europe for memorials, gravestones and the like. In such cases, the shield of the deceased would be placed in the centre of the memorial, and down either side would be shown all the shields of arms of the parents, grandparents and sometimes great-grandparents, both on the male and female side. These heraldic pedigrees in stone can still be seen in many European churches.

COMPLEX QUARTERING

This chart gives an example of how quarters accumulate over the generations, as heiresses marry into the family, and yet more quarters are added to the shield.

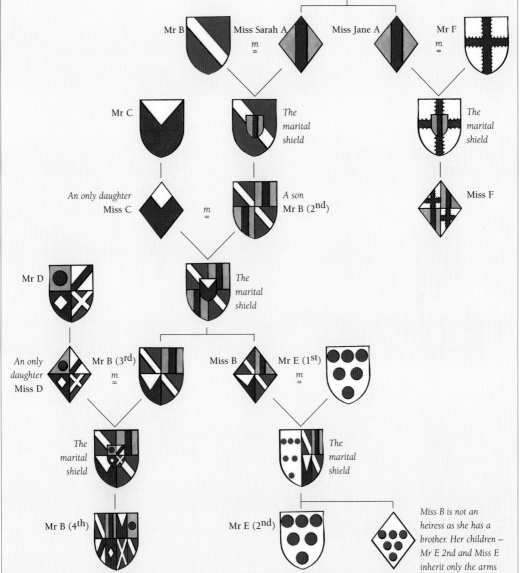

Mr A

Mr A *has no sons, his 2 daughters are termed co-heiresses and can equally impart their family arms to their children as a quartering.*

Mr B

Miss Sarah A

m
=

Miss Jane A

m
=

Mr F

Mr C

The marital shield

The marital shield

An only daughter
Miss C

m
=

A son
Mr B (2nd)

Miss F

Mr D

The marital shield

An only daughter
Miss D

Mr B (3rd)

m
=

Miss B

Mr E (1st)

The marital shield

The marital shield

Mr B (4th)

Mr E (2nd)

Miss B is not an heiress as she has a brother. Her children – Mr E 2nd and Miss E inherit only the arms of their father

DIFFERENCE MARKS AND CADENCY

It is said that the *raison d'être* of heraldry is its ability to celebrate the individual's identity in visual terms, so that the coat of arms can be thought of as the pictorial signature of the bearer. Just how individual the arms are, in fact, depends on the nationality of the user. For instance, in Poland an identical coat of arms may be borne by many different families with no blood relationship because it is used by a whole tribe, or *ród*. In some countries, personal shields are distinguished only between branches of royal houses. In Scotland families update their heraldry through a process of rematriculating their arms through the court of Lord Lyon. The distinguishing features used for this are known as "cadency" or "difference marks".

▼ *English cadency marks, as set out in the 6th edition of John Guillim's* A Display of Heraldry *(1724).*

SONS AND DAUGHTERS

Much of heraldry can be accused of sexism, as daughters are not considered as important as their brothers. In England, until recently, they were afforded little notice at all unless they were classed as heraldic heiresses. Even then, should there be several daughters and no sons, the daughters had no marks of difference or cadency between them, each bearing an identical lozenge of their father's arms. On the Iberian peninsula the situation seems to be much more sensible, and the female side of a family is considered every bit as important as that of the male. In Portugal anyone is entitled to choose their surname and arms from whichever side of the family they wish, and a system of difference marks denotes from which side of the family the arms are derived and whether they come from parents or grandparents.

The newest national heraldic authority,

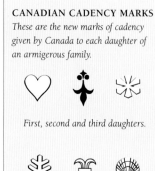

CANADIAN CADENCY MARKS
These are the new marks of cadency given by Canada to each daughter of an armigerous family.

First, second and third daughters.

Fourth, fifth and sixth daughters.

Seventh, eighth and ninth daughters.

that of Canada, has also given difference marks to each daughter in the same way that sons have their coats differenced.

MARKS OF CADENCY

While difference marks may be applied to a variety of family and heraldic relationships, cadency tends to be used to indicate sons. It is very much the preserve of English heraldry, in which a set of small marks are placed upon the shield for male children up to the ninth son. The heraldic writer Beryl Platt sees their origin in the symbols adopted by the heirs of Charlemagne. She belives that the Count of Boulogne, whose family used these marks, had set great store by the dialogues of the Emperor Charlemagne with his confessor Alcuin, and would have found references there to heavenly and natural symbols as inspirational devices. In Boulogne the sun stood for the Count, the crescent for his second son, the star for his third son, and the bird for his fourth son. The cadency marks of later children could also have been taken from Charlemagne's dialogues. The most important and fre-

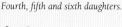

The First House.

The Second House.

The Third House.

The Fourth House.

The Fifth House.

The Sixth House.

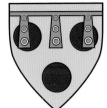
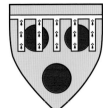

▲ *Medieval difference marks for members of the Courteney family of Devon, England.*

quently used mark is the "label". It is an addition to arms not only in English heraldry, but also in Scotland, France, Spain, Portugal, Belgium and Italy. In England it has long been used as the mark of the eldest son, and a plain white label is given to the heir apparent of the sovereign.

The origin of the label might be found in the sculpted shield of a 13th-century English knight, probably Sir Alexander Giffard, in Boyton, Wiltshire. The shield bears the ancient arms of Giffard – Gules three lions passant Argent. Over the whole shield there is the label, most probably representing a cord stretched over the charges on the shield. From the cord were attached several ribbons, and at this early stage their number seems not to have been of any significance (Sir Alexander's shield shows five ribbons). By the late 15th century, how-

ever, three ribbons or "points" seem to have been fixed as the number for an eldest son. Such is the finesse of the stone carvers' work at Boyton, the contrasting crudeness of the label shows clearly its deliberately temporary nature. It would seem that the eldest son was expected to remove the label when he became head of the house.

Other sons, from the second to the ninth, all have their own cadency marks, but there is no rule about the use of such marks (which are usually placed in the centre chief point). It is possible for sons of sons of sons to place their own cadency mark on a cadency mark, and so on, but this may become an absurdity as the mark becomes so small as to be useless. Furthermore, should any quarterings be added by a family branch (through marriage to a heraldic heiress) this would in itself be considered sufficient difference as to negate any need for a cadency mark.

Adopted children may use the arms of their adoptive parents (after a royal licence has been granted to do so), charged with two interlaced links of a chain. In certain cases, an English family may assume the arms of another through royal licence, usually because of a so-called "name and arms clause" in the will of the last of a line. Often this was done when the father of an heiress wished to see his family arms and name continue, as on the shield of Vere Fane-Bennett Stanford of Preston, England. His wife's arms appear twice, once on an escutcheon and also as the first quarter of the main shield, differenced by a cross crosslet, as there was no descent by blood.

Recently English married women have been allowed to bear (if they should wish to) their own family arms alone on a shield, as opposed to their marital arms. This is made clear by the inclusion of a small blank escutcheon on the main shield, as seen on the arms of Margaret Thatcher.

▼ *The shield of Sir Alexander Giffard of Boyton, showing how the first labels might have been temporarily constructed.*

▼ *A blank escutcheon in the arms of Baroness Thatcher denotes that these are her own arms, rather than her husband's.*

▼ *The arms of Vere Fane-Bennett Stanford, who assumed the arms of his wife's family, differenced by cross crosslet.*

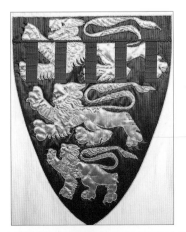

HOW A MEDIEVAL FAMILY USED ITS ARMS

*S*i monumentum requiris, circumspice ("If you would see his monument, look around"): these words, carved above the north door of St Paul's Cathedral in the City of London, refer to the cathedral's designer, Sir Christopher Wren. Yet the very same words could have been used by many men centuries before Sir Christopher's age, who, through heraldry on castle and in church, sought to ensure their family's and their own immortality.

One medieval family of the West of England, the Hungerfords of Farleigh Castle, afford an example of the none too subtle way in which the nobility of Europe sought to stamp its authority over vast tracts of land and all that lived upon it. In stone, stained glass, parchment and needlepoint, the Hungerfords and many of their kind used heraldry to make a statement: "I am my arms. Hurt them and you hurt me – at your great peril be it."

▼ *On the ruins of Farleigh Hungerford Castle, the family arms above the main gate still proclaim the Hungerfords' lordship.*

ASSERTION OF IDENTITY

The Hungerfords were not remarkable in any way, but were typical of their times: sometimes cultured, sometimes violent, self-made, monied, landed, immensely proud, medieval in thought and deed. The family enjoyed its heyday in the late 14th and early 15th centuries, just at the time when the rival royal houses of York and Lancaster were flexing their muscles. It also happened to be the peak of that English heraldic phenomenon, the badge or cognizance; and the Hungerfords made the fullest possible use of their own device – a sickle or, its variation, three interlaced sickles – in many different ways.

Heraldry played a large part in the noble family's daily life. The Hungerfords stamped their arms on seals, barns, outbuildings and chantries, and set their sickles on seats, ceilings and church towers. Walter, 1st Baron Hungerford, a friend and adviser to the Lancastrian kings, had his arms set, as was his right as a Knight of the Garter, within the Chapel of St George in Windsor Castle itself. At court

▲ *A roof boss in St Thomas' Church in Salisbury denoting the trappings of patronage. It was the Hungerford family's large donations that helped to pay for the church's restoration in the early 1600s.*

he would probably have donned his great collar of "Ss", the livery collar of the dynasty he served so faithfully.

THE ACQUISITION OF ARMS

Although not perhaps remarkable in their class and time, the Hungerfords are intriguing in their use of arms, possibly taking as their own the arms of the Heytesbury family (Per pale indented Gules and Vert a chevron Or), whose

▼ *The quartered arms of Heytesbury and FitzJohn (Hungerford) appear in an elaborate medieval tiled floor from their former property at Heytesbury.*

▲ *The much-used sheaf and sickle crest of the Hungerfords is carved in stone on the roof of St Thomas' Church, Salisbury.*

▼ *The Hungerfords made full use of heraldic seals. The top seal, of Sir Robert Hungerford before 1449, differences not only the arms but the banners, crest and badge of his father, Lord Walter, while the bottom one also includes the supporters.*

heiress had married a Hungerford. They also seem to have done the same with the arms of another family, FitzJohn of Cherhill (Sable two bars Argent in chief three plates), which later became the acknowledged arms of Hungerford.

The Hungerford crest of a "garb" (a wheatsheaf) between two sickles may also have been adopted from that of another family, Peverell; such arms of alliance were not unusual at the time. The Hungerfords had most probably originated as lower gentry and were non-armigerous, becoming so through marriage with the heiresses of more well-to-do families. Even the nature of the garb in the Hungerford arms has an element of mystery about it – is it in fact a sheaf of wheat or pepper, a play on the name Peverell? The Hungerfords delighted in the use of their sickles, often charging their memorials and property with interlacings of sickle, a design well suited to many household ornaments and items of furniture.

In the will of Lord Walter Hungerford, Knight of the Garter (proved at Croydon, 21 August 1447), his son Robert was left

▲ *Along with other families of their time, the Hungerfords took the arms of more influential families for their own. In time the bars and roundels of the FitzJohns became the accepted arms of Hungerford. They also changed their crest from the talbot's head to the garb of the Peverells.*

"2 altar cloths of red crimson velvet, with diverse compresses de sykeles curiously embroidered…my great alms dish of silver having on each side a lion supporting my coat of arms; and a pair of silver dishes bearing knots of sickles". Sir Robert Hungerford was, according to his father's will, to bequeath these items to his heir.

The Hungerfords, proud and privileged as they undoubtedly were, lived in a troubled age. In the records of the time we can read of a rising in 1400 against King Henry IV, during which the rebels took several of the King's "lieges" (lords) prisoner. They compelled Lord Walter, "the King's Knight, to go with them and robbed him of the King's Livery called 'Colere' [the collar of Ss] which he was wearing, worth £20", an enormous sum in those distant days.

▲ *Like his father, Robert, 2nd Baron Hungerford was a staunch supporter of the House of Lancaster, and proudly wore the collar of Ss of that house.*

Times were to get better for Lord Walter, for in December 1418 he was rewarded with the Lordship of Homet in Normandy in return for an annual fee of a lance to which was attached a fox's brush (tail), one of the heraldic badges of Henry IV. However, a large part of the Hungerford revenues which arose from the acquisition of spoils in the French wars were used to bail out Lord Walter's grandson, Sir Robert, who was taken prisoner at the Battle of Castillon in 1453, a battle which brought the Hundred Years' War to a close with defeat for the English. One of the members of the deputation sent over to France to treat with Sir Robert's captors was Chester Herald – fulfilling one of the many duties undertaken by the heralds of the time.

HERALDRY AND ETERNITY

The Hundred Years' War, the Black Death and death in childbirth were among many perils the Hungerfords had to face, just as they reached the peak of their power in the English West Country. Beyond death, there was Purgatory, that period in which souls were lodged in Heaven's waiting room, waiting for their family to purchase a promotion heavenwards through prayer and good deeds. Here too, heraldry had its part to play. The Hungerfords, in common with many of their peers, endowed "chantries", chapels where the priests were employed solely to sing or chant daily masses for the noble benefactors. The wills of the latter make frequent mention of the trappings of their chantries and the priests that served

them. Presumably it was hoped that, if God in his Kingdom was looking down, he would notice the arms and badges of the noble family concerned and be grateful for the display. That, at any rate, must have been the thinking of Lord Walter, when he gave to the Abbey Church of Bath a cope of red velvet patterned with waves, and two other copes of gold damask velvet, that was "worked with myne armes for better memory".

The theme was taken up in the will of Lord Walter's daughter-in-law, the formidable Margaret Botreaux, Lady Hungerford. In the document she bequeaths to the Priory of Launceston (in Cornwall) a pair of vestments of red and green (the Hungerford livery colours) with the arms of Hungerford and Botreaux on the cross, and a further new pair of vestments to be worked with the arms of Hungerford, Beaumont and Botreaux. At

▼ *The finesse of the medieval craftsman is apparent in this complex seal design of Margaret Botreaux, widow of Robert, 2nd Baron Hungerford.*

▲ *Heraldry could be used in the most mundane ways. Here it embellishes the lock plate of the family vault at Farleigh Hungerford.*

▲ *Ever the self-publicists, the Hungerford family placed its heraldry on all kinds of property. This interlaced sickle badge was uncovered recently above a false ceiling in a farmhouse, some five centuries after its crude manufacture.*

▼ *Keeping the money in the family, a Hungerford marries his cousin. The crescent, centre left, denotes the younger branch on these impaled arms.*

Salisbury Cathedral, the wonderful altar cloths that the Lady Margaret gave included several bearing Lord Hungerford's crest and arms. Even the chantry chapels themselves, as in the case of the Hungerford Chapel in Wellow church, near Bath, might be brightly painted in the family livery colours.

On Salisbury Plain, over the borders of Wiltshire into Somerset and Gloucester and far and wide in the West Country, the Hungerford name spread itself. Whenever they acquired land, and wherever they had their souls prayed for, they stamped their authority through heraldry. Even on their last journey, entombed in their coffins, the Hungerfords could still afford a final nod to their arms, as the lock panel on their own family vault at Farleigh Castle was charged with the Hungerford shield. So famous were they in the West Country that other noble families in the area were keen to show an attachment to them through arms. In the 18th century, long after the Hungerfords had left the Plain, the Pleydell-Bouveries chose to use Lord Walter's chantry chapel in Salisbury Cathedral for their own pew, decorating it with over 50 shields of arms recording the Hungerford marriages and their descent from that family.

▲ *The priest of the Hungerford family, at Wellow church, Somerset, was surrounded by the heraldry of those he was expected to pray for, from the family arms to their red and gold liveries used as ceiling patterns.*

▼ *In common with others in that exalted band, the Knights of the Garter, Walter, 1st Lord Hungerford's arms appear on his stall plate in St George's Chapel, Windsor.*

PATENTS OF ARMS

From the late medieval period, those who were granted arms usually received them by way of a document, written on parchment, vellum or paper. The earliest form of patent was quite simple, a single sheet with the seal authorizing the grant suspended from it by a cord. The arms of the recipient were portrayed in colour, either in the margin or in the centre of the document. A legally worded text, in Latin or the language of the issuing authority, described the arms and to whom the grant was made.

Patents of arms gradually became more elaborate, and their decoration might include the armorial bearings of the sovereign or heraldic authority. In English patents, the leading capital letter might enclose a portrait of the king of arms who had signed and sealed the document. The borders and headings of the patents

▲ *A detail from the Deissel grant shows the fine workmanship of the trained miniaturists responsible for much of the heraldic art of 17th-century Austria.*

▼ *A grant of arms for Jacob Johann Deissel, an Austrian doctor, who was ennobled in 1663 by Emperor Leopold I. It is a typical example of 17th-century arms produced for the scientific, military and government personnel who served the imperial household. The grant was presented in a unique iron case and a wooden sealbox.*

became heavily embellished with scrolls and strapwork, interspersed with birds, flowers, beasts and allegorical devices. Sometimes the actual coat of arms appears almost as an afterthought.

While English and Scottish grants have kept much to their original format (on a

single sheet), those of other nations generally assumed book form, with one page devoted to a painting of the armorial bearings (often within a landscape) while other pages describe the grantee's genealogy, titles and personal history. The cover was often of leather or velvet, embossed with the arms of the sovereign.

Today, those national heraldic authorities that still exist keep in the main to the traditions set down centuries ago in their particular country. When drawing up patents of arms, therefore, the book form of the patent still exists in Spain while the single sheet form is still framed in England, Scotland, Canada, and the Netherlands. Ireland has more recently taken up the book form of the patent.

The selection of patents and grants shown on these pages date from the 17th to the late 19th century, and are from a collection in the possession of the celebrated Dutch heraldic artist and engraver, Daniel de Bruin. The collection offers a remarkable glimpse into the artistic traditions of several major European heraldic authorities. It also offers an insight into how heraldry continued to reflect the political affiliations of the individual states, the rewards given by rulers to their loyal subjects and servants, and the continuity of a heraldic tradition. The grants also show the charm and expertise of the artist's work in attempting to make a standard document personal.

Sadly, the wonderful tradition of the illuminated patents came to an end with the fall of the monarchies after World War I, but by that time most such documents had evolved to a standard printed form where only the armorial bearings were

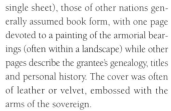

▶ *An Austrian patent of nobility of 1819, presented to Karl von Rodiezky Freiherr von Weizelbrag, a military officer who fought against Napoleon. The imperial arms are flanked by those of the provinces in which Rodiezky served. The style of the grant, with its spirit of conservatism, is typical of those produced in early 19th-century Austria.*

◄ *This Dutch grant of 1829 by King William I of the Netherlands to the family Van Herzeele, maintains the medieval form of patents: it is drawn up on a single sheet, with the text run around a depiction of the arms and a seal at the base.*

painted and the letters handmade. Yet, in recent years the College of Arms in London has returned to the more ancient form of having elaborate illuminated borders

▼ *The cover of a grant of arms by Emperor Franz Josef of Austria, c1867, employs the imperial eagle. The wax seal is protected by a metal seal cover.*

included in the patent or grant. This form of illustration has led to a flowering of artistic talent and style, which echoes that of the late medieval period through to the 18th century. Provided the client can afford the required fee, a patent's border may bear a collection of flowers and foliage, individual badges and charges taken from the arms of the grantee, fanciful creatures, or birds and animals found in the grantee's home or locality.

This wide choice of pictorial elements in the grant happily continues the tradition illustrated by the 1663 grant to the Austrian doctor Jacob Deissel, in which the local flora of his land is depicted and his profession symbolized; while in the grant of 1795 to the Hungarian Georgievies brothers, the left hand corner shows a local scene that probably includes a picture of the brothers' family mansion.

▶ *A 1745 patent of Maximilian III, Elector of Bavaria, to Philipp Paret. The pages of the book patent record the brave conduct of the ennobled Paret during his time as an officer in the imperial Wallonian Dragoon Regiment.*

▲ *A grant of 1795 to the Georgievies brothers by Emperor Francis I, King of Hungary. The arms of the provinces decorate the canopy.*

▶ *A grant of 1767 by Empress Maria Theresa of Austria to a Dutch banker, C. A. Verlugge. The imperial arms are flanked by the arms of Hungary and Bohemia.*

TANDEM BONA CAUSA TRIUMPHAT

APPLICATIONS
OF HERALDRY

—

HERALDRY HAS ALWAYS APPEALED TO THE PROUD, THE ROMANTIC
AND THE RICH. AS A RECORD OF LINEAGE, IT WAS AN INTRINSIC
PART OF THE PAGEANTRY OF ROYALTY, BUT IT WAS NOT THE
EXCLUSIVE PROVINCE OF THE NOBILITY. IT HAS BEEN ADAPTED TO
SERVE RELIGIOUS FOUNDATIONS, CITIES AND PROFESSIONS.
DURING THE AGE OF EXPLORATION THE FASHION FOR ARMS WAS
CARRIED AROUND THE WORLD, AND IN TIME DISTINCT NATIONAL
STYLES AROSE. THROUGH ITS ABILITY TO ADAPT TO CHANGING
TIMES AND NEW USES, HERALDRY REMAINS ALIVE AND WELL, AND
MORE ARMS HAVE BEEN GRANTED IN THE LAST CENTURY
THAN IN ANY PREVIOUS AGE.

◄ *A manuscript from the 15th century shows the*
Holy Roman Emperor and the imperial arms, sur-
rounded by the seven electors and their arms.

TIBI FIDELIS

ROYAL HERALDRY AND NOBILITY

The heraldic achievement presents a picture of the family history and
alliances that have placed a monarch on the throne or a duke and duchess
in their castle. Royal and noble families have always been keen to display
this effective indicator of their lineage and title, and occasions of state
ceremonial provide welcome opportunities for the full splendours of
heraldry to be seen and enjoyed. Much of the pomp of such occasions
derives from the strict observance of distinctions of rank; as heraldry has
developed its refinements have included numerous details that define
positions in a social hierarchy, whether of royalty, nobility, military
order or the church.

◄ *The arms of a British peer, Lord Howe, with the
supporters, coronet of degree and helm allowed by
his rank – that of baron.*

ROYAL HERALDRY

For centuries royalty has been seen as the fount of all noble titles and grants of arms, so it is not surprising to find that monarchs availed themselves of heraldry. Yet crowns, sceptres, orbs and other royal trappings were latecomers to the world of heraldic accoutrements. Until the late 15th century, there was seldom anything to differentiate the heraldic achievement of a king from that of a knight. However, on seals of the late 13th and early 14th centuries, crowns were sometimes depicted over the shields of royal individuals.

CROWNS

Heraldic crowns were imitations of actual headgear worn by monarchs. By the late 16th century royal crowns were often depicted with crimson or purple caps within them, and were embellished with raised "arches", decorated with gems and pearls, rising from the circlet and crossing over the head. In some royal families the number of arches was reduced for lesser members. While the English sovereign's crown has two intersecting arches, for

example, the coronet of the Prince of Wales has only one. Other members of the royal family have coronets without any arches.

▼ *The coronation of the English King Henry IV in Westminster Abbey, 1399. The royal arms are held by officials before the dais.*

▲ *The arms of Anne, Princess Royal of Great Britain. The supporters and lozenge are both charged with a personal label (labels are used by both male and female members of the British royal family). The coronet is that of a son or daughter of the sovereign other than the heir apparent.*

▲▼ *Subtle differences of rank can be shown by coronets surmounting the royal arms. Above is the coronet for a Swedish royal prince, below, that of the heir to the throne.*

▲ *The arms for the Counts of Rosenborg, the title given to Danish royal princes who married morganatically – marrying outside royal rank.*

▲ *The Portuguese Duke of Coimbra (d1449) bears a label taken from the arms of his maternal family, the Dukes of Lancaster.*

▲ *The white label of the royal line of Orléans on the arms of France was further differenced by crescents for the Counts of Angoulême, a junior branch.*

The crown of the dauphins of France, after 1662, had arches formed of dolphins, taken from the charges in their arms.

Elsewhere there was less differentiation between family members. In Austria, for example, the emperor bore a curiously shaped crown with high arches enclosing jewelled "horns", but the crown prince and all the other archdukes bore identical crowns of more conventional appearance.

Today, some republics still retain the trappings associated with former royal powers. In Hungary, the 1,000-year-old

▼ *The personal arms of King Matthew Corvinus of Hungary (1458–90) are placed over quarters for Hungary ancient, Hungary modern, Dalmatia and Bohemia, and surmounted by St Stephen's crown.*

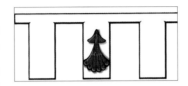

▲ *The label of Prince William of Great Britain. The escallop is taken from the arms of the Spencers, his mother's family.*

crown of St Stephen, considered one of the finest examples of the medieval goldsmith's craft, is such a symbol. The crown's history is remarkable: having many times been hidden, stolen, lost and found, after World War II it was spirited out of Hungary to America, where it was kept safe from the Hungarian communist authorities. It was returned in 1978 and is now in the National Museum in Budapest.

The absence of a crown can be just as telling. The Swiss, proud of their freedom from any royal authority, often placed the peasant's hat of William Tell over a shield bearing the arms of the various cantons.

Although the crown is the most obvious sign of royal rank, the arms of the sovereign are often accompanied by a pavilion or robe of estate strewn with crowns or charges taken from the royal arms, and the shield is surrounded by the orders of chivalry specific to the monarchy. The pavilion is a domed tent surmounted

by the crown, with its sides drawn back to display the royal arms placed within it. Though it is common to the arms of most sovereigns, it has never found favour in British royal arms.

ROYAL DIFFERENCE MARKS

In Britain particularly, marks were added to the shields of sons and other relatives to distinguish them from the head of the family. The descendants of British kings also bore such marks, which were known as "brizures", which mainly consisted of labels, bordures and bends. For centuries the heir apparent to the sovereign has borne a three-pointed label. The earliest example seems to have been Azure, and the number of points could vary, but during the lifetime of Edward the Black Prince (1330–76), it became normalized as three points Argent. The Black Prince was created Prince of Wales in 1343, and the same label is still borne to this day by the heir apparent to the sovereign.

Other children of a British sovereign use labels bearing small charges that are mainly taken from royal badges, such as roses or crosses of St George. For some centuries the grandchildren of the sovereign have borne five-pointed labels, but the most recent label to be assigned to a royal grandson – that of Prince William, eldest son of

▲ *The foundation document for Henry VII's Chapel in Westminster Abbey, London. The royal arms are supported by the red dragon of Cadwallader, a badge of the Tudors.*

▼ *The arms of the Emperors of Austria and their major dominions – the arms of the Kingdom of Hungary bear the crown of King Stephen, with its bent cross.*

the Prince of Wales – has only three points. The central point is charged with an escallop taken from the arms of his mother's family, the Spencers, whose arms include three escallops Argent.

The French royal family was divided into numerous branches, each of which differenced the royal arms with their own particular brizures. These included the white label used by the House of Orleans and the red bend of the Bourbons. When the lesser branches of these lines in time put out their own branches, each differed the brizure of their branch with smaller charges. The Counts of Angoulême, for example, charged the white label of the House of Orleans with red crescents.

In Russia, members of the Romanov dynasty tended to difference their arms by means of supporters to show their proximity to the throne.

2. Oberösterreich.

3. Niederösterreich.

4. Salsburg.

5. Steiermark.

6. Kärnten.

7. Tirol.

8. Mähren.

9. Böhmen.

1. Kleines Reichswappen von Österreich.

10. Ungarn.
(Das ungar. Gesamtstaatswappen z. auf Textbeilage.)

11. Krain.

17. Dalmatien.

▶ *The arms of the monarchs of Europe in the late 18th century. This plate, taken from a French work on heraldry, places the Catholic kingdoms first, and the Protestant states lower down the page.*

ROYAL QUARTERINGS

As with most ancient families, the arms of the ruling dynasties of Europe often started with the simplest designs. The Hohenzollerns started with a shield quartered in white and black; their neighbours the Habsburgs had a red lion rampant on a gold field. At the height of their powers, when the Hohenzollerns were Emperors of Germany and the Habsburgs were Holy Roman Emperors, both were able to sport shields of many quarterings: each quarter represented a lordship, county, principality or kingdom over whose fortunes the emperor held sway. Yet at the heart of each grand design could still be found the red lion of the Habsburgs and the simple quarters of the Hohenzollerns.

Some monarchs, such as those of France, made relatively little use of quarterings in their arms. The fleurs de lis of France are thought by some to be symbols of the Virgin Mary, by others to be three toads. The creatures of the English kings, which have at times been thought of as

DANGEROUS DIFFERENCES

It seems incredible that the display of arms alone would be enough to topple men of power and influence. Yet during the reign of Henry VIII this was the fate of Henry Howard, Earl of Surrey and his near relation Edward Stafford, Duke of Buckingham. Henry had a paranoid suspicion of anyone with a claim to his throne, and while both men had the right to bear differenced versions of the royal arms, they were rash in their ostentatious use of royal heraldry. It was even suggested that the Earl of Surrey had removed the difference marks from his arms, asserting his claim to be more royal than the King. Whether guilty or not, the two aristocrats were executed.

---

either lions or leopards, were of equally ancient and mysterious origin. The English monarchs quartered the French royal arms with their own to back up their claim to the throne of France, even placing the French arms in the most prominent quarters (1 and 4), and the fleurs de lis remained in the British royal arms as late as the 19th century. British monarchs kept their arms simple by displaying only quarters representing their kingdoms: England, Scotland, Ireland and France. But when the British throne passed to the House of

Guelph (Hanover) in 1714 the royal shields became more complex, including quarters for Brunswick, Lüneberg and Hanover. Over the last three was a small escutcheon charged with the crown of Charlemagne, indicating the office of Archtreasurer of the Holy Roman Empire, held by the British monarch as Duke of Brunswick and Lüneberg.

Members of the Swedish royal family include as quarterings the arms of the province from which they take their ducal title, for example Varmland or Uppland.

THE BRITISH NOBILITY

Evolved over a millennium, the British nobility has developed a multitude of mannerisms, styles of address, dress, insignia and duties so complex and contrived that few outside its ranks understand them. While noble families no longer wield the power and wealth they once commanded, even a Labour government continues to see a need for lords and ladies of sorts: although it removed most of the hereditary holders of peerages from the House of Lords in 1998, it offered some ordinary citizens the chance to become "people's peers", and deck themselves out in scarlet and ermine.

Naturally, members of the nobility do not go around from day to day wearing their robes and coronets. In fact most of them will now have little chance of wearing their robes officially ever again, unless it is for the coronation of a sovereign. However, at least one of their number was, until quite recently, given to having his daughter dress up in his coronation robes and thrill impressionable visitors by processing down corridors when his ancestral home was open to the public.

PEERS AND PEERESSES

The word "peer" is derived from the Latin *pares*, meaning "equal" and it refers to the collective nature of the upper aristocracy. This is because despite their different ranks – from duke to baron – all holders of peerage titles were until recently entitled to a seat and vote in the House of Lords, one of the two chambers of the British Parliament. Only a few of these hereditary peers are still chosen to sit and vote in the upper House. Since the passing of the House of Lords Act, 1998, the majority of those entitled to such a seat and vote are holders of a life peerage, and their titles become extinct upon their death.

RANKS AND TITLES

The British peerage is divided into five ranks. In order of seniority, these are duke, marquess (or marquis), earl, viscount, and baron. Life peers rank as barons, and are entitled to wear the robes and coronet of that rank. Many people assume that a British lord has to live on, or own, the estate from which he derives his title: that the Duke of Somerset must own that county, or that the Earl of Plymouth lives in that city. This is certainly not the case, though in the medieval period such men may well have derived their titles from the land they governed on behalf of the king.

Of the five ranks, the highest, duke, derives its name from the Latin *dux*, or war leader. Dukedoms have always been bestowed sparingly and there have been

◀ *Until the 18th century, the funerals of the nobility were occasions for a prominent display of heraldry. The funeral trappings included the hatchment, a diamond-shaped board bearing the arms of the deceased. This impressive hatchment is that of John, 1st Duke of Atholl, d1722.*

to a nobleman of high repute. In the Holy Roman Empire, a count of the marches, or *Markgraf*, was responsible for guarding the easternmost borders.

The middle rank, that of earl, is the oldest of the five. It derives from the *earldorma*, the Anglo-Saxon official appointed to administer a shire on behalf of the monarch. The equivalent rank in the French nobility was the *comte* (or count), and in Germany, *Graf*. The administrative duties of the earl or count meant that he was a busy man and would often have needed a deputy or "vice-count" to assist him. From this subordinate office the rank of viscount arose.

The lowest rank of the peerage, that of baron, was introduced by William I from France into England. By the 13th century the barons were "summoned by writ" to take their place in the King's Council, or Parliament. The Scottish equivalent of this rank is a "lord of Parliament", or simply a "lord". In Scotland the title of "baron" is feudal by nature, and occasionally it may be purchased; it does not now give the bearer a seat in the House of Lords but does have certain heraldic insignia.

periods since 1448, when the first non-royal dukedom was conferred, during which no holder of the rank was living. In Britain, where the rank of prince is not used outside the royal family, all male children of the sovereign are styled prince, and their daughters, princesses. It has also long been the case that the younger sons of the sovereign are each given a dukedom, those of York, Kent and Gloucester being reserved for the royal family.

David Lloyd George, British Prime Minister from 1916–22, complained that a fully equipped duke was as costly to maintain as two dreadnoughts, and less easy to scrap. Those who upheld the peerage system countered by saying that a British duke "in full sail" was twice as effective as any battleship and much more difficult to sink.

The rank below duke is marquess. It derives its name from a guardian of the marches, or borders – a sensitive and strategic office entrusted by the sovereign

▲ *The Parliament of Edward I (1272–1307) in session: the parliamentary robes worn by the lords sitting opposite the bishops are very similar to those of today's peers.*

▼ *At his 1991 introduction to the House of Lords, Lord Runcie (centre) is flanked by Garter King of Arms and Black Rod (left), and two peers of the same rank (right).*

FORMS OF NOBLE ADDRESS AND COURTESY TITLES

The wife of a duke is a duchess. The wife of a marquess is a marchioness; that of an earl, a countess; that of a viscount, a viscountess; and that of a baron, a baroness. All holders of a peerage, up to and including marquesses, are addressed in speech as "My Lord" or "Your Ladyship", and their wives as "My Lady". A duke and duchess are both addressed as "Your Grace".

In the British peerage, only the head of a family bears the title (as opposed to the practice of some other nations, where many members share the rank). However, the eldest son of a duke, marquess or earl may, during his father's lifetime, use one of his father's lesser titles (often accrued before the senior title). Such a title is known as a "courtesy title" because of its acknowledgement by the royal court, though it has no legal standing. Should the "courtesy lord" have children of his own, his eldest son may use another of his grandfather's lesser titles. For example, the Duke of Leinster's eldest son is known as the Marquess of Kildare, and in turn his eldest son is styled the Earl of Offaly; the

▼ *The Earl and Countess Mountbatten of Burma in their coronation robes, at the coronation of Elizabeth II in 1953.*

eldest son of the Marquess of Zetland is styled the Earl of Ronaldshay, and his eldest son is Lord Dundas.

A younger son of a duke or marquess is given the style of Lord, followed by his name: for example, "Lord Charles Brown". A daughter is styled "Lady Jane Brown". The younger son of an earl, or any son of a viscount or a baron, is styled "the Honourable Charles Brown". A daughter is "the Honourable Jane Brown", or "the Honourable Mrs Brown" if married. In conversation or informal correspondence, "Hons" are addressed as Mr, Miss or Mrs.

The eldest son of a peer is permitted to use his father's supporters – differenced by a label and with the consent of Garter King of Arms – only if he is summoned to Parliament in the lifetime of his father. However, there are many examples to be found of eldest sons bearing their father's supporters and even coronets of rank, despite never having received such a summons. All this is very confusing, not only to foreigners trying to understand the most complex honours system in the world, but also to the British themselves. Such arcane intricacies were dismissed by Oscar Wilde in a letter to Robert Ross:

…I have written to him [Lord Alfred Douglas] to tell him that… for him to try and pose as your social superior because he is the third son of a Scotch marquis and you the third son of a commoner, is offensively stupid. There is no difference between gentlemen. Questions of title are matters of heraldry – no more.

Peerages normally pass through the male line by direct descent, or sideways through brothers and their issue. Certain titles (usually ancient baronies or earldoms) can pass through the female line, and should the holder of such a title be a woman she is said to be a peeress "in her own right".

RIGHTS AND PRIVILEGES

The privileges of a British peer have been eroded by time, especially since 1998, when most of the "hereditaries" lost their right to sit in the House of Lords. They

▲*The Earl Marshal of England, His Grace the Duke of Norfolk in 1998. He wears his parliamentary robes and holds his gold baton of office.*

used, for example, to be entitled to trial by their peers, presided over by the Lord High Steward. The last case of this kind was that of Lord Clifford, who was accused of manslaughter in 1935. Peers are still able to claim the right of direct access to the sovereign, but the present Queen has probably not been much bothered by any lords or ladies seeking her advice.

Before the 1998 House of Lords Act, there were over 850 hereditary peers who were entitled to a seat and a vote in the House of Lords. Although those times have gone, for many the House of Lords is still the most exclusive of all London's clubs. In past centuries that sense of belonging was sometimes marked in pompous ways by the peers themselves. In the 16th century for example, Elizabeth I's Lord Chancellor, Sir Christopher Hatton, erected replicas of the arms of every one of his fellow peers at his home at Holdenby, Northamptonshire, while Lord Burghley decorated his mansion with a map showing the arms of every major landowner in the country.

ROBES AND CORONETS

There are two types of peers' robes: those worn for Parliament and those worn at a coronation. Parliamentary robes, known since the late medieval period, are worn when the peer is introduced into the House of Lords and during the state opening of Parliament. They are made of fine scarlet cloth trimmed with white fur. Each peer's rank can be deduced by the number of rows, or "guards", of fur borne on the front. The robe of a duke is "powdered", or decorated, with four guards of ermine, spaced equally, with gold lace above each row. The robe of a marquess has four rows on the right and three on the left, each with gold lace. An earl's robe has three rows of ermine and gold lace. The robes of a viscount and a baron are identical, each having two guards of plain white fur and gold lace.

Peers' robes are made by Messrs Ede and Ravenscroft, the court tailors, in London. Few people today – even peers of the realm – can afford real ermine, and rabbit fur or "coney" tends to be used instead, dyed to imitate the black spots of ermine. If the peer should take pity on the rabbit or ermine, he or she may prefer to have synthetic fur. A baron's parliamentary robe at the time of writing would cost the new peer £2,000 (US$3,000), although one enterprising peeress ran hers up on her own sewing machine, using fabric purchased in the local market. For gold lace she used gold foil patterned with the

▲ *Peers' robes charge the arms of the London firm of Ede and Ravenscroft Ltd, which has made robes for the British peerage for centuries.*

▼ *The arms of Lord Mowbray, Segrave and Stourton. As a baron, his coronet of rank bears six balls on the rim, of which four are visible. It appears surmounting his arms without helm or crest.*

points of a comb. Coronation robes are much more costly and are, of course, seldom seen, unless they happen to be placed on public display in the peer's country house. The official description states that these robes or mantles:

>...are created out of crimson velvet, edged with miniver [white fur], the cape furred with miniver pure, and powdered with bars or guards of ermine according to their degree:
> Barons: 2 guards
> Viscounts: 2 guards and a half
> Earls: 3 guards
> Marquesses: 3 guards and a half
> Dukes: 4 guards
> The said mantles or robes to be worn over full Court dress, or regimentals.

If a duke were to ask the court tailors to make him a set of coronation robes today, he would probably have to pay more than £10,000 (US$15,000).

The wives of peers, and peeresses in their own right, wear coronation robes or mantles powdered with guards in number according to their (or their husband's) degree. The robe or mantle also has a train, which varies in length from one yard for a baroness, to two yards for a duchess.

While in other nations coronets of rank are simply heraldic ornaments, the unique distinction of the British peerage is that they do get to wear actual coronets according to their degree, albeit only on one rare occasion – at the exact moment the monarch is crowned. Coronets of rank are officially described as follows:

>The coronets to be silver gilt; the caps of crimson velvet turned up with ermine, with a gold tassel on the top; and no jewels or precious stones are to

be set or used in the coronets, or counterfeit pearls instead of silver balls.

• The coronet of a Baron to have, on the circle or rim, 6 silver balls at equal distance.

• The coronet of a Viscount to have, on the circle, 16 silver balls.

• The coronet of an Earl to have, on the circle, 8 silver balls raised upon points, with gold strawberry leaves between the points.

• The coronet of a Marquess to have, on the circle, 4 gold strawberry leaves and 4 silver balls alternately, with latter a little raised on points above the rim.

• The coronet of a Duke to have, on the circle, 8 gold strawberry leaves.

The coronets worn by the peers' wives are smaller variants of those of their husbands.

Although no precious stones or pearls are now permitted to adorn peers' coronets, those borne by medieval earls would almost certainly have been heavily jewelled. Most aspects of coronet design were set in the 17th century; before that time, barons did not wear coronets at all but were permitted to wear only a cap of scarlet and ermine.

▼ *The arms of Francis Russell, 2nd Earl of Bedford c1580. Little except the helmet of degree has changed since then in the composition of a peer's arms.*

CHE SARA SARA

▲ *The full splendour of the arms of a modern British peer, Baron (Lord) Howe, with supporters, coronet of degree and helm.*

THE HERALDRY OF PEERS

Peers of the realm enjoy the right of supporters and a depiction of the coronet of their degree. The latter is placed directly above the shield and not upon the helmet, which is placed above it with the crest. The helmet of a peer is silver, garnished with gold, and set in profile showing five bars. However, it is not necessary for the helmet itself actually to appear in the achievement, which is often simplified to include only the coronet – with or without its cap – and the crest. The peer may also place a robe of estate in the armorial achievement, but this is seldom done. A Scottish peer bears crimson mantling lined with ermine.

Should a married woman be a peeress in her own right, the situation becomes more complicated. The complete marital achievement uses two sets of arms, with the husband's on the dexter side and the wife's on the sinister side. Traditionally,

peeresses in their own right have been, by their nature, heraldic heiresses. The peeress's husband therefore martials his arms in the normal fashion, with an escutcheon

▼ *The marital achievement of a peeress in her own right, married to a commoner, her arms appear on the right, her husband's shield with her escutcheon on the left.*

of pretence of his father-in-law's arms in the centre of his shield. The escutcheon is "ensigned", or surmounted, with the correct coronet of rank for his wife. Should the husband himself be a peer, he uses the complete achievement of his degree, with supporters, coronet and so on. If he is a gentleman he simply uses the arms of that degree. In both cases, to the sinister of the husband's achievement is that of the peeress on a lozenge borne by supporters and ensigned with her coronet. If the peeress is Scottish, she can also bear in her achievement the crest of her family.

In recent years many women have been made life peers. They are thus peeresses in their own right but – provided they have brothers to carry on their family arms – not heraldic heiresses. If such a peeress is married, her husband impales his and his wife's arms on the shield, with his wife's complete achievement alongside.

When the husband of a peeress in her own right dies, she shows her situation by bearing two lozenges, the one to the dexter with the marital coat, the sinister remaining as before. The widow of a peer who is not a peeress in her own right uses the dexter achievement only – the marital arms martialled on a lozenge – but this is still "protected" by the supporters and coronet of her husband's peerage. The wife of a lord, knight or baronet enjoys her husband's title, being "Lady So and So", yet if plain Mr Jones marries a peeress in her own right, he remains plain Mr Jones.

THE BARONETAGE

There is one other rank in the British nobility that is hereditary yet does not entitle the bearer to a seat or vote in the House of Lords. This rank, which manages to confuse many, is that of baronet. In effect, the holder of a baronetcy is treated as a hereditary knight. He is therefore known as, say, Sir John Smith, and can place "Bt" after his name. Coming somewhere in precedence between knights and peers, the baronetage was considered by some to be particularly associated with "new money". It is said that Queen Victoria found it a useful way of ennobling members of the working class. At one point in the 19th century, so many wealthy brewers were members of the baronetage that it was nicknamed "the beerage".

The baronetage had its origins with James I (1603–25), who created the degree of baronet as a way of raising funds. The title was granted on payment of a fee of £1,095 – the sum required to maintain 30 infantrymen in Ulster for three years – and the first 100 letters patent were ready in 1611. A similar idea was promulgated for Scotsmen prepared to finance the settlement of Nova Scotia. The Baronets of Nova Scotia bear the arms of a British knight (with helm affronty with visor open), augmented with the arms of Nova Scotia. This can be borne on a canton or inescutcheon, or as a badge suspended below the shield by a tawny ribbon. Baronets of Ulster – and more lately of the United Kingdom – bear in similar fashion the red hand of Ulster on a white field.

TITLES FOR SALE

The selling of baronetcies raises the question of whether it is possible to buy other titles. At certain periods the sale of knighthoods and peerages was all but blatant. It seems that anyone who could afford it could advance themselves to the ranks of knights and lords if they wished. Certain courtiers, often favourites of the sovereign, saw it almost as their duty to obtain – at a price – titles for their friends or family. Sir Robert Peel was driven to write: "The voracity of these things quite surprises me. I wonder people do not begin to feel the distinction of an unadorned name."

By Victoria's reign the business had been somewhat tightened up, but there was one more scandal over the sale of titles in the 1920s, when the Liberal Party, then in power under Lloyd George as Prime Minister, saw the sale of titles as a possible means of augmenting party funds. It was claimed that costs would vary from £10,000 for a knighthood to £100,000 for a peerage, and the go-between chosen to sound out likely clients was the "peerage broker" J. Maundy Gregory. The furore created by this shady dealing in titles for political ends ultimately assisted in Lloyd George's fall from office and the passing of the Prevention of Abuses Act (1925). This made it an offence to accept "any gift, money or valuable consideration as an inducement or reward for procuring…the grant of a dignity or title of honour".

There are few chances of seeing peers in their finery, except from the House of Lords visitors gallery when a new peer is introduced. On such an occasion, the new peer is dressed in parliamentary robes and accompanied by two fellow peers of the same rank. Garter King of Arms leads them into the chamber in full ceremonial uniform, complete with tights, tabard and chain. The centuries-old ceremony involves much bowing and doffing of hats.

▼ *The shield of a baronet of the United Kingdom is charged with an escutcheon bearing the red hand of Ulster, and the helm is that of a knight (with its visor open).*

THE ORDER OF THE GARTER

The rise in chivalry brought with it messages of loyalty, heroism, glory and brotherly love. It was seized upon by the princes of Europe, who saw it as the ideal stratagem with which to bond men of rank and military expertise, creating elite brotherhoods – the chivalric orders – that would serve them in both war and peace. One of these was the English Order of the Garter. Medieval and romantic writers, inspired by the ethos of chivalry, drew on the stories of King Arthur and the Round Table, the English connections of which served Edward III's political ambitions when he instituted the Order of the Garter. The year has been disputed but is believed to be 1348, although it has also been suggested that the Order was founded some four years earlier, when the King set up a round table for knights who had taken part in a great tournament at Windsor.

INSIGNIA OF THE ORDER

The original members of the Order were the King and the Prince of Wales (Edward the Black Prince), together with 24 companions, who each took a blue garter as their device. It has been suggested that the

garter was intended to represent a sword belt, but the more romantic story concerns an incident at a ball held in Calais, when a garter fell from the leg of Joan, Countess of Salisbury. Seeing the smirks of the courtiers and the Countess's discomfort, King Edward picked up her garter and uttered the words, "Honi soi, qui mal y pense" ("Evil be on him who thinks it").

It may be no coincidence that the colours of the Garter – blue and gold – were also those of the French arms, when at the time of its foundation Edward III was making a claim to the French throne. Although the earliest depictions of the Garter robes show them to have been murrey (maroon) strewn with garters, by the 15th century they were blue and bore a single garter on the left shoulder. Members of the order have also always worn an actual garter on the left leg below the knee.

Gradually the insignia were increased. Henry VII (1485–1509) introduced the splendid collar, consisting of gold knots alternating with red roses encircled by garters. From this is suspended the George, a mounted figure of St George slaying a green dragon. The star of the Order was

LADIES OF THE GARTER

During the late Middle Ages, ladies were associated with the Order and although they did not enjoy full membership they were apparently entitled to wear a garter on their left arm. Effigies of Ladies of the Garter can be found in the churches of Ewelme and Stanton Harcourt, both in Oxfordshire. One of the last to be so honoured was Henry VII's mother, Margaret Beaufort. After her death in 1509 the Order became exclusively male, except for female sovereigns, until 1901, when Edward VII made Queen Alexandra a Lady of the Garter. Since then, several reigning queens have been members. In 1987 women were made eligible for the Garter in the same way as men, styled as Lady Companions of the Most Noble Order of the Garter.

▼ *The effigy of Alice, Duchess of Suffolk. The Duchess is shown wearing the Garter around her left forearm.*

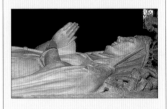

▼ *A splendid design of 1589 showing the arms of the knights of the Garter from 1486–1589, enclosed on the Tudor Rose.*

▼ *The Garter has been used to encircle not only the arms of the knights but also the prelates and chancellors of the Order.*

instituted by King Charles I in 1629. It bears the red cross of St George, encircled by the garter and surrounded by silver radiating beams.

THE INSIGNIA IN HERALDRY

Since the Tudor period it has been the norm for a Garter knight to place his arms within the garter. It is also permissible to place the arms within the collar of the Order, although this is seldom done today, possibly because the collar is such a complex item to paint accurately. Other British orders of chivalry follow this pattern, and

▲ *Roger Mortimer, Earl of March (d1398) in robes of the Garter. The portrait is taken from a 15th-century document.*

remains, so that the earliest of these date from the late medieval period.

The shields of the Garter knights hang in St George's Hall, also in Windsor castle, and many were destroyed during a fire in 1992. The replacement shields met with disapproval among heraldists, as the work was given to a sign painter (who afterwards said that he never wanted to see another shield in his life). The shields of those appointed since 1999 have been created by a full-time heraldic artist.

The other British orders of chivalry also have chapels attached to them. The Chapel of King Henry VII in Westminster Abbey, London, is home to the Order of the Bath, and contains the stall plates of such famous members as Lord Nelson, the Duke of Wellington and Lord Kitchener of Khartoum. The Order of St Michael and St George has a chapel in St Paul's Cathedral. St Paul's also houses the Chapel of the Order of the British Empire in its crypt, although there are no stall plates there and the banners all relate to the Royal Family. The Royal Victorian Order has its home in the Queen's Chapel of the Savoy. Its stall plates include that of Sir John Miller, showing Sir John himself – not once but twice – as supporters to his own shield.

▼ *The late Major General Sir Hugh Sykes, Knight Grand Cross of the Most Exalted Order of the Star of India, encircled his arms with the collar of that Order.*

their members place their arms within a circlet bearing the motto. Knights Grand Cross may place their arms within the collar of their order. Knights (and baronets) show their degree by placing above their shield a steel helmet with a plain visor, fully open.

When a knight of a chivalric order displays a marital achievement of arms, two shields (or ovals) are depicted side by side. That on the dexter has the knight's arms alone within the circlet or collar of his order, that to the sinister has the full marital achievement of husband and wife (impaled or with escutcheon of pretence) within a wreath. The helmet of degree sits

at the junction between the two shields. The two coats show that the knighthood was conferred on the man and not his wife, but she through courtesy enjoys her husband's title and is addressed as "Lady" (followed by her husband's surname).

In Britain, when a woman is awarded with the equivalent of a knighthood, she is called a dame (Dame Grand Cross or Dame Commander), and may place her lozenge within the circlet of the order.

DISPLAYS OF ARMS

During his lifetime, the banner and crested helmet of each Garter knight is hung above his stall in St George's Chapel in Windsor Castle. At the back of each stall is an enamelled metal plaque bearing the knight's arms, and while the banner and crest are taken down on his death, his stall plate

THE ORDER OF THE GOLDEN FLEECE

The earliest orders of chivalry in Europe were religious, formed with the intent of creating bands of military men to fight in the Holy Land. As the structure of society in western Europe changed during the 14th century, with the dominance of the Church giving way to royal power, a number of temporal orders of chivalry were founded to strengthen and glorify the position of kings. Perhaps the most glorious of these royal knighthoods belonged to the Duchy of Burgundy, whose dukes were as powerful and wealthy as any king of Christendom.

Seeing the prestige of Edward III's Order of the Garter, Philip the Good, Duke of Burgundy (1419–67) decided to create a similar institution to bond together the highest nobles of his own realm. He gave each male member of his house, and his most trusted counsellors and friends, a bejewelled golden chain, the forerunner of the collar of the Golden Fleece. The Order of the Golden Fleece (La Toison d'Or) was founded in 1430 in celebration of Philip's marriage to Isabella of Portugal. As with the Garter knights, Duke Philip exacted a vow from the Knights of the Golden Fleece to defend the Church and his ducal house from all malignant foes.

CHAPTER MEETINGS

In common with other orders of chivalry, the knights were to meet in a chapter, which was to be held every few years in one of the great cities of Burgundy. The first chapter was held in 1431 at Lille (now in northern France) and 25 knights were installed on that occasion. As with the

▲ *The 15th-century Burgundian court was "the richest in Christendom". Here, Charles the Bold, Duke of Burgundy (1466–77) presides over his council. The border around the scene bears the arms of all his territories.*

Garter, stalls in the chapel of the Order were decorated with the armorial achievements of the knights. However, in the case of the Golden Fleece, where chapter meetings were held in various Burgundian cities, sets of arms dating from separate meetings can be found in churches across northern France and Belgium. The chapter meetings often coincided with other lavish spectacles laid on by the Dukes of Burgundy. These events were the envy of the princes of Europe, few of whom were able to equal Burgundian opulence.

At a meeting of the chapter the Duke of Burgundy sat as Grand Master. On either side of him, the knights would take their places, each wearing the collar of the

◀ *The arms of the Dukes of Burgundy on the tomb of Charles the Bold in Bruges. The quarters are 1st and 4th Burgundy modern, 2nd Burgundy ancient with Brabant, 3rd Burgundy ancient with Limburg. The escutcheon bears the arms of Flanders.*

Order. The chapter meetings were administered by officers, each with a specific duty. The Chancellor of the Order, normally a high-ranking prelate, was responsible for the great seal. He organized the meetings and reported to the Grand Master on any wrongdoings of the knights. He also spoke the funeral oration after the death of a knight. The Treasurer looked after the statute books and the collars of the Order, each of which was numbered and returned on the death of a knight. The Secretary wrote down the minutes and recorded the martial deeds of the knights.

As with most orders of chivalry, the Golden Fleece had its own herald called, appropriately, Toison d'Or King of Arms. This officer wore a badge of office, a

▲ *The stall plate of Philip II of Spain, Sovereign of the Order of the Golden Fleece, placed in St Baaf's Cathedral, Ghent for the 23rd chapter meeting of the Order in 1559.*

DIVISION OF THE ORDER

The male line of the house of Burgundy came to an end in the 15th century, when all the fortunes of that extraordinary land fell to the great heiress, Mary of Burgundy, the sister of Charles the Bold. Mary married the Habsburg Archduke Maximilian, who became Holy Roman Emperor in 1493. Mary and Maximilian's grandson, Charles, eventually succeeded to the throne of Spain in 1516.

When the Habsburg bloodline became extinct in Spain, the Austrian Emperor, Charles VI (1711–40), claimed sovereignty of the Golden Fleece from the Bourbon monarchs of Spain, and in 1713 re-instituted the Order in Vienna. From that time the Golden Fleece continued separately in each of the two countries. The Austrian branch admitted only Catholics, but the Spanish branch became a civil order in the 19th century, and current members include Queen Elizabeth II of Britain.

Despite the fall of so many European monarchies in the first half of the 20th century, several of the great temporal orders of chivalry survive, among them the Order of the Garter and the Order of the Thistle. Two Scandinavian orders, the Danish Order of the Elephant (1462), and the Swedish Order of the Seraphim (1748), maintain splendid displays of heraldry relating to current and former knights of the orders.

▼ *The collar of the Golden Fleece, shown in its full form in a Flemish armorial of the late 16th century.*

version of the collar of the Order known as the "potence", decorated with the arms of all the knights at a particular chapter meeting. The herald was responsible for much of the ceremonial associated with the Order and for making sure that the knights' heraldry was correctly marshalled.

INSIGNIA OF THE ORDER

The shield of arms of each knight of the Golden Fleece is enclosed within the collar of the Order, each link of which depicts the device or badge of the Dukes of Burgundy – a steel within a flint emitting showers of sparks. Suspended from the central flint in the collar is a representation of the golden fleece, and a line from Philip's speech: "I will disperse my enemies and strike before they are ready." One of the theories mooted for the choice of the golden fleece as the Order's device is an allusion to the wool trade, source of Burgundy's great wealth; another is that it referred to the Argonauts, whose quest for the golden fleece embodied the qualities that Philip sought in his own knights.

The potence of the King of Arms and the robes of a knight of the Order are displayed in the Kunsthistorisches Museum in Vienna, and many other museums have fabulous examples of the insignia.

HERALDRY IN THE CHURCH

Heraldry was adopted by the Church not very long after its birth on the battlefield. It hardly needed to be shown what to do with arms, since its hierarchy tended to be drawn from the nobility, the class that had already adopted heraldry. Although princes of the Church were supposed not to take part in war, two of the most militant men on the battlefield of Hastings in 1066 were Odo, Bishop of Bayeux, who was the half-brother of William of Normandy, and Geoffrey, Bishop of Coutances. These fighting prelates used their weapons in as terrible a fashion as any other Norman warrior.

Ecclesiastical users of heraldry developed their own methods of displaying their arms, tending to place them on the oval seals they had used since long before heraldry appeared. Whereas the military man displayed himself on his seal in a warlike manner, a proud prelate would show him or herself – abbesses often made use of armorial seals – in the act of blessing, accompanied by a shield of his or her personal arms. The seal of an abbey, cathedral or other institution often bore its patron saint together with the arms of the institution (if used) as well as those attributed to the saint. This is still the case for many dioceses and monastic institutions. During the

▲ The arms of cardinals portrayed in a 15th-century window of Toledo Cathedral, Spain, are surmounted by their red hats.

period when heraldry was being used in its true form by medieval knights in warfare, western Europe knew only one Church. The heraldry of the Catholic Church has since provided the model for other Christian denominations, including the Protestant clergy, although they tend to use simplified forms.

PAPAL ARMS

The Pope places his family arms on a shield ensigned by the papal tiara. Behind the shield are placed the keys of St Peter: a gold key points to the dexter, symbolizing papal power extending up to heaven, and a silver key points to the sinister, symbolizing power over the faithful on earth. The keys are often joined together by a red cord. During the period between the death of a pope and the election of his successor (known as the interregnum or sede vacate), the keys pass to the cardinal-camerlengo (the papal treasurer), who bears them in saltire beneath another emblem peculiar

to the Catholic Church, the pavilion known as the "ombrellino", which is, in fact, an umbrella. Both keys and pavilion are usually placed above the shield of the camerlengo, indicating that it is his duty to watch over the rights of the holy see until the election of the new pope.

THE CARDINAL'S HAT

Since the 13th century, the rank of cardinal has been distinguished by the wearing of a red hat, adorned with cords intended to be tied under the chin. It was long the custom for a cardinal's hat to be hung above his tomb, and you can often still see these dusty insignia hanging in cathedrals in Catholic countries. The red hat found its way into heraldry, where it ensigned the cardinal's arms. The cords hung down on either side of the shield and were often

▲ The arms of Pope John Paul II, as used for papal notepaper, display the symbols of the papacy: the crossed keys and tiara.

▲ *The oval seal design typical for a religious institution or individual here shows the punning arms of Milton Abbey, Dorset, England: a mill on a tun (barrel).*

ornamented with tassels. Their number was not fixed at first, but under Pope Pius VI (1775–99) it became the custom to set 15 tassels on either side.

▼ *Great events in the Church calendar could be recorded through heraldry. This page from the Chronicle of the Council of Constance (1414–18) shows the arms of the great clerics who sat for the election of Pope Martin V (elected November 1417).*

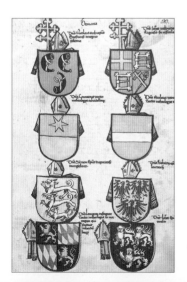

ARCHBISHOPS AND BISHOPS

Resident archbishops may make use of the "pallium". Originally a toga-like vestment, this shrank to a Y-shaped band worn over the shoulders. It is often used as a charge in the arms of archiepiscopal dioceses.

Archbishops can also make use of a double transfixed cross behind their shield, while bishops place a simple cross behind theirs. High prelates of the Protestant Church may choose a shield of arms ensigned with a precious (jewelled) mitre. Sometimes a crozier and cross is placed in saltire behind the shield.

In northern Europe, and especially in Britain, it is quite common for archbishops, bishops and abbots to marshal their personal arms with those of their diocese or abbey. In British dioceses, the shield is impaled (as in a marriage): the dexter half bears the arms of the see and the sinister half the arms of the bishop. As Protestant clergy are allowed to marry, the hatchment of a bishop or archbishop often shows two shields of arms, that on the dexter with the arms as just described, that on the sinister bearing the personal arms further impaled with those of the wife's family.

ECCLESIASTICAL PRINCES

For centuries, archbishops, bishops, abbots and even abbesses were able to rule over certain territories in the Holy Roman Empire. These mighty princes of the Church often used achievements of arms every bit as grand as any other ruler. Some did not even bother to show any mark of ecclesiastical dignity, preferring to use mantles, princely hats or coronets of rank. More often they combined both ecclesiastical and lay insignia, and adorned their palaces and churches with some of the grandest achievements of arms ever seen.

Their arms often include not only the symbols of their pastoral duties, such as the crozier and cross, but a sword. This seems a most unlikely object to find in the arms of a churchman, or even a churchwoman, but it signifies that they literally had power of life or death over their subjects. A sword can even be seen in the arms of Abbess Elizabeth Antonia of Saxe-Meiningen (1713–66). Though Abbess

▲ *The modern achievement, including a mitre and robe, of an archpriest of the Ukrainian Orthodox Church in Canada, the Very Revd Waldemar Kuchta.*

Elizabeth's jurisdiction was confined to the cathedral and convent of Gandersheim in Lower Saxony, and her subjects numbered fewer than twenty, she asserted her independence from the Dukes of Brunswick by placing the imperial eagle behind a cartouche of the abbey's arms. These were divided Per pale Sable and Or, the imperial colours commemorating the early abbesses of Gandersheim, who were imperial princesses.

In Britain the sword-in-arms of prelates was virtually unknown, except in the arms of the Bishops of Durham. Durham Cathedral appears in many ways to be more castle than church, and a real castle stands right behind the great church. The prince-bishops of Durham were given palatinate status by the medieval English kings, making them virtually sovereign rulers in their diocese, because they were expected to maintain their own standing army and keep vigil against the invading Scots. The prince-bishops maintained the unique distinction of placing their mitre within a ducal (or heraldic) coronet. Earlier bishops also included in their mitre an ostrich plume, thus combining a bishop's hat with a warrior's crest. Their seals showed them as knights, charging into battle, with swords held aloft.

RELIGIOUS ORDERS OF CHIVALRY

Medieval Europe was dominated by two powers, the knights and the Church. While the Church often railed against the excesses of troublesome knights, who were not averse to sacking the odd abbey, it was into the local church that the knights' bodies were eventually carried. These violent characters were the same men whose memorials often appeared in due course in the stained glass windows of the church.

THE FIRST CRUSADE

Pope Urban II (reigned 1088–99), saw a way to channel the violence of the military. Rather than beseeching men to stop fighting, he encouraged them to take their aggression out on the principal bugbear of the Christian world – the Muslims. His rough and ready evangelism appealed to the fighting men of Europe: they saw the possibility of achieving not only eternal glory, but also earthly riches.

Urban used the symbolism of the crucifix during his rallies of 1095, announcing that it should be the token of their cause. The message immediately took effect, as men tore up strips of coloured cloth and stitched crosses on their tunics. Despite many setbacks, the First Crusade (1096–99)

▼ *Arms of the Hoch- und Deutschmeister (Grand and Teutonic Master) of the Teutonic Order.*

▲ *A seal showing two impoverished Templar knights frugally doubling up on one horse.*

achieved its aim: Jerusalem was captured and its inhabitants – men, women and children – were murdered in an orgy of brutality.

While the prospect of riches was an obvious draw, there were some of high rank who espoused the noblest aims of chivalry. For several years prior to Jerusalem's capture, a group of knights had acted as protectors to pilgrims to the city. At the time of the First Crusade they lived near the Temple of Solomon in Jerusalem. In 1119 Hughes de Payns and Geoffrey de St Omer incorporated the group into a religious order, the Poor Knights of the Temple of Solomon, usually known as the Knights Templar. So poor did the early Templars claim to be that their seals often depicted two men riding a single horse. The

idea of priest-knights soon caught on and led to a flowering of other military orders of chivalry. Among them were the Knights of the Order of St Lazarus of Jerusalem, who maintained leper hospitals, and the Knights of the Hospital Order of St John of Jerusalem (the Knights Hospitallers), formed to aid sick and weary pilgrims. Some of the great dormitories they built still survive. The Hospitallers and the Templars acquired great wealth and built vast castles. There was little love lost between these two powerful orders, and when not fighting the "infidel", they were apt to fight each other.

INSIGNIA OF THE ORDERS

Each religious order of chivalry settled on a cross of a particular form and colour, and some of these symbols are still familiar today, none more so than the white eight-pointed cross of the Hospitallers, now called the Sovereign and Military Order of St John of Jerusalem, and known as the Order of Malta. The British branch of the Order became the Most Venerable Order of St John, whose members are famed for their voluntary relief work as the St John's Ambulance Brigade.

The Prince Grand Master of the Order of Malta quarters his family arms with those of the Order, and his shield is placed on an eight-pointed white cross surrounded by a rosary. The whole is placed on a black princely mantle and ensigned by a princely crown of degree. Other high-ranking prelates (notably Bailiffs Grand Cross) are entitled to bear a chief of the Order – Gules a cross Argent – and have a banner of the Order carried in procession.

▼ *Left to right: The arms of the Order of the Knights Templar, the Order of St Lazarus, and the Sovereign and Military Order of St John of Jerusalem (the Order of Malta).*

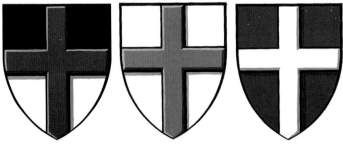

▲ *Arms of the 78th and current Grand Master of the Sovereign Military Order of Malta, Fra Andrew Bertie. From medieval times the grand masters have quartered the arms of the Order with those of their family.*

Protestant chapters of the Order were formed in the late 16th and 17th centuries. Their heraldry conforms in the main to the Sovereign and Military Order of St John of Jerusalem, except that various national symbols are added to the decorations, arms and banners.

Of the other religious military orders, the most famous were the Teutonic Order of Germany and the Orders of Santiago and Calatrava, both of Spain. The crosses of each order have often found their way into the heraldry of their members. The Teutonic Knights, who maintained their fighting traditions by opposing pagan tribes along the eastern Baltic, displayed a black crutched cross (cross potent) which told of their origins caring for sick and wounded knights and pilgrims who came from their homelands.

Until the 14th century, there was at least one nation – Lithuania – which the Teutonic Order could still attempt to convert through the sword, but in 1386 Grand Duke Jagiello of Lithuania converted to Christianity (having married Jadwiga, heiress to the Polish throne). However, the Order continued to invade his borders and tried his patience so much that in 1410 he exacted a terrible revenge. At the Battle of Grunwald, hundreds of the Teutonic

Knights were killed. Some, it is claimed were roasted in their armour on spits by the victorious Poles.

It is sometimes supposed that in the arms of Jerusalem the gold crosses borne on a white field were originally red. This version is used by the Order of the Holy Sepulchre, which originated when knighthoods were conferred on Crusaders visiting the Church of the Holy Sepulchre in Jerusalem. It is said that the knights of the Order were dubbed with the sword of Godfrey de Bouillon, a leader of the First Crusade. Its members may place their shields on the main cross potent and include the four small crosses couped around the edge or, like the members of the Order of Malta, they can place the cross alongside their achievement of arms, as best befits the design. The highest ranking members can quarter the crosses with their personal arms.

The Knights of St John left their mark through their heraldry wherever they went, especially on Malta, where the arms of the Grand Master can be seen on many buildings. In the former Conventual Church of the Order, now the Pro-Cathedral of St John in Valetta, a collection of 400 tesselated floor plaques in multi-coloured stone indicates by their arms the burial places of many members of the Order of Malta.

▲ *A medieval miniature shows the Knights of St John receiving orders from their Grand Master, Pierre d'Abusson (whose arms appear on the building top right), during the Siege of Rhodes by Muhammad II in 1486.*

▼ *One of the finest displays of heraldry in the world is to be found on the floor of St John's Pro-Cathedral in Valetta, Malta, where the arms of many officers of the Order of St John are executed in marble.*

CIVIC AND
STATE HERALDRY

Most people feel the need to belong, whether it be to a football team, a
town or a nation. Identification with such an entity engenders a sense of
security and strength, and from that strength comes pride. The emblems
adopted by the sovereigns of Europe in the late Middle Ages soon became
identified not so much with the rulers themselves but with their entire
realms. The English were united behind the strength of the royal leopards,
the French were protected beneath their golden lilies. As the nation state
became a reality during the medieval period, the major cities and city states
of Europe also grew in wealth and power, believing themselves as rich and
mighty as any ruler or dynasty.

◀ *The civic seal, or sigil, from 1336, for the Italian*
town of Cividale.

CIVIC AND NATIONAL ARMS

Like the Church, whose religious and chivalric orders had embraced heraldry on a corporate basis, the towns and cities of Europe united their people behind devices that often reflected the protective nature of civic government. Their shields bore stylized views of municipal fortifications, with battlemented walls and turrets, or a gateway with its portcullis and other defences, asserting the defensive power and strength of the corporation.

Many early civic arms incorporate older devices found on the council's official seals. These often depicted not only the fortifications of the place, but also its patron saint, an important figure in the town or city's history. Not every town felt the need to put its protection in the hands of its patron saint alone. Where a municipality was under the influence of a local magnate or prince, who might or might not have a residence in the town, the arms of the ruler often filled the space within the gateway on the municipal shield. A combination of the arms or figures of the saint and the ruler was also common.

◄ *Many civic seals emphasized the safety of their city walls, and this was soon translated into heraldry.*

CIVIC ARMS AND EMBLEMS

As with personal arms, in the early stages of heraldry civic arms were usually adopted at will. It was only in the 15th and 16th centuries that towns started to be granted arms in a formal way, by letters patent issued on behalf of the sovereign. Provinces and counties tended to be known by the arms of their rulers, or used arms based upon theirs. Many are still in use, although major land reforms and boundary changes throughout Europe in the 19th century resulted in widespread reform of regional district heraldry.

In Britain any corporate body, from a city to a company, is entitled to apply for arms, but many towns, district councils and county councils that are not armigerous are adopting logos rather than arms, to represent themselves as dynamic and forward-looking. Perhaps this is because many of the arms granted in the 20th century were not the most imaginative of designs, with over 70 per cent having as a principal charge a blue and white wavy line to represent some local water feature. The use of supporters is reserved for civic authorities viewed by the heralds as having some special eminence or distinction.

In Britain there is technically no such thing as "county" or "city" arms, as the arms are considered to belong to the body corporate: that is, the council or corporation in whose name they are granted. In Scottish heraldry, corporations are given a special type of helmet, called a "sallet", to differentiate them from personal arms.

NATIONAL ARMS

The need for a device representing national unity has been recognized for centuries, by both republics and monarchies. Some of the earliest republican arms must be those of the Swiss cantons. Instituted during the late medieval period, they were borne on the banners under which the famous Swiss troops marched. Swiss-trained bands were prized by other states for their prowess and discipline. Among the most famous of the cantonal arms were the white cross on red of Schwyz, the black ox head of Uri and the black bear of Appenzell.

When they were not fighting for other nations, Swiss troops kept in training by fighting those of the neighbouring cantons. One of the many disputes that arose between the cantons of Appenzell and Uri occurred when the people of Appenzell derided those of Uri by claiming – through the use of their arms – that they were as thick-headed as an ox. The inhabitants of Uri got their own back by taunting the Appenzellers, flourishing the latter's arms with the black bear missing its genitals. This was too much for the Appenzellers, who attacked Uri to avenge the insult.

WORLDWIDE HERALDRY

From the late medieval period onwards, heraldic writers gave arms to nations and rulers who had never actually encountered heraldry. To the writers this was no matter. Such was the nature of sovereignty that all

▼ *The arms of two Czech towns, Prague New Town (left) and Tábor (right) show how the motifs of civic seals were translated on to heraldic shields. Both include emblems of the kings, emperors and dynasties under which the towns prospered.*

monarchs, whether Christian or heathen, alive or dead – and their realms – were of noble status and deserving of heraldry. Thus the Shah of Persia was given a shield charged with a sun in splendour surrounded by stars, and the Sultan of Turkey was granted the Ottoman crescent, with the shield ensigned by a turban.

In time, as Europeans settled in all continents as a result of trade or conquest, heraldry was adopted by their rulers. Today, some eight centuries after the birth of heraldry in Europe, many nations and their rulers have achievements of arms. They range from the kings of Jordan to the republics of Indonesia and Bolivia. As far south as Antarctica itself, heraldry has made its mark. The English heralds designed arms for the Falkland Island Dependencies on 11 March 1952, and in 1963 the crest of the Antarctic research ship *Discovery* was added to the arms.

▲ *Arms of the major European monarchies at the beginning of the 20th century (left to right, top to bottom): Prussia, Austria, Hungary, Bavaria, Russia, Germany, Britain, Saxony, Italy, Spain, Württemberg. At the end of World War II all but two were extinct.*

▼ *The boroughs (contrades) of Siena in Italy attempt to outdo each other in magnificence at the opening procession of the festival of the Palio. This early 17th-century painting portrays the prosperity, independence and pride of the city-state.*

THE GARTER SERVICE

There are two annual events at which the full panoply of British state ceremonial can be observed by the public, and each has its own unique display of heraldry. The first is the service of the Order of the Garter in St George's Chapel, Windsor, which takes place on a Monday in mid-June, with a spectacular procession.

INVESTITURE

The investiture of new Knights of the Garter is held on the morning of the service in the Throne Room at Windsor. Two officers of the Order – Garter King of Arms and the Gentleman Usher of the Black Rod – bring in the knight or lady elect. He or she is brought, between two knight sponsors, to the sovereign, who personally invests him or her with all the insignia of the Order. For men, a garter is tied around the left leg and is held there by Garter King of Arms while the following admonition is read out, recalling a time when members of the Order formed the backbone of the monarch's military command structure:

> To the honour of God Omnipotent and in Memorial of the Blessed Martyr, St George, tie about thy leg, for thy renown, this most Noble Garter. Wear it as a symbol of the Most Illustrious Order, never to be forgotten or laid aside, that thereby thou mayest be admonished to be courageous, and having undertaken a just war, with which thou shalt be engaged, thou mayest stand firm, valiantly fight courageously and successfully conquer.

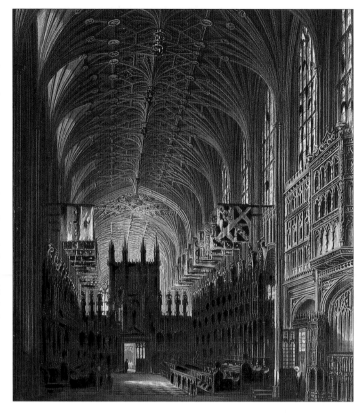

THE PROCESSION

After the investiture follows lunch, after which the Garter Knights assemble in their robes in St George's Hall, the largest room in the castle, before processing to their service. They walk from the royal apartments to St George's Chapel, which lies at the foot of the hill inside the castle's outer

▲ *St George's Chapel, Windsor Castle, seen in an engraving of 1810. The stalls of the Knights of the Garter are dominated by their armorial banners, helms and crests.*

▼ *An etching by Marcus Gheeraerts the Elder, showing the procession of the Knights of the Garter in 1576.*

bailey. The first part of the procession is headed by the Constable and Governor of Windsor Castle, whose uniform includes insignia unique to his office, including a depiction of the castle's Royal Tower.

The Military Knights of Windsor follow, in their scarlet uniforms. They are the successors of the 26 impoverished ex-soldiers originally appointed as "bedesmen", people who were employed to pray for the souls of the Garter Knights. According to the letters patent instituted by Edward III in 1348, and subsequent statutes, each bedesman was to wear a red cloak with a small shield bearing the cross of St George. The cross still forms part of the insignia of the Military Knights, who also wear a silver cut Garter star and crown.

The Military Knights are followed by the officers of arms in their tabards and Tudor

MILITARY AND NAVAL KNIGHTS OF WINDSOR

All retired military officers, the Military Knights live in lodgings allocated to them in the 16th century: a row of houses built against the inner side of the castle wall opposite St George's Chapel. Apart from attending the Garter ceremony, they continue to fulfil the duties imposed on them in 1348 by attending chapel every Sunday to pray for the sovereign and the Knights of the Garter. Once known as Poor Knights, their name was changed in the 19th century, after rude and satirical verses about their alleged infirmity had been broadcast about the town of Windsor.

Between 1795 and 1892 there were also Naval Knights of Windsor. However, such was the nature of the old sea-dogs that there was much discord, not only amongst themselves, but also with the Military Knights. Far from leading a "virtuous, studious and devout life", they were wont to frequent taverns and bawdy houses in Windsor and were known to belabour each other with their crutches and wooden legs.

bonnets, bearing a crowned Tudor rose, worn especially for the occasion. Behind the heralds come the Garter Knights in full robes, bonnets with ostrich plumes and the collars of the Order. Next are the Princes of the Blood and finally the officers of the Order leading the sovereign's procession. As with all the officers of the British orders of chivalry, each man has insignia of office, the most famous being the black rod borne by the Gentleman Usher of the Black Rod. The Garter officers wear cloaks bearing a shield with the cross of St George.

Next come the sovereign and consort, with the trains of their mantles held up by pages in the royal livery. On the sovereign's mantle is a large representation of the Garter star instead of the normal badge of the Order. The sovereign's party is followed by the Yeoman of the Guard. As the entire procession weaves its way to St George's Chapel, the festival atmosphere is maintained by military bands and the processional route is lined by troopers of the Household Cavalry. The pouches they wear on their cross belts bear the royal arms and their helmets continue the theme of the day by sporting the star of the Garter within a wreath.

The procession is met at the chapel by the clergy, and yet again the pageantry and pomp associated with royalty is manifest. The various members of the sovereign's ecclesiastical household are entitled to wear scarlet cassocks. Royal chaplains are

▲ *The standard of the Yeomen of the Guard, as approved by King George VI on 27 June 1938. It includes the badge of the House of Windsor (bottom right), newly created to appear on this standard.*

identified by a badge consisting of a silver-gilt wreath, crown and the sovereign's cypher; priests-in-ordinary wear a similar badge in silver. The steps to the chapel are lined by the officers of arms, and at the moment of the sovereign's entrance a fanfare sounds. If a new knight has been invested in the morning he will be led to his stall by Garter King of Arms. The Chancellor of the Order then calls out the knight's name, and there follows a service, after which the royal party and the rest of the participants return to the castle.

▼ *The Military Knights of Windsor leaving St George's Chapel after the Garter Service.*

THE STATE OPENING OF PARLIAMENT

The ceremonial meeting of the British sovereign with parliament has its origins over 1,000 years ago, when the king consulted with his peers – other aristocrats in many ways as powerful and wealthy as he. In time the sovereign became more remote from his subjects, until events such as the signing of Magna Carta, the Civil War and the Revolution of 1688 brought the monarchy back into line.

Before the ceremony can proceed, a detachment of the Yeomen of the Guard, in their Tudor uniforms, search the cellars of the Palace of Westminster. They are looking for would-be terrorists following the example of Guy Fawkes who, on 5 November 1605, attempted to overthrow James I and his government by exploding barrels of gunpowder hidden in the cellar.

THE ROYAL PROCESSION

The sovereign is preceded by the royal regalia, which are allocated a coach of their own. In addition to the Imperial Crown, these include the Cap of Maintenance symbolizing the monarch's religious orthodoxy,

▼ The arrival of Queen Victoria at the House of Lords to open her first Parliament. The scene includes the Lord Chancellor, with his purse, and Garter King of Arms.

and the Sword of State which indicates his or her duty to defend justice. The sovereign follows in the Irish State Coach, escorted by the Household Cavalry.

At the moment the sovereign enters the Houses of Parliament the royal standard is raised on the Victoria Tower. The sovereign is greeted by the Earl Marshal of England, the Duke of Norfolk (or his deputy), who carries a gold baton tipped with ebony. Also present is the hereditary Keeper of the Palace of Westminster, the Lord Great Chamberlain. He wears a uniform of scarlet and gold, with blue collar and cuffs. Suspended from a hip pocket is his gold key of the Palace of Westminster, and in his right hand he bears his wand of office. Also in attendance are the Officers of Arms in their tabards. The sovereign is escorted up the royal staircase to the Robing Room. The staircase itself is a heraldic feast, its walls covered with the arms of sovereigns and their cohorts going back to the birth of heraldry.

In the Robing Room the sovereign is vested with the Imperial State Crown and dons the crimson Robe of State, whose train is carried by four pages dressed in the royal liveries, before the procession moves off. Amongst the many details to be noticed are the sticks carried by Gold Stick

▲ At the state opening of Parliament in 1958, Queen Elizabeth II processes to the Lords Chamber, preceded by the Lord Great Chamberlain. The Yeomen of the Guard line the processional route.

in Waiting and Silver Stick in Waiting, two senior officers in the Household Cavalry. Their office dates from Tudor times, when the sovereign was constantly protected by two chosen guards, who even slept outside the bedroom door. Charles II commemorated their devotion to duty by presenting sticks bearing either a gold or silver head inscribed with his cypher. The cypher of the current sovereign also appears in the badge of office of the Mistress of the Robes, the senior lady of the royal household.

The scene is further enhanced by the Yeomen of the Guard and the Honourable Corps of Gentlemen at Arms, who have their origin in the Band of Gentlemen Pensioners, a personal guard drawn from the king's confidants. The Gentlemen at Arms carry poleaxes with blades engraved with the royal arms. Their uniform has a scarlet coat with gold epaulettes and belt, blue trousers and brass helmet topped by white feathers. The helmet plate bears gilt royal arms quarterings within the Garter, mounted on a silver cut star. Their badge of a portcullis appears on their uniform and on their standard, devised by the

▲ *The Standard of the Honourable Corps of Gentlemen at Arms, with battle honours and the portcullis badge of Henry VIII, in whose reign the bodyguard was formed.*

English College of Arms in 1936. While it is based on the tapered shape of a cavalry standard, that of the Yeomen of the Guard is almost square. It bears the badges of the various dynasties it has served, from the crowned hawthorn bush of Henry VII to the badge of the House of Windsor, a representation of the Round Tower of Windsor Castle.

▼ *The Palace of Westminster is a haven of heraldry. Here, an artist restores the painted arms of the Chiefs of the General Staff on the Peers' Staircase.*

On the way to the House of Lords the royal procession passes by numerous armorial achievements, reflecting not only the history of the Houses of Parliament, but the leadership of the nation. At the top of the Peers' Staircase are the arms of Chiefs of the Imperial and General Staff, and at the bottom the arms of former Speakers of the House of Commons (since 1700) who have become peers.

In the Lords Chamber, the windows are set with the arms of peers and below them appear the arms of the Lord Chancellors. Much of the detail of the chamber is heraldic, from the ceiling bosses to the posts that support the curtain running around the gallery. Like much of the Palace of Westminster, the room dates from after the fire of 1834.

THE GRACIOUS SPEECH

The chamber's grandest feature, the throne, stands on a golden platform set with royal emblems. The royal party take their places and in front of them sit the peers. The Lords Spiritual (the bishops) are in their ecclesiastical robes, the Law Lords in robes and wigs, and the Lords Temporal (life peers and representative hereditary peers) in their parliamentary robes.

The Lord Chancellor approaches the sovereign holding his own insignia of office, the Lord Chancellor's Purse, embroidered with the royal arms within a border of cherub's heads. The purse formerly contained the matrix of the Great Seal of the Realm, but today it holds the text of the speech which the sovereign will read to the assembled Lords and Commons.

The sovereign is not allowed to enter the Commons, so they are commanded to attend by the Gentleman Usher of the Black Rod, who wears his chain of office and carries the Black Rod itself. The Speaker leads the Commons to the Lords, and when all are assembled in the Lords Chamber, the sovereign begins the Gracious Speech, which sets out government policy for the coming year.

THE YEOMEN OF THE GUARD

Enhancing the pageantry of the state opening of Parliament are the Tudor uniforms of the Queen's Bodyguard of the Yeomen of the Guard. They wear the plant badges of the United Kingdom on the breast of their tunics: the combined rose, thistle and shamrock, on a background of scarlet and gold, the royal livery colours. Not to be confused with the Yeomen Warders who guard the Tower of London and wear a similar uniform but without the cross belt, the Queen's Bodyguard of the Yeoman of the Guard is the oldest royal bodyguard in existence, having served for more than 500 years. They can be observed not only at the state opening of Parliament but also at the annual Garter service in Windsor.

MILITARY HERALDRY

The military forces of the world have long been custodians of heraldic tradition. Amalgamations and changes of rulers, governments and commanding officers, have kept the heraldic designer busy devising new badges, standards or uniforms. While the medieval knight's horse bore a "trapper" or saddle-cloth resplendent with the arms of its rider, its modern equivalent – the tank – is likely to bear the heraldic liveries of a regiment.

The history of military heraldry is of course as old as heraldry itself. The military are upholders of tradition, and can give the heraldist a splendid insight into national heraldry and history. Although centuries have passed since military men wore full plate armour in battle, reminders of that remote age remain. British army officers of senior rank still wear "gorget patches" on their collars that once supported the steel gorget, or throat guard, of the medieval knight. In certain armies, some officers (normally guard commanders) still sport the gorget itself, which may bear the arms of the monarch or state.

PERSONAL LIVERIES

For centuries the military forces of Europe were recruited according to the feudal system. Lords agreed to support their leader during war through "liveries and maintenance", in return for estates with which they met the great expense of maintaining private armies. The wearing of a lord's heraldic colours and badges (liveries) was a striking aspect of the medieval scene, especially during the period of inter-dynastic strife in England now known as the Wars of the Roses (1455–85).

As late as the 19th century, certain European armies still included regiments paid for and equipped by "colonel proprietors": rich men or women, normally of high rank, who saw such private troops as liveried retainers. They naturally expected the troops to wear their heraldic colours, albeit as "facing colours" on the cuffs and collars of their uniforms. There was much jostling between the nobility to outdo not

▲ *The arm badge of the Royal Svea Lifeguards of the Swedish Army, showing the regimental arms.*

▲ *Military badges. Left, a pocket badge for the Swedish district staff of Norlands. Right, a Danish army heraldic collar badge.*

only the enemy, but also their fellow colonels, in the most recherché styles. The tradition of the colonel proprietor survives today in a muted form, in the honorary commanders of certain regiments. Even in republican France, some regiments bear the arms of former commanders from the days of the *ancien régime*.

European monarchs have long had a habit of swapping splendid uniforms with each other, making their cousins honorary colonels of regiments. By this means, almost a century after the "collapse of the eagles", these symbols of the Prussian and Austrian monarchies are still borne by British soldiers. The double-headed eagle of the Habsburgs (with their arms on its breast) is worn by the 1st The Queen's Dragoon Guards on their cap badge.

FLAGS AND STANDARDS

The medieval tradition of a military unit going into battle under the standard of its commander is now obsolete (although Lord Lovat's piper famously led the Lovat Highlanders in the attack on D-Day in 1944, bearing His Lordship's pipe banner). However, as late as World War II, British tanks sported pennons of their regiment when going into battle.

Like all military insignia, unit flags differ from nation to nation. Some armies, notably those of republics, utilize the national flag with the addition of unit title

▼ *The shape of the standard favoured by medieval noblemen is still maintained in the flags of certain British Army units, especially artillery units.*

▲ *The simplicity of Norwegian military heraldry is exemplified in the badge of the Norwegian Army 6th Division (left) and a cap cockade (right) for the Norwegian King's Guard during the reign of Olav V.*

and battle honours. Others, as in the Swedish and Finnish armies, use the regimental badge and colours.

In the British Army, the small medieval badge-bearing flag – known as the "guidon" – has its modern equivalent in the company colours of the regiments of Foot Guards and the pennons of the regiments of the Royal Artillery. In each case the flag is long, narrowing at its end into one or two tails. Royal Artillery pennons are crossed by diagonal bands bearing the regimental motto, with the regiment's badges set in the segments between the bands, similar to the standard of a medieval English nobleman. Each company of Foot Guards has its own heraldic emblem, most of which are taken from well-known royal badges or "cognizances".

NATIONAL ARMY INSIGNIA

King Gustavus I of Sweden (1523–60) is widely credited with the formation of the first truly national army, based on a system by which each prince maintained an infantry and a cavalry regiment. By the early 19th century its units were bearing provincial arms on their helmet plates and other insignia. From the late 1970s, Swedish army units were also given formal achievements of arms, with the shield of the province surmounted by a royal crown.

Many European armies retain their national colours in the form of a metal cockade, maintaining a tradition dating back three centuries or more, of troops wearing a cloth cockade in the livery colours of their commander on their headgear. The armies of Denmark, Finland,

Norway and Sweden are all known by their cockades, splendid variants of which are worn by the troops of the guards regiments in Oslo and Copenhagen. The full military cockade worn by these troops usually comes in two parts or "buttons": the top button bears the national colours and the lower bears the national arms.

The arms of countries, provinces or districts provide the theme for many regimental badges, whether in uncoloured metal – as in the collar and shoulder insignia of the Finnish, Danish and Swedish armies – or in full colour, as on the shoulder patches also worn in the latter two forces. The Danish armed forces also wear striking heraldic collar badges, including a medieval knight on his charger and a plumed war helmet.

The insignia adoped by the Norwegian Army follow the tenets set by the leading heraldist Hallvard Trætteberg, using a shield with just two tinctures and in most cases only one charge (single or multiple), such as the crossed retorts of the NBC (nuclear, biological and chemical) Unit, or the wolf's head of Brigade North. One exception was the badge of the Royal Guard (HM Kongens Garde) during the reign of King Olav V. It bore the king's monogram (V) between two knives (swords), and was known as "the dinner service" by members of the unit.

REGULATORY SCHEMES

The two World Wars saw what amounted to a free-for-all in unofficial insignia, as soldiers sought to inject some humour, often of a bawdy and derogatory kind, into the mud and chaos of modern warfare and to enliven their drab uniforms.

Eventually, various nations came up with regulatory schemes. One of the most interesting suggestions, in 1935, was for units of the French Army to bear shields taken from the arms of the places in which they were located. However, the French government disliked the designs that we produced, in which time-honoured, pre-revolutionary symbols relating to royal and imperial power were prominent, and the scheme was shelved. Since World War II, the French Army has sought to regulate all

military insignia so that they follow certain heraldic tenets. Ideas for a unit badge normally start with the unit itself, and the suggested design is sent to the Service Historique de l'Armée de Terre in the Château of Vincennes (which maintains a collection of 15,000 unit badges), to ensure that it conforms to the ideals of clarity and sobriety cherished by the service. The insignia will often be allowed to include the arms of the local town or province. If acceptable, it is passed to the French defence ministry to be formally approved, and is given an authorized number. For a badge worn by a fighting unit the number is prefixed by the letter G (for *guerre*); for a "brevet", or specialist badge,

▼ *The pocket badge of the French 1st Parachute Hussar Regiment bears the arms of its founder, Count Ladislaus Bercheny.*

▼ *The pocket badge of the French Army's 1st Transport Regiment bears the arms of the city of Paris, where it is based.*

▲ *The heraldic beret flash and crest (now superseded) of a unit in the 172nd Infantry Brigade (Alaska) in the United States Army.*

the prefix is GS. There is even a specialist badge for a French Army war artist, which bears a shield and helm as its design.

The United States Army has its own Institute of Heraldry, which lays down specific patterns for military insignia. Each unit or battalion at regimental level is entitled to a coat of arms that is formally granted by the Institute. The grant shows the achievement of arms in full colour with its formal blazon, and also explains the symbolism behind the design.

Each colour-bearing unit in the army is entitled to its own crest as well as shield, but for new units without battle honours the crest is omitted, with the idea that, at a later date, some event in its war service will give rise to a suitable crest. The shield should be the standard shape, as on official drawings, and the design upon it true heraldry, of a simple uncluttered nature. Embattled lines of partition are reserved for organizations that have captured a fortified objective. For National Guard units the crest is normally that of the state to which the unit belongs, and units in the Army Reserve are entitled to bear the crest of a "minuteman proper" (one of the militiamen of the fledgling Republic, so named because they undertook to be ready for action at a "minute's notice").

The unit badge is normally described as a "crest", although this refers to the complete design. Worn by enlisted men on side caps and shoulder straps, it is officially known as "distinctive insignia", or DI. Each regiment or comparable unit in the US Army has its own branch colour, upon which is embroidered the arms of the United States, with the national shield and crest replaced by those of the unit.

It is stipulated that the unit motto should not include "anything of a sordid, malign or malevolent character, implying animosity or partiality towards nations or groups of nations, or which stresses the destructive nature of warfare", although many unofficial unit badges of the Vietnam era certainly did not follow this advice – "Peace", "Hell" and "Bomb Hanoi" were popular themes, as well as "Kill".

Much official American military heraldry is of excellent quality and combines the best of ancient and modern heraldic styles. For instance, the arms of the 152nd Field Artillery Battalion are blazoned: Gules, on a canton of the same, fimbriated Or a projectile (artillery shell) bendwise, scintillant of the last. In addition to the heraldic tinctures, corps colours may also be used, as in the arms of the 201st Engineer Battalion: Per bend wavy Buff and Azure [the colours of the Quartermaster Corps] a fleur de lis Argent.

The fleur de lis is found in the arms of those units deployed in France in either or both of the two World Wars. The Institute of Heraldry designates other charges for particular campaigns, such as tomahawks for the Indian Wars or a cactus for Mexican campaigns. As an armorial charge indicative of a certain campaign, the fleur de lis can also be found in the arms of regiments of the Italian Army, which have distinctive pocket badges. The trident from the arms of the Ukraine and the lion of Abyssinia are among other charges used.

FULL ACHIEVEMENTS OF ARMS

Spanish Army units have their own achievements of arms, although only the shield tends to be used for uniforms while the full achievement is kept for more formal occasions. The insignia are regulated by the Spanish Army's Institute of History and Military Culture.

Each major unit of the Spanish Army has its own arms, a full achievement accompanied by the following exterior ornaments: the branch insignia placed in

▼ *The full armorial achievement for the 20th Anti-aircraft Regiment of the Spanish Army.*

▼ *In the arms of Bravo Group, KFOR, of the Portuguese Army, a "plate engrailed" makes an excellent parachute canopy.*

▼ *The Portuguese Army Archives Department is represented by a magpie and a shield division suggesting bookshelves.*

saltire behind the shield (such as the crossed batons of a *capitan general*, for the army headquarters). Above the shield is placed a royal crown. Any decorations worn by the unit are placed below the shield, but if the unit has the distinction of the *laureada*, the highest decoration it can win, this appears as a laurel wreath ornamented with sword blades encircling the shield. The achievement is complete when accompanied by scrolls bearing the regimental title, its nickname (if it has one), the *cri-de-guerre* (if borne) and the regimental battle honours.

The resulting arms are some of the most splendid heraldic compositions in modern military use. They show a fascinating diversity of themes, with each *tercio*, or unit, of the Spanish Foreign Legion bearing the arms of a famous warrior, such as Don Juan of Austria or the Gran Capitan Don Gonzalo Fernandez de Cordoba. The Special Operations Groups each have an animal in their arms associated with ferocity, or some means of attack: for example, SOG Valencia has a black bat, taken from the arms of Valencia but also indicating the unit's speciality – night attacks.

Other units take part or all of the arms of their home base or area of recruitment. The 50th Motorized Infantry Regiment "Canarias" includes, as well as charges taken from the arms of its base Gran Canaria, a dragon pierced by lances representing "the expulsion from the island of the English pirate, Admiral Francis Drake".

Finally, a happy combination of ancient and modern symbolism makes up the arms of Regional Engineer Unit 21. Its shield bears a bulldozer in front of a cross composed of a road intersection, while the border features the traditional punning charge of the ancient kingdom of Granada, the pomegranate.

Portuguese military units are also granted full achievements of arms, and many of their designs are simple but striking, such as a parachute canopy, which is heraldically interpreted as a "plate engrailed". The device used for the shield of the Portuguese Army's General Archives Department – books arranged on shelves shown as Paly per fess counterchanged –

is accompanied by that legendary collector, the magpie, as a crest.

In the German Army, the Bundeswehr, some freedom is allowed in insignia design. Formality is observed in the design of the arm badges of major units – divisions, brigades, corps and schools – which often bear the arms of the province in which the unit serves, but the pocket badges of smaller units are left to the commander. If he has little interest in heraldry, the designs, though always on a shield, can be complex and distinctly non-heraldic.

The matter has, however, been corrected in many cases by the "education" of unit commanders by one man with an extensive knowlege of heraldic design – Lt Col Herbert Lippert. His designs range from Teutonic Knights (from Marburg, the unit's home town) firing into the air with a bow for Air Defence Battalion 340, to a double-headed griffin (the vigilant custodian of treasure) for Direction and Replacement Battalion 855. He has made extraordinary use of counterchanging, with four semi wolves courant, for Field Replacement Battalion 24 (stationed in the town of Wolfhagen).

COMMEMORATIVE BADGES

In areas of eastern Europe that formally came under the influence of Imperial Russia, there has been a continued tradition of military insignia, much of it heraldic. The designs have a common origin in the splendid breast badges worn from the latter half of the 19th century until 1917 by units of the Imperial Russian

▲ *On a badge worn by Russian airborne troops, a parachute appears on the breast of the double-headed eagle, a legacy of the tsarist era.*

Army. It was the tradition in that army for a commemorative badge to be awarded to individuals, not so much for regimental identification but on meeting certain requirements, such as length of service. These regimental commemorative badges, made from enamelled metal, often bore imperial symbols, cyphers of the Russian sovereign and the imperial eagle, accompanied by the arms of the province or city from which the regiment recruited.

As for today's Russian Army, once again the double eagle appears on much of its insignia, both official and non-official. However, the peaked caps of the military now bear two badges – the lower one has the red star with the hammer and sickle, and the upper badge bears the double-headed eagle charged on the breast with St George and the dragon.

Between 1918 and 1939 Poland was once again a free and independent nation. The Polish Army reorganized and made use of commemorative breast badges in a similar fashion to the Imperial Russian Army. These often contained the monograms of former monarchs or *hetmen* (traditional commanders), and the arms of the town, city or province from which the regiment took its title.

◄ *A fascinating example of counterchanging in the badge of the German Army's Field Replacement Battalion 24.*

NAVAL HERALDRY

As with the armies of the world, the other fighting services have adapted their national heraldry to suit the ways in which it could be displayed on their equipment and uniforms. Warships traditionally bore the arms of the sovereign splendidly carved on their sterns. Figureheads were usually associated with the vessel's name, but could also be fashioned to hold a cartouche of arms.

The sterns of the great warships built between the 16th and 18th centuries were platforms for some of the grandest displays of heraldry ever seen. A spectacular example can be seen on the stern of the 17th-century Swedish flagship, the *Vasa*, raised from Stockholm harbour in 1961, which bears the complete achievement of arms of the sovereign, Gustavus Adolphus, for whom it was constructed. A model of a 17th-century Danish warship, in the Naval Museum in Copenhagen, shows that the ship itself bore not only cartouches of arms for all the Danish territories but also those of the Duchy of Brunswick-Lüneburg for Sofie Amalie, the Queen of Frederick III (1648–70).

ROYAL NAVY INSIGNIA

Many modern navies model their insignia on those of the British Royal Navy. As with army regiments, naval badges often started life unofficially, devised by ship's companies and their captains, and might be displayed on anything from a gun tampion to the ship's stationery. Though the Navy tried to impose some order, the Badge Committee set up in 1914 soon lapsed.

In 1916 Major Charles Ffoulkes RM, founder of the Imperial War Museum in London, was asked by the shipbuilders, Swan Hunter, to design badges for 20 ships they were building for the Royal Navy. Ffoulkes subsequently offered his

▲ *Ships were considered apt platforms for heraldry, and some figureheads, such as this one on HMS* Victory *at Portsmouth, England, bore the royal arms.*

▲ *Pictures from earlier centuries suggest that flags flown from ships could be vast, like this royal standard flying from a French warship of the 18th century.*

services free to the Admiralty, and the Ships Names and Badges Committee was set up on 10 December 1918.

Between 1918 and 1937 Ffoulkes designed 550 ships' badges for the Royal Navy, and many contained heraldic charges associated with the ship's name and taken from

◄ *For centuries the seals of admirals bore their arms on the sails of ships of the period. This fine example is the seal of Richard Duke of Gloucester (later King Richard III of England), Admiral of England, c1480.*

▶ *A model of the 17th-century Danish naval vessel,* Sofie Amalie, *named after the Queen of Frederick III of Denmark. The white horse of Hanover is surrounded by shields of arms of the kingdom of Denmark and the Dukes of Brunswick-Lüneburg.*

personal or civic arms. The first was for HMS *Warwick* and bore the bear and ragged staff device of the Earls of Warwick. The badge of the cruiser HMS *Effingham* had a demi lion pierced through the mouth, taken from the "Flodden augmentation" of the Howard family, of which the Earls of Effingham were a branch. Other

badges incorporated puns, such as a flying dove in front of a shakefork (a heraldic charge in the shape of a letter Y) for HMS *Dovey.* The symbol was placed within a frame of plaited rope, with a plaque above bearing the ship's name, surmounted by an imperial crown. The frame differed in shape for each type of vessel: battleships took a circular frame; cruisers, a pentagon; destroyers, a shield; auxiliaries, sloops, aircraft carriers and shore establishments, a diamond. During World War II the shapes were revised, and now all ships and Fleet Air Arm Squadrons take circular badges; shore establishments have diamonds and Royal Fleet Auxiliaries, pentagons.

The Royal Netherlands Navy follows the theme closely. Its badges are round, surrounded by a plaited rope tied at the base in a reef knot. The shield is surmounted by a naval crown, of the kind placed on memorials to Dutch naval heroes. Any motto is placed beneath the shield. Behind are placed crossed anchors, a device of the Dutch Admiralty since the 17th century. The anchor device is popular across the world: the Royal Danish Navy and the Royal Norwegian Navy favour a single anchor in pale behind a shield of arms, with a royal crown surmounting the shield.

One of the more bizarre RNN designs, for the gunboat *Flores,* was designed a year

▲ *The badge of the former Royal Netherlands Ship,* Flores, *depicts the tree of skulls from the island whose name it shares.*

▲ *Some Royal Netherlands Navy ships, such as the frigate* Bloys van Treslong, *have badges charged with naval heroes' arms.*

after the boat's decommissioning in honour of its service during World War II. The charge is a stylized version of the extraordinary *scheldenboom,* or "tree of skulls", traditionally erected on the island of Flores and hung with the skulls of the islanders' vanquished enemies.

HERALDIC SHIPS' BADGES

Dutch naval badges are often fully heraldic in that they bear the arms of naval heroes such as Tromp or de Ruyter, or of towns, provinces or cities. United States Navy

▼ *The badges designed for ships of the British Royal Navy still follow the pattern set in the first half of the 20th century.*

▼ *The USS* Winston S. Churchill's *badge, named after Britain's wartime leader, bears charges from the Churchill family arms.*

badges also often bear the arms of naval heroes, presidents, or other famous people. They may show the full arms or a made-up device taken from the arms of an eminent person. The badge for USS *Winston S. Churchill* (the first US Navy ship to be named after a British politician) contains a fleur de lis, cross of St George and lion passant guardant – all charges referring to Churchill's personal arms, and those of England. The ships of the Federal German Navy have maintained their own tradition of bearing the arms of cities, provinces and famous commanders on their prow, initially on the warships of World War II such as the *Graf Spee, Bismarck* and their class.

In recent years the Russian Navy has replaced the Soviet naval ensign bearing the hammer and sickle with one of the oldest war ensigns still in existence, the cross of St Andrew (blue on white), first adopted in about 1700 by Peter the Great. Peter also adopted for his own navy a reversed variant of the British jack, which he knew from his time spent with the Royal Navy.

An extraordinary manifestation of the tumultuous changes that have taken place in Russia may be seen on the conning towers of the nuclear submarines of the Russian Navy. These now bear the double-headed imperial eagle, with St George and the dragon on its breast.

AIR FORCE INSIGNIA

During World War I, fuselage art on aircraft showed a flair for design influenced by the most modern art of the age. Sometimes the individual unit markings designed by the pilots themselves extended along the entire length of the aircraft. French crews devised some of the most innovative air force "heraldry", and squadrons of today's Armée de l'Air bear many of the unofficial badges adopted then, amongst them the Sioux Indian chief's head chosen by the Lafayette squadron.

While the French still allow a free hand in the design of unit insignia, other air forces, such as those in Britain and the United States, maintain a much stricter control and have official authorities to design and monitor the use of formal badges. In the US Air Force, squadrons must have a pictorial device displayed on a disc, while the emblem of a flag-bearing unit (with a

▼ Aircraft of the United States Air Force tend to bear the badges of wing, squadron and command.

headquarters component) should be armorial, with the device on a shield. Unit insignia must be prepared in two versions: full colour, and subdued (olive green and black) for use in combat. Despite such strictures, towards the end of the Vietnam War there was a proliferation of non-authorized insignia, such as the badge chosen by a USAF base hospital in Korea specializing in the treatment of venereal diseases, which depicted a VD germ in a white coat bearing a syringe.

Just as close co-operation with the Royal Navy set the pattern for the insignia of various other navies, the same was the case with the allied air forces during World War II. The insignia of the Royal Flying Corps – the forerunner of the Royal Air Force – began unofficially, but an Inspector of Royal Air Force

▲ Two examples of pocket insignia of French Air Force airbase units: that of BA106 (top) bears the arms of Bordeaux, that of BA118 (bottom), Mont-de-Marsan.

▲ The badge of 22 Squadron, Royal Air Force, with its pi symbol for "22 over 7".

Badges was appointed in 1936, and the connection with traditional heraldry was acknowledged by the selection of an officer of arms to fill the Inspector's post, as is the case today.

Every RAF badge consists of a circular frame in the form of a laurel wreath, in which the title of the unit appears, ensigned by the royal crown and bearing a motto on a scroll beneath the badge. The central plaque often contains a heraldic allusion to the unit's history and location. One of the simplest and most original charges is the pi symbol in the badge of 22 Squadron. In 1916 the squadron was based for a time with No 7 Wing and when the wind lay in a certain direction its aircraft had to take off over the roof of No 7 Wing's headquarters – hence 22 over 7, or the pi symbol.

Commonwealth air forces maintained the RAF pattern, though the laurel wreath was usually replaced by plants of national origin, such as the maple leaf for Canada, fern for New Zealand or lotus for India. Other nations have also followed this scheme. The wreath of unit badges in the Royal Netherlands Air Force is constructed

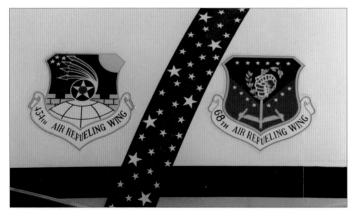

out of orange leaves and fruit – the badge of the House of Orange. The Royal Danish Air Force has a coat of arms for each unit, and replaces the wreath with a wing.

Some RAF units, notably schools and colleges, have a full achievement of arms. The crest of the Central Flying School is a pelican vulning itself (feeding its young with its own blood). The arms of the former Royal Aircraft Establishment

▼ *The arms of a Royal Danish Air Force Squadron painted on an aircraft fuselage.*

symbolized its research into early flight with a pterodactyl, while the Empire Test Pilot School, at Boscombe Down in Wiltshire, had a crest of an eagle rising from an astral coronet, fondly known by the students as the "chicken in a basket". (The College of Arms grants this coronet to institutions associated with aviation, as well as senior ranks of the RAF.) Although the ETPS has been absorbed into the Defence Evaluation and Research Agency, the crest is still retained in outline on the tailfins of the school's training aircraft.

▲ *The air forces of the world tend to adopt a flamboyance not met with in navies and armies. Here a Tornado fighter bomber of the German Air Force, elaborately painted for an air show, still bears the cross of the Teutonic Knights, dating back to the time of the Crusades.*

▼ *The Empire Test Pilot School at Boscombe Down in Wiltshire, England, uses the crest from the unit's arms on its aircrafts' fuselage or tail. It shows an eagle rising from an astral coronet.*

THE POLICE AND SECRET SERVICES

So many police forces have direct or indirect connections with their nation's military forces that it is not surprising to see a marked resemblance between their insignia. However, the United Kingdom appears to be unique in that its heraldic authorities have on several occasions granted full heraldic achievements to police authorities.

POLICE INSIGNIA

The uniform worn by British police forces was standardized in 1934, although many new items of clothing have been added since then. Nearly all bear the insignia of the particular force. Many use armorial bearings or the county arms, and tend to feature the royal cypher within a circlet and star. The most prominent armorial achievement of any British police force must be that of the Metropolitan Police in Greater London, whose portcullis is distinctively featured on its police cars. The arms also include a double tressure flory counter-flory taken from the Scottish royal arms, symbolizing the Met's world-famous headquarters, Scotland Yard.

Like several other police forces that possess arms, the Metropolitan Police does not actually use them on its cap and collar

▼ This badge follows the pattern set by the Canadian Heraldic Authority for Canada's police badges. The municipal arms and provincial flower are standard elements.

badges. The Wiltshire Constabulary was granted full armorial bearings in 1989, but does not use them in any form on its insignia and vehicles, although it has gone to the trouble of having a splendid heraldic standard manufactured, which is borne at formal parades. Its design includes the crest of a bustard, the county bird, holding a truncheon. The arms of various other British regional forces feature cap bands, police dogs and even the pavements pounded by policemen "on the beat".

The French and German provincial police bear their provincial or department arms on arm and helmet badges, as do many other regional and municipal police forces worldwide, from New South Wales to Maryland. In France the three fleurs de lis of the Bourbon dynasty, symbols proscribed by the revolutionaries of the First Republic, now serve the police in the Paris (Ile de France) region. In recent years the Canadian Heraldic Authority has granted formal heraldic badges for Canadian municipal police services. All the designs conform to a standard pattern, which includes a shield of arms in its centre.

The police are not the only public service to make use of armorial bearings, whether their own or those of their locality. British ambulance and fire services often sport arms in their insignia, on both uniforms and vehicles. In 1995 the South Wales Fire Service was granted full armorial bearings, which are used on the service's fire engines. The design of the shield is an adaptation of the three chevrons in the arms of the de Clares, the

▲ The design for the cap badge of the South Wales Fire Service, appropriately charged with its heraldic badge.

ruling family in the area during the Middle Ages. In the Fire Service design, the chevrons are differenced by being "rayonny" (in flames); above and below the chevrons are "gutty de larmes" (drops of water), and the crest is a lion bearing another heraldic charge, a "water bouget" (leather water bottle) with which to extinguish the flames.

SECURITY SERVICES

The world's so-called secret services are not so secret as to want to remain heraldically invisible. Even the USA's clandestine Phoenix Programme (set up to assassinate Viet Cong collaborators) adopted that mythical bird as its device. The Phoenix

▼ When on formal parade, the Wiltshire Constabulary fly their standard which includes the crest of the bustard with a truncheon.

▲ *The patrol cars of Scotland's Lothian and Border Police sport the force's full arms, including the sallet helmet given by the Scottish heralds to corporate organizations.*

Programme was said to be the Central Intelligence Agency's action army during the Vietnam War, and while the phoenix insignia was unofficial, the CIA itself has had armorial bearings since 1950. The shield, Argent a compass rose of sixteen points Gules, and the crest, Or a wreath

▲ *The warning eye of the American bald eagle keeps watch over the shield of the CIA.*

Argent and Gules an American bald eagle's head erased, are officially interpreted as follows: "The American Eagle is the national bird and is a symbol of strength and alertness. The radiating spokes of the compass rose depict the coverage of intelligence data from all areas of the world to a central point." The CIA arms are displayed in many forms, both in the organization's headquarters building and on its medals: the Distinguished Intelligence Medal places the arms on the breast of the national eagle, as befits US governmental institutions.

The old and much respected foe of the CIA, the Soviet Union's Komitet Gosudarstvennoi Bezopasnosti, or KGB, also maintained its own insignia. Its mission as the sword and shield of the state was to protect the hammer and sickle of communism, and it even had its own branch colour, royal blue, the sight of which on its arms, shield and cap bands was enough to put fear in all but the bravest hearts. Its present-day successor, the Federal Security Service, has managed to keep the sword and shield in its insignia, while replacing the hammer and sickle with the old tsarist symbol of the double-headed eagle displayed.

The KGB's most loyal friend, the East German Staatssicherheitsdienst – better known as the Stasi – used the GDR's state arms on its flag and breast badge in a typically militant socialist fashion. This was cynically known amongst Soviet conscripts as "hurrah art".

In Britain the Secret Intelligence Service (MI6), has not bothered to obtain a heraldic device of its own, but has permission to use the royal arms. However, its colleagues in the Security Service (MI5) do use their own heraldic badge designed by the College of Arms. It features a winged sea-lion, reflecting the Service's association with the armed services, and portcullises, symbolic of Parliament, which allude to its function of upholding Parliamentary democracy. The portcullises are interspersed with the rose of secrecy and green cinquefoils, whose five petals refer to MI5,

▲ *The badge of the British Security Service, otherwise known as MI5.*

◄ *The breast badge of the Russian Federal Security Service, successor to the KGB. The design keeps the shield and sword used by the KGB, but replaces the hammer and sickle with the imperial double-headed eagle.*

and whose colour has been associated with intelligence at least since World War I. The Security Service's motto is *Regnum defende*, "Defence of the realm".

▲ *The dreaded East German Security Ministry, better known as the Stasi, included in its insignia the state arms with hammer and compasses.*

INSIGNIA OF OFFICE

Since the late medieval period it has been common for a man or woman of high rank who holds an official position, usually at court, to wear or carry some form of insignia as an emblem of his or her high office. The earliest form of insignia seems to have been a wand or staff, which may have had its origin in ordinary staves such as those carried by shepherds, and examples can be found in the scenes of daily life painted on the walls of Egyptian tombs. Paintings dating from the Old Kingdom (c2700–c2150 BC) depict bailiffs or tax collectors using a form of truncheon when attempting to exact payment from recalcitrant farmers. Wooden batons have also been found in the tombs of Egyptian temple officials, bearing inscriptions asking for long life, prosperity and good health.

OFFICIAL INSIGNIA IN ARMS

Some of the earliest heraldic insignia of office are depicted on the seals of medieval admirals. These use the motif of a sailing

▼ Under the Bourbons, French court officials placed their insignia, including bottles, horns and wolves' heads, beside their shields.

ship, with the arms of the officer placed on the ship's sails, flags and streamers. By the 17th century admirals tended to show their office by placing anchors behind their shields of arms. In France, where many insignia of office originated, even rank was indicated by them: admirals of France had a pair of anchors in saltire, the cross bars strewn with fleurs de lis, vice-admirals had one plain anchor in pale behind the shield, and admirals of the galleys placed a grappling anchor behind their shield.

There is no hard and fast rule regarding the bearing of insignia of office. Some appear only as heraldic accoutrements, while others are actual objects, borne on ceremonial occasions. The French court of the 17th and 18th centuries made use of a splendid array of heraldic insignia, ranging from the

▲ The arms of justice of the hereditary Constables of Navarre are proudly borne at either side of the shield of the Dukes of Alba.

crowned batons semy de lis of the Master of the Royal Household, to the extraordinary wolves' heads placed on either side of the shield of the Grand Louvetier (Grand Wolf Huntsman).

THE CONSTABLE

As the highest-ranking officer in the medieval army, one of the constable's duties was the overseeing of martial law, including the passing of the death penalty. In time, the shields of the high constables were placed between two "arms of justice" – arms in armour issuing from clouds holding their sword of office. On taking his office, the Constable of France was presented with the sword itself, in a sheath of royal blue, semy de lis. One of the greatest Constables of France was Bertrand du Guesclin, who held the office from 1370–80. When he knew that he was dying, he sent the great sword back to

Grand Boutelier Echanson
André de Guynde
Supprimée.

Grand Pannetier
Jean Paul Timoleon de Cossé
Duc de Brissac.

Grand Veneur
Louis Jean Marie de Bourbon
Duc de Penthievre.

Grand Fauconnier
Louis Cesar de la Baume le Blanc
Duc de la Vallière.

Grand Louvetier
le Marquis de Flamarens
le Comte de Flamarens en Survivance

Grand Mareschal de Logis
Louis Michel Chamillart
Comte de la Suze.

▲ *A painting of the thanksgiving service for George V and Queen Mary, 1935. The Lord Chamberlain leads the Court with his staff of office, and the route is lined by the Yeomen of the Guard in their Tudor tunics.*

Charles V, saying: "Take it and return it into the King's keeping, and do you tell him that I have never betrayed him or it." This the King knew, and remembering du Guesclin's loyalty gave him the rare honour for a commoner of burial in the Abbey of Saint Denis, the traditional resting place for French royalty.

In recent years the constableships of two nations, Navarre and Scotland, have been in the hands of noblewomen. In the former case, the Duchess of Alba (who is the most titled lady in the world) places her shield between the arms of justice, the clouds bearing the arms of Navarre. Her shield quarters the royal arms of the British House of Stuart in a bordure compony (a border divided into segments) signifying illegitimacy, since the Dukes of Alba are descended from a natural son of James II.

THE MARSHAL

In practice, many of the duties of the medieval constable devolved on his deputy, the marshal, who carried a black gold-tipped baton as the insignia of his office. In France, by the reign of Philip IV (1285–1314), the marshal sat in judgement on certain cases at a great marble table in the Palais de Justice in Paris, administering a blow, or *bastonarde*, to the guilty with his baton.

By the 18th century, the baton seems to have passed wholly into heraldic usage in France, for when Marechal de Duras (1715–89) attempted to try the anti-revolutionary lawyer and historian Simon-Nicolas-Henri Linguet, he threatened to use the baton to condemn him, whereupon Linguet retorted, "Monsieur le Marechal, you would not know how to use it." The marshal did not share the constable's right to the arms of justice in his heraldic achievement: instead he placed crossed batons behind his shield, a practice taken up by marshals throughout much of Europe, including the Earl Marshal of England.

The Riksmarskalsk (Marshal of the Court) of Sweden still has a staff with a maroon shaft decorated with gold crowns, which appears in the armorial achievements of recent holders of the office.

In England, where the hereditary title is held by the Dukes of Norfolk, the Earl Marshal was for centuries unable to exercise his office personally because he was a Catholic, and it was common for his duties to be administered by a deputy, who placed one baton in bend behind his shield. Such a device can often be found in the margins of patents of arms (mainly from the Georgian period). The hereditary constableship, long held by the family of Stafford, Dukes of Buckingham, was abolished by Henry VIII after the attainder of the third Duke on grounds of treason in 1521. The office is revived temporarily for the coronation of the sovereign, its ceremonial duties being undertaken on other occasions by the Earl Marshal. Conversely, in Scotland, the hereditary post of Earl Marshal, long held in the family of Keith, was lost through attainder. The hereditary constableship of Scotland is alive and well, and is held by the Hays, Earls of Erroll.

▼ *The plaque of a Knight of the Swedish Order of the Seraphim. Behind the shield are the batons of the Marshal to the Royal House and of the Chancellor of the Order.*

THE CHAMBERLAIN

At the Danish court, the Chamberlain has a staff decorated with golden leaves and bears on his court uniform the insignia common to all chamberlains, a gold key – a reminder of the time when such officers were trusted by sovereigns with the keys to their private apartments. Such keys usually have the sovereign's cypher in the bow (the ring at the top of the key). Chamberlains of the British royal household wear the key on Garter blue ribbon.

In heraldry, most chamberlains place crossed keys behind their shield, but in England a Lord Great Chamberlain places the white wands of a high court official in saltire behind the shield, while the key is placed in fess below it. (The title of Lord Great Chamberlain is hereditary but it is not a full-time post, whereas the office of Lord Chamberlain is not hereditary but the holder is involved in the day-to-day running of the royal household.)

THE STAFF OF OFFICE

A wand or staff of office was common to most court officials, and apart from marking their status, it was a useful tool for fending off the common people. Usually

▶ *Proud of his status at court as well as in the Church, Cardinal Wolsey is portrayed here holding the baton of the Lord Chancellor of England.*

▼ *Originally the key to a sovereign's personal apartments, the chamberlain's key – the highest sign of trust – has been worn on his court uniform since the Middle Ages.*

made of wood, or perhaps of ivory, it could be a short baton or as tall as the man who bore it. It was ceremonially presented to the official by his master or mistress when he took up his office, and – equally ceremonially – was broken in pieces when he relinquished the office, or on the death of those whom the officer had served.

Today, the staves of office of the British royal household are little changed from those their predecessors used centuries ago, except for one innovation: a silver ferrule halfway up the shaft, bearing the title of office, has a screw thread that allows the staff to be "broken" ceremonially when the officer relinquishes his post. The two halves are then handed back and can be screwed back together to give the ex-officer a memento of his former position.

The breaking of staves was a popular allegorical theme in former centuries. Elizabeth I of England, during one of her royal progresses around her realm, was "accosted" by a savage man covered in moss and ivy, bearing an oaken staff in his

▼ *The staff of an officer of the royal household is fitted with a screw, allowing it to be re-assembled after its ceremonial "breaking" when the officer retires from his post.*

hand. After regaling the Queen with words in praise of his patron – her favourite, Robert Dudley – the "savage" broke his staff in half, "like a dismissed Chamberlain", and threw away the pieces, unfortunately hitting the Queen's horse on the head with one of them. The ceremonial breaking of the wand of office is made much of in an account of the funeral in 1574 of Edmund, Earl of Derby: "The Steward, Treasurer, and Comptroller, when the body was buried, kneeling on their knees, with weeping tears, brake their staves and rods over their heads, and threw the shivers of the same into the grave."

OFFICIAL BADGES

While much European court ceremonial disappeared, along with the courts themselves, after the end of World War I, little changed in the British royal household. The splendid uniforms of the officers of state were retained, and upon them the jewelled badges and the great golden keys.

Among the most fascinating of the badges is that of the Marshal of the

▼ *The badge of a former Master of Ceremonies to the English court bears the olive branch of peace on the front and the sword of war on the reverse. Nowadays, such a badge is worn by the Marshal of the Diplomatic Corps at the Court of St James.*

Diplomatic Corps, with its oval pendant. On one side it bears a hand grasping an olive branch, and on the other a hand grasping a sword. The story goes that in times of peace the olive branch was turned to the viewer, but when war was declared with another nation, its ambassador would receive an ominous visit from the Marshal – or rather his predecessor the Master of Ceremonies – who by this time would have swivelled his badge around to the martial side. Today, this badge may be glimpsed through the carriage windows when the Marshal of the Diplomatic Corps accompanies a new ambassador on his way to present his credentials to the Queen.

Another badge with a picturesque history is that worn by members of the Corps of Queen's Messengers. These gentlemen attend to the diplomatic mail that passes between British embassies and the Foreign Office, and the nature of their duties has given rise to many tales of bravura and adventure. Their neck badge is an oval bearing the sovereign's cypher within the Garter. Below it runs a little silver greyhound: did this originate from one of the heraldic supporters of the House of Tudor,

▼ *A delicate silver greyhound, perhaps one of the most romantic of all insignia, hangs from the badge of a member of the Corps of Queen's Messengers.*

or did it start life as one of the stands of a silver bowl used by Charles II in exile in the Netherlands? The tale is told that, as he gave his orders to his secret messengers, one asked, "How shall we be known?" King Charles snapped the little greyhounds off the bowl, giving one to each messenger and saying, "This will be your badge."

Neither the badge of the Marshal of the Diplomatic Corps, nor that of the Queen's Messengers, is used in an armorial achievement. In Scotland, however, castle governors, the Lord High Constable and many other high officials are still granted armorial insignia.

The need to be recognized and honoured lies deep within the psyche, a fact remembered by such modern institutions as the burger-bar giant McDonald's, which awards stars to its workforce to be worn as evidence of "rank". Each star has a different design – starting with crossed mop and brush and passing on through burger bun and chip fryer to smiley face (for good customer relations) – and with it comes an increment in pay. In all, five stars can be awarded, making the bearer the equivalent in military rank of a field marshal.

▼ *Doormen in the Palace of Westminster wear the badges of royal messengers. The figure of Mercury below this badge denotes a door keeper of the House of Commons.*

HERALDRY IN UNIVERSITIES AND SCHOOLS

Although they came later to the heraldic scene than towns or ecclesiastical bodies, universities and other major teaching establishments throughout Europe did take up heraldic devices. Often these tended to be limited to seals, but where arms were granted to or assumed by universities and schools, it was common to adopt the heraldic device of the establishment's founder and link it to a symbol of learning.

COLLEGE FOUNDERS

While most universities have arms or a seal common to the entire establishment, the colleges of the major English universities have individual arms which often have ancient origins, again usually with some obvious reference to the founder.

Amongst the most interesting arms are those of Clare College and Pembroke College, both in Cambridge. In the case of Clare College the arms of the husband and wife have been reversed, as Elizabeth, daughter of Gilbert de Clare, 3rd Earl of Gloucester, was considered far more important in estates and degree than her first husband, William de Burgh, Earl of

▲ *Margaret Beaufort's arms grace the entrance to Christ's College, Cambridge.*

Ulster. Her family arms therefore took the heraldically more important side (dexter of the marital shield). Elizabeth outlived three husbands, a fact remembered by the tears of mourning placed on a black border around the arms.

Pembroke College was founded in 1347 by Marie, daughter of Guy de Chastillon, Comte de St Pol, and wife of Aylmer de Valence, 2nd Earl of Pembroke. The

college arms have preserved the practice of dimidiation: the coats of de Valence and de Chastillon are cut down the middle and the dexter half of Valence is wedded to the sinister half of de Chastillon.

The grandest displays of heraldry in Cambridge must surely be the arms of Margaret Beaufort (1443–1509), mother of Henry VII. This proud and pious lady founded two colleges: Christ's and St John's. Both sport the Beaufort arms, complete with their yale supporters. The ground beneath the yales' hooves is scattered with Margaret's cognizance, the daisy flower or marguerite.

Oxford University is not to be outdone in heraldic honours by its younger rival. Among the shields that speak of extraordinary times in English history are the arms of that pompous prince of the Church, Cardinal Thomas Wolsey, Archbishop of York and Lord Chancellor, who founded Christ Church College. Included in the Cardinal's arms are many allusions to the institutions and individuals to which he owed his fortunes. His birthplace, Ipswich, is represented somewhat grandly by the arms of families that

◀ ▶*The cloisters of the University of Padua are richly decorated with the arms of noble students of previous centuries, which have long outlived their bearers.*

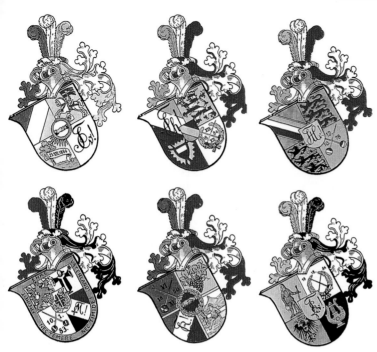

▲ The arms of Stephen Coombs, of the Katarinaskolan in Uppsala, Sweden, include the school arms (lower right) and those of his old college, Balliol, Oxford (top

▲ The arms of student fraternities from the University of Heidelberg often bear duelling swords (epées), which can be seen crossed in three of these shields.

at one time held the Earldom of Suffolk: de la Pole (leopards' faces Azure) and Ufford (a cross engrailed). The lion passant guardant on the cross represents Pope Leo X, from whom Wolsey received his cardinal's hat. The rose stands for Wolsey's position as a royal minister and the Cornish choughs are a reference to his namesake, Thomas à Becket.

Each college displays its arms to full effect in many different places, from the façade of the building to the silver on the table. More often than not they will be encountered along with those of benefactors, ancient and modern. In Oxford, the arms of all the colleges can be seen on the doors of the Bodleian Library.

STUDENTS' ARMS

Some European universities made much of the arms of students, since many came from noble families. The finest display of students' arms appears in the precincts of

the University of Padua, in northern Italy. Although it dates mainly from the 19th century, many shields still decorate the university's ancient courtyards and testify to the prestige it enjoyed all over Europe.

A unique feature of German heraldry is the arms of student fraternities displayed in the universities. These fraternities were famous for their duelling societies, and scars on the faces of young noblemen were considered a sign of honour. Each fraternity's members tended to come from the same region, so their arms included not only duelling swords, but also charges taken from the arms of their homeland. The centre of the arms often bore an inescutcheon upon which was placed a motto, or monogram, such as VCF for "Vivat, Crescat, Floreat" (Live, Flourish, Flower).

SCHOOLS

Though school arms are common in Britain, they are unusual elsewhere in Europe. The tradition does exist in Sweden, where schools display heraldic flags of their municipality. In 1993, the Katarinaskolan (St Katherine's School) at Uppsala assumed arms that were registered

in the Skandinavisk Vapenrulla (the Scandinavian Roll of Arms). They were the suggestion of Stephen Coombs, the Chairman of the Board of the School's Educational Foundation, and take as their badge a Catherine wheel surmounted by a cross formy. The wheel with its spikes refers to the martyrdom of St Katherine, but is also identified with Little Karin who, according to a Swedish folk song, was laid in a barrel with spikes.

▲ Religion was central to the medieval scholar's life and often a school or college looked to a particular saint for patronage. The arms of Eton College, for example, are charged with the lilies of the Virgin Mary.

MEDICAL HERALDRY

Most corporate heraldry contains a number of common symbols or charges that are particularly related to the profession or institution concerned. These charges can get very repetitive, but they do provide a clue to identity. They are a phenomenon chiefly related to British and Commonwealth heraldry, and are not often found elsewhere. The charges that frequently appear in arms related to medicine are good examples of this kind of usage.

Some medical arms, such as those of St Bartholomew's Hospital in London, have no such charges. William Wakering, Master of the Hospital from 1423–62, used the armorial bearings Per pale Argent and Sable a chevron counterchanged. These arms were not granted to Wakering or his family but because he was Master for such a long time they became associated with the hospital and are recorded as such in a 16th-century roll of arms.

SNAKES AND OTHER BEASTS

A good example of a "themed" charge is the snake, which almost invariably has a connection with medicine and is frequently used by medical institutions as well as in the personal arms of medical practitioners. For centuries the snake was thought to possess wisdom and mysterious healing powers. Temples used by ancient healers included pits of harmless snakes, thought to have healing properties.

▼ The gates of Bristol General Hospital, bearing fine representations of the city arms.

▲ Lord Leycester's Hospital in Warwick, England, maintains a fine display of heraldry, including the bear and ragged staff of the Earls of Warwick and the shield of the Dudley family above it.

As snakes periodically shed their skin, appearing to be reborn, they were seen as vehicles of immortality.

Snakes were also associated with Aesculapius, the Greek and Roman god of medicine. A legend told that as he was examining a patient, a serpent crept in, climbed his staff and imbued him with wisdom. In heraldry, the snake is usually depicted twined about a rod, known as the staff of Aesculapius. Snakes can also be found in other attitudes, such as knotted, or devouring their own tails, and may be

entwined about other charges. A particular species may be blazoned occasionally, such as the red-bellied black snake of the Royal Brisbane Hospital, or the Children's python (*Liasis childreni*) in the arms of the Australian Royal Children's Hospital Board.

Two mythical creatures more or less exclusive to medical heraldry are the caladrius and the opinicus. The caladrius, a bird found in ancient bestiaries, was credited with therapeutic powers. It was pure white, and the lower part of its leg was reputed to "purge" diseases of the eye. The opinicus had lion's legs, dragon's wings, pointed ears, a long bill and a camel's tail. It was granted as a crest to the Barber Surgeons of London in 1561.

INANIMATE CHARGES

Surgical instruments have been used as heraldic charges from early times. Perhaps the best known is the fleam, a form of lancet used for blood-letting. In heraldry it resembles an elaborate figure seven. It was used in the arms of the Company of Barbers of London in 1451. A spatula was included in the badge of the Fellowship of Surgeons of London in 1492, and both instruments were incorporated in the arms of the Worshipful Company of Barber Surgeons of London in 1569.

In its arms granted in 1672, the Royal College of Surgeons of Edinburgh has a bordure charged with seven surgical instruments which, though not specified individually, are described as "several instruments indicative of the art". Scalpels, ophthalmascopes, inhalers, dental and mammary probes and syringes have all been used as charges.

The shield of the Royal College of Pathologists (1971) is Argent a bar wavy Gules between in chief two torteaux and in base a benzene ring Sable. The use of straightforward charges illustrates the four disciplines of pathology: the red wavy line suggests histopathology, one torteau represents a red cell for haematology, and the second stands for biology. Microbiology is represented by the benzene ring.

▲ *In the arms of the British Association of Urological Surgeons, the compartment is appropriately strewn with sweet peas.*

▲ *In the arms of The Faculty of Accident and Emergency Medicine, a wounded supporter sports a multitude of injuries.*

Plants naturally have a place in medical heraldry by virtue of their curative properties. The foxglove, opium poppy and cocaine plant are all associated with anaesthetics or painkillers. The mandrake is found in the crest of the Association of Anaesthetists of Great Britain and Ireland (1945). A poisonous plant of southern Europe, it was used in the Middle Ages as a sedative and painkiller. Its knobbly, forked roots were thought to resemble the human figure, and when pulled from the ground it supposedly emitted a piercing shriek that sent people mad. The pome-

▼ *The Urological Society of Australia's charge of a view up the neck of the bladder when peered at through a cystoscope.*

granate is usually depicted in heraldry as split, showing its many seeds, and is used to represent fertility. It was used in the arms of the Royal College of Physicians by Garter Barker in 1546. In more modern times, a British institution serving urologists has been granted arms in which the compartment is strewn with sweet peas.

SUPPORTERS

The supporters of medical arms include mythical beasts, real animals and birds, and real people as well as gods and goddesses. The latter, in addition to Aesculapius, include his daughter Hygeia, goddess of health. She is shown holding a bowl with a snake entwined about her arm drinking from the bowl. Machaon and Podalrius, sons of Aesculapius, are also often used. They were said to have been Greek surgeons at the Siege of Troy, where Machaon removed an arrow from the wounded Menelaus. Machaon is usually seen holding a broken arrow in his hand. Egyptian deities are represented in British arms by the goddess Isis, who appears in the arms of the National Institute of Medical Herbalists, and by Imhotep, the god of medicine, seen in the arms of the Institute of Health Service Management.

The patron saints of surgeons, Cosimo and Damian, support the arms of the Fellowship of Surgeons, and St Barbara, the patron saint of the injured, supports the shield of the Institute of Accident

Surgery. Hippocrates, founder of medical ethics, appears in several achievements.

More recent medical figures include William Harvey (1578–1657), who discovered the circulation of the blood and supports the arms of the British Medical Association, and Dr Benjamin Golding, founder of Charing Cross Hospital in 1818. British anaesthetists, Dr John Snow (1813–58) and Dr Joseph Clover (1825–82) support the shield of the Royal College of Anaesthetists. The sinister supporter of the Arms of the Royal College of Paediatrics and Child Health is Thomas Phaire, author of the first book on paediatrics written in English in 1553.

Anonymous figures include nurses in uniform and – for the Royal Victoria Eye & Ear Hospital, Australia – a surgeon gowned and ready for the operating theatre. A boy and a girl support the shield of the Australian Royal Children's Hospital.

The horn of the unicorn was believed to possess healing as well as aphrodisiac properties when ground down, and when hollowed out and used as a cup it was thought to combat poisonous substances. The horn of the rhinoceros was thought to possess similar properties, and both are displayed as the crest and supporters of the Society of Apothecaries.

▼ *The shield of a 19th-century English doctor, Thomas Smith, combines the hand feeling a pulse of the College of Physicians, with the rod and serpent of Aesculapius.*

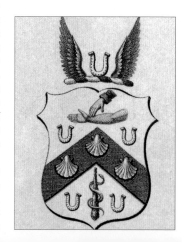

GUILDS AND LIVERY COMPANIES

In the late medieval period the growing wealth and power of the mercantile classes, and the guilds and fraternities to which they belonged, allowed them to make inroads into the preserves of the aristocracy. Naturally, the latter were none too happy about this chipping away of their prerogatives by the self-made men who had their power bases in the cities of Europe. However, various laws that attempted to safeguard the dress and other attributes of the nobility were of little use: the money of the merchants could not be ignored by lords or even kings.

Merchants and craftsmen organized themselves into guilds that safeguarded their trades, which were in some ways the forerunners of modern trades unions. A member who had served as an apprentice in his craft, and who had paid his dues and been initiated into the rites and mysteries of the guild, could expect a degree of protection against the hardships of medieval life. On his death he would know that the other guild members would give him a splendid funeral, complete with heraldry.

The wealth of the guilds, and of the individuals who made up their numbers, was vast. Merchants were often richer and lived in greater splendour than any petty European prince. It is not surprising that among the earliest English patents of arms are those of several guilds. The very same arms – such as those of the Mercers, Vintners, and all the other trades that helped to make the living in London among the richest in the medieval world – may still be seen in the annual Lord Mayor's Procession through the city. Each guild, or livery company, makes its presence known through its own particular arms and colours, or liveries.

▲ Heraldry has come a long way from the medieval battlefield to the Nottinghamshire coalfield of Manton Colliery.

◄ The traditional procession in Siena, Italy, of the city's guilds, where the participants dress in medieval costume.

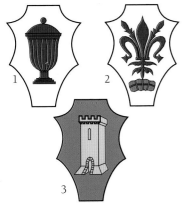

▲ *The officers and magistrates of the city state of Florence enjoyed their own arms of office, including: 1 Masters of the Salt, 2 members of the Mercantile Tribunal, 3 officers of the monte comune (the public debt).*

CRAFT SYMBOLS

All over Europe the pride men took in their professions and civic status was made manifest in symbol and colour. If he had not yet become armigerous, the merchant could content himself by showing off his individual mark, possibly placed on a shield. Many churches and houses from England to Switzerland were decorated

▼ *In 1715 Thomas Doggett, a staunch Hanoverian, instituted a rowing race on the River Thames. Six royal watermen still compete for the coat and badge, shown here, which bears the white horse of Hanover.*

with such marks, often in the form of initials and crosses. In England, merchants of the wool trade, or "staple", used such devices not only on their homes but also to mark their wool bales.

The arms of the guilds often included some obvious symbol of their craft, such as a pretzel for the bakers and an ox and axe for the butchers. The guild's patron saint was also often included, although after the Reformation in England several livery companies adopted new arms more attuned to the times, and any symbols overtly associated with Catholicism were judiciously shelved.

From such fraternities, other organizations emerged, such as the freemasons, in whose ceremonial heraldry plays its part.

▲ *A medieval grant of arms to the Tallow Chandlers of London, 1463. The power of the city guilds was made manifest through the splendour of their arms.*

Their insignia apes that of a royal household, with keys and staves of office like any court chamberlain. The "jewels" of lodge officers often include not only the arms of the town or region from which the lodge members come, but also the arms of influential local families, who may have provided past masters of the lodge.

▼ *In procession in Bruges, Belgium, the guilds still make a fine showing of their arms, most of which include motifs alluding to their particular trades.*

GLOBAL HERALDRY

Although heraldry uses an international language, achievements of arms have always been devised and regulated by national authorities. The royal heralds, around whom the various heraldic institutions grew up, were in the service of individual monarchs, and over the centuries many nations developed their own distinct heraldic styles. From its beginnings in northern Europe, heraldry spread all over the world during the eras of global exploration and conquest. While some countries no longer maintain their own heraldic authorities, the tradition is thriving in many parts of the world, and new ideas and artistic innovations continue to invigorate the heraldic realm.

◀ *The arms of the Jewish congregation of Shaar Hashomayim in Canada, with the crest borne on a helmet in the style of the Maccabeans.*

SCOTLAND

No country has a more diverse and fascinating application of heraldry than Scotland. It is one of the few nations with a true heraldic institution that can boast a continuous history going back centuries. Although smaller than the English College of Arms, the Court of Lord Lyon is every bit as adventurous and innovative when it comes to heraldic interpretation and application.

THE COURT OF LORD LYON

In Scotland the chief herald is Lord Lyon King of Arms. In the old kingdom of Scotland, Lord Lyon was a Privy Councillor and minister of the crown. The nature of kinship, which permeated Scottish society at all levels, gave rise to a regiment of men known as "sennachie", or bards, who called out the pedigrees and histories of the chiefs of clans and "septs" (other families loyal to a clan) at formal gatherings. Lord Lyon was Chief Sennachie of the royal line, and it was his duty to recite the king's pedigree during a coronation.

The new Lord Lyon, appointed in 2001, is considered to be more attuned to the legal side of his duties than to the heraldic side. This reflects the fact that he is concerned with many matters attached to Scottish clanship, and may often be

▼ *Scottish Officers of Arms make a proclamation in Edinburgh.*

involved in the judging of genealogies. The sacrosanct nature of heraldry in Scotland means that Lord Lyon's roar can be very loud. In recent years Sir Malcolm Innes, when Lyon, pursued anyone who presumed to bear arms not officially registered, from ice cream vendors and football teams to the owner of Harrods. In January 2000, Mohamed Al Fayed was ordered to remove the arms of the Chief of Clan Ross, which he had erected on his Scottish castle, Balnagowan, the ancestral home of the Ross family.

That case pales into insignificance compared with a 1958 grant of arms to the English town of Berwick-on-Tweed, which until 1482 was part of Scotland. The town council petitioned the English heralds for a coat of arms, but seemed to dislike the design. The townspeople then petitioned Lord Lyon, since in Scotland ancient arms are a form of heritable property, and it was held that Berwick had established an ancient right to arms in Scotland.

The heraldic author Lt Col Robert Gayre stated that Scotland could look upon Berwick as occupied territory, wrested from its own country and held as a base for further pretentious aggression against Scotland. The arms Lord Lyon matriculated included not only the bear and wych-elm, but also chained bears for supporters and the coronet and compartment applicable to a Scottish royal burgh. Eventually, the

▲ *The arms of Berwick-upon-Tweed as matriculated with the Scottish heraldic authorities in 1958.*

controversy died down and Berwick received a patent from the College of Arms in 1977: this time they ensured that the bear and wych-elm had prime position.

With the exception of Lord Lyon and Lyon Clerk, the Scottish heralds are paid only nominal fees and pursue full-time careers elsewhere, often in spheres appropriate to their heraldic duties, such as in law firms and museums or as artists. There are three heralds in ordinary: Marchmont, Rothesay and Dingwall, and four pursuivants in ordinary: Dingwall, Kintyre, Carrick and Unicorn. There are also two pursuivants extraordinary: Falkland and March. In addition, some Scottish peers of ancient title are entitled to their own private officer of arms: the herald of the Earls of Erroll, Hereditary High Constables of Scotland, is called Slains Pursuivant and bears a tabard of his master's arms, Argent three escutcheons Gules.

The Scottish officers of arms can be seen wearing their tabards and badges of office on such occasions as the installation of the Governor of Edinburgh Castle, when the standard of the Governor is unfurled above the Castle gates. The standard bears both the arms of his office and his personal arms. Also on view are the six Scottish State Trumpeters, with the royal arms of Scotland embroidered on their trumpet banners. The State Trumpeters also attend Lord Lyon at the reading of royal proclamations at the Mercat Cross in Edinburgh.

THE ARMS OF SCOTLAND

The red lion rampant within a double tressure flory counter-flory, was first used on a seal of Alexander III of Scotland in 1251, although the red lion was probably previously used by William I, "The Lion" (1165–1214), and a border of fleurs de lis was used in the arms of his son, Alexander II (1214–49). When James VI of Scotland acceded to the English throne in 1603 after the Act of Union (as James I), the ramping lion of the Scots was placed in the second quarter of the royal arms. When the British sovereign visits Scotland the quarters are reversed, Scotland taking the first quarter.

The British royal family is, in effect, the chief clan of Scotland and uses certain heraldic insignia as with any other clan. Royal Stewart tartan and its variants are worn, and the royal crest for Scotland may at times be observed. The sovereign's eldest son has his own heraldic banner for use in Scotland, where he is Duke of Rothesay, Earl of Carrick, Baron Renfrew, Lord of the Isles, Great Steward of Scotland. He uses a plain label in conjunction with his Scottish arms.

THE ORDER OF THE THISTLE

Scotland's own order of chivalry is the Most Ancient and Most Noble Order of the Thistle, founded in 1540, and its Knights in their dark green mantles take their places in the stalls of the Chapel of the Order, attached to St Giles Cathedral in Edinburgh. The Chapel, inaugurated in 1911, is full of heraldic symbolism, and attached to the stall backs are the stall plates of the Thistle Knights, while their banners are grouped around the pillars in the body of the Cathedral.

THE ROYAL COMPANY OF ARCHERS

In Scotland the sovereign's bodyguard is formed by the Royal Company of Archers. Originating as a private archery club in 1676, it received a royal charter from Queen Anne, for which the "reddendo", or service in return, was to present the sovereign, when requested, with a pair of barbed arrows (an archer's "pair" numbering three). The Company's field uniform is dark green with crimson piping for men, gold for officers, and its insignia includes the reddendo of arrows and the star of the Order of the Thistle. The officers also have collar badges. Their bonnets are decorated with eagles' feathers: one for men, two for officers and three for the Captain General. The Secretary outclasses them all, by wearing a Malayan condor's feather.

BLAZON OF THE ROYAL ARMS

As Queen of the Scots, Elizabeth II bears Quarterly 1 and 4 Or a lion rampant Gules armed Or and langued Azure, within a double tressure flory counter-flory of the second [Scotland]; 2 Gules three lions passant guardant Or [England]; 3 Azure a harp Or stringed Argent [Ireland]. Encircling the shield is the collar of the Most Ancient and Most Noble Order of the Thistle. The crest is an imperial crown proper surmounted by a lion sejant affronty Gules imperially crowned holding in his dexter paw a bared sword and in his sinister a sceptre, both proper. On a compartment vert with thistles proper are the supporters: dexter a unicorn Argent armed tufted and langued Or imperially crowned proper and gorged with an open crown chain reflexed over the back Or and supporting a banner of St Andrew; sinister a lion rampant guardant Or imperially crowned proper supporting a banner of St George. On a scroll above is the motto *In defens*; and in the compartment the motto of the Order of the Thistle, *Nemo me impune lacessit*.

▲ *The jacket of an archer in the Royal Company of Archers, topped with the bonnet of an officer, with two feathers.*

▼ *The hat of the High Constable of Holyroodhouse, with black cock's feathers and the silver stag and cross of Holyrood.*

▶ *The baton of office of the Hereditary Master of the Household in Scotland, a position held by the Dukes of Argyll, has at its head the lion that surmounts the crest of the Scottish royal arms.*

THE SCOTTISH CLAN SYSTEM

The clan – the word stems from the Gaelic for "children" – is an enlarged family unit. It ensures that all within its ranks are equal. The common kinship of the clan, whether real or nominal, knits together every Highland community. While official records refer to the Earl of Argyll, the Lord of the Isles or Lord Lovat (as they would be known in Edinburgh), in their own lands these lords are simply called the MacCailean mor (son of great Colin), the MacDonnal (son of Donald), or the MacShimidh (son of Simon).

Although predominantly a Highland phenomenon, the clan system was also found in the Lowlands, amongst great names such as the Douglases. The terrible feuding between Highland and Lowland clans reached the highest levels of Scots society and had many victims within the royal house itself, as kings were often merely the pawns of other great families. It is a theme often reflected in heraldry. Even a playing card, the nine of diamonds, is called the "curse of Scotland" because nine lozenges appear in the arms of John Dalrymple, 1st Earl of Stair, who instigated

▼ *At a gathering of Clan Donald at their ancestral seat, banners of the chief and chieftains are much in evidence.*

the massacre of the Macdonalds at Glencoe in 1692. The hammer in the arms of Naesmyth and the oak tree and frame saw in the crest of Hamilton both refer to incidents during which family members had to disguise themselves as workers to avoid discovery by enemies pursuing them during Scotland's more turbulent moments.

CLAN INSIGNIA

Personal heraldry in Scotland is closely linked with the clan system, and stringent rules protect armigers and their heraldic status. The full panoply of clan insignia can be seen at annual clan gatherings, at events such as the Highland Games. Apart from wearing the clan tartan, of which there may be several versions, clan members wear on their bonnets a silver badge (or for women, a brooch) of the chief's crest within a strap and buckle, which also bears the chief's motto, slogan or war cry.

The crest on the badge is not that of the wearer but the property of the clan chief. Armigers may display their own crest within a plain circlet bearing motto or slogan, and place this behind the badge on a silver feather. The head of a large clan branch, officially recognized as such by the Lord Lyon, may bear crest, circlet and motto with two feathers. A clan chief

▲ *The arms of the late Sir Fitzroy Maclean include a feudal baron's cap and insignia of the hereditary Keeper of Dunconnel.*

places three feathers behind the badge, and a peer may add the appropriate coronet of rank. Even members of the royal family keep to this tradition, wearing the Scottish royal crest on Balmoral bonnets.

HERALDIC FLAGS

At a clan gathering a selection of heraldic flags will be on display, representing the clan chief, chieftains (the heads of family branches) and other senior figures. Such flags are closely regulated by Lord Lyon and come under his legal jurisdiction through an Act of Parliament of 1672. All are recorded on the matriculations of arms of those entitled to such honours.

The most important flag to look out for is the standard, which is granted only to those who have a "following", such as a clan chief. One of the most splendid heraldic accoutrements in use today, the Scottish standard has an unbroken history from the feudal standard of the late Middle Ages. It is viewed as a headquarters flag

and does not necessarily mean that the chief is present: this is indicated by the square personal banner displaying his own arms. Ancient Scottish standards normally had the saltire on the hoist (the section of the flag nearest the pole), but modern standards more often bear the owner's personal arms in this area. The remainder is divided into two tracts of the livery colours for chiefs of clans or families, three tracts for very major branches – chieftains – and four for others. The standard is very long, ranging from 7 metres (8 yards) for the sovereign to 3.5 metres (4 yards) for knights and barons. It is tapered and split into two rounded ends (for peers and barons), or unsplit with a rounded end for non-baronial chiefs. It usually bears the owner's crest and heraldic badges, which include the clan's plant badge separated by transverse bands bearing the owner's motto or slogan. If the owner is a peer or feudal baron, the flagpole may be ensigned by a coronet or chapeau of degree.

The guidon is similar to a small standard, one third shorter than the standard assigned to feudal barons. It is assigned to

▼ *The Braw Lads Gathering, Galashiels – one of several "ridings" in Scotland where heraldry is much in evidence.*

lairds (the rough equivalent of English lords of the manor) who have a following.

The fourth type of flag to look out for is the "pinsel". This triangular flag denotes a person who represents the chief in his or her absence. On the chief's main livery colour is his or her crest within a strap of the second livery colour and a buckle (gold for full chiefs) bearing the motto. Outside the strap and buckle, a gold circlet is inscribed with the chief's or baron's title. On top is the coronet of rank or baronial cap. The flag also bears the plant badge and a scroll inscribed with the motto.

FEUDAL BARONIES
The clan chief or chieftain may also be a feudal baron. Lands that have been vested by charter from the Crown (or, rarely, by other high nobles) give the possessor special rights, including certain forms of public justice not normally found on ordinary estates. The holders of such feudal baronies are termed barons or baronesses. (The Scottish equivalent of an English baron is a lord of Parliament.) Before 1587, feudal barons were also entitled to sit in the Scottish Parliament, so the holders of Scottish feudal baronies enjoy certain heraldic honours akin to those of the peerage. These include a chapeau or cap of maintenance, which is placed directly above the shield between it and the helm. The colour of the chapeau shows the particular form of barony:

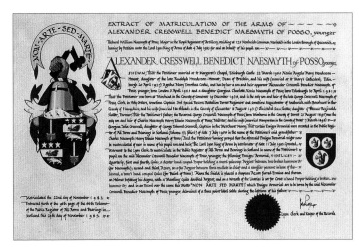

▲ *A matriculation of arms for Alexander Naesmyth of Posso, from the Court of Lord Lyon. This includes the feudal chapeau for an heir of a barony not in possession.*

1 Chapeau Gules, furred ermine: baron of the kingdom of Scotland still in possession of the barony.
2 Chapeau Azure, furred ermine: the heir to such a barony, not in possession.
3 Chapeau Gules, furred ermines (contre-ermine): a baron of Argyll and the Isles, or one of the older earldoms still in possession.
4 Chapeau Azure, furred ermines: the heir to such a barony, not in possession.

Scottish barons place behind their shield a feudal-baronial mantle, Gules, doubled of silk Argent, fur-edged of miniver and collar ermine, and fastened on the right shoulder by five spherical buttons Or.

The heirs of barons possessed of a barony before 1587 are entitled to clan heraldic supporters (this may also be the case for barons before 1627, but the point is not fully resolved). Feudal barons may also display a baronial helmet, "of steel with a grille of one or three grilles garnished with gold". A barony implicitly has a baron court, of which the presiding judge is baron-baillie and the executive officer is the baron-serjeant. Each has his own insignia and is entitled to heraldic mention of these when matriculating arms.

WALES

Over the centuries British monarchs have maintained in their shields heraldic references to the major nations over which they ruled: the "leopards" of England, the ramping lion of the Scots and the harp of Ireland. Yet one nation, Wales, has seldom figured within their achievements. There never was a king of all Wales, the country was split for centuries into kingdoms, principalities and lordships, and the Welsh had their own names for each degree. Under the English crown Wales has always been called a principality.

Not surprisingly, the Welsh themselves have often seen this as an example of the desultory way in which the government in London regards them. It is telling that the name "Wales" comes from an Anglo-Saxon term for "stranger". The strangers in this case were the Celtic inhabitants of the British Isles who took refuge from the Anglo-Saxons in the hinterland of Wales.

After 1066, the Welsh gained new neighbours, the Normans, who in time made inroads into Wales itself. The Norman and Plantagenet kings often gave the borderlands to their most trusted nobles, who marked out for themselves semi-independent territories. One of the most imperious of those Anglo-Norman dynasties was the family of de Clare, Earls of Pembroke and Gloucester. They were early enthusiasts of heraldry, and it was through the de Clares and other Norman magnates that it spread to Wales.

Although it was not as widespread and popular as among the English nobility, heraldry was certainly being used by the middle of the 13th century. In Gwynned, for instance, two sons of Llewelyn the Great used arms quartered with four counterchanged lions passant, gold and red being the favourite colours.

THE IMPORTANCE OF LINEAGE

Anyone in medieval Wales, of whatever status, was expected to be able to recite his or her own lineage for five generations. Surnames were not used, except among the English settlers. A man was Evan, son

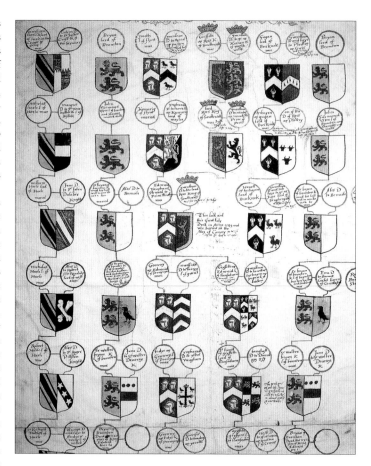

▲ The Welsh interest in genealogy is demonstrated by this pedigree of 1593 for Anne Harle, showing descent from Edward Vaughan, Lord Steward of all Wales.

► This 19th-century bookplate for a Welsh family includes many of the arms attributed to the princes and noble tribes.

of Howel, son of Llewelyn, and so on. The close-knit nature of Welsh society meant that no further recognition was needed, and the local bards could always be called upon to recite a full lineage.

The all-powerful figure in Welsh lineage was the antecedent known as the noble progenitor. Most of these dated from the

in general, it seemed that they would have been of armigerous status whenever they lived, and that their descendants were automatically entitled to the arms – whether real or attributed – of their noble progenitor. Such arms were invented, often using symbols taken from the potent store of bardic poetry and story-telling.

Many Welsh families still proclaim their descent from one or more of those warrior lords. One such ruler was Hywel Dda (Hywel the Good), "The Law Giver", whose 10th-century realm covered much of South Wales. Among many sensible and pragmatic laws he made was this: "It is required of those of noble descent, that their lineage be proclaimed to all in prominent places about their dwellings."

An extraordinary interpretation of this command was made around 1909 by Mrs Ada Lansdown-Williams, who used heraldry to display not only her own lineage but that of her husband, in her manor house on the Welsh coast. The house, now a hotel, contains a display of painted tiles illustrating a lineage going back to the times of the Law Giver himself. She seems to have completed her heraldic scheme in time for the 1,000th anniversary of Hywel Dda's accession. It is a glorious reminder of the staying-power of Celtic lore.

▲ *Heraldry was introduced into Wales by the late 13th century and its style was often adapted to suit Celtic taste, as here on the gravestone of Madog ap Gruffudd, Vale Crucis Abbey, Clwyd.*

▼ *One of Ada Lansdown-Williams' modern painted tiles displaying her lineage in her house near St Davids.*

Dark Ages, when the power vacuum left after the collapse of Roman power was filled by the rule of tribal leaders, strong men whose character bound the people together in desperate times. Some were real men, others semi-legendary. It has been suggested that King Arthur himself was an amalgam of several rulers. To the Welsh people of the late medieval period, men like Cilmin Troed-ddu (Cilmin of the Black Foot) of Caernarvonshire, or Hedd Molwynog of Denbighshire, were most certainly real people and a proud ancestry to be preserved and honoured.

As heraldry filtered into Wales through warfare, trade and even inter-marriage, arms were assumed by some Welsh magnates, such as Gruffyd ap Llewelyn (the Great). More often, they were attributed to chieftains who had ruled in pre-heraldic times. To the bards, and to Welsh society

THE DRAGON OF WALES

Linked with King Arthur, the red dragon was also said to have been the emblem of Cadwalader, a Welsh prince of the 7th century. The Tudor dynasty used Cadwalader's dragon in their armorial bearings, notably as a supporter, and to this day the badge of the Prince of Wales is a red dragon.

IRELAND

The Irish came late to heraldry. It had little place in Gaelic culture, which had its own rich tradition of symbols. When heraldry did arrive from England, it was seen as yet another foreign import, baggage associated with the hated Anglo-Norman adventurers who managed to gain a foothold on Ireland's south-east coast during the 12th and 13th centuries. The narrow stretch of land, with its capital in Dublin, was termed "the pale": within this area the Norman lords and merchants felt secure from the native Irish who were, literally, "beyond the pale".

The arrival of heraldry in Ireland was associated with the English elite. Families such as Butler and Fitzgerald, who in time became more Irish than the Irish, spent as much time feuding against each other as

they did fighting their Gaelic neighbours. The simple arms of these two families – Argent a saltire Gules for the Fitzgeralds, Or a chief indented Azure for the Butlers – reflects their early adoption.

IRISH CHARGES

In time the indigenous Gaelic nobility did become curious about heraldry, although often in a somewhat desultory fashion. Symbols that had formed part of a pre-heraldic tradition found their way on to shields of arms, where they often seem ill-placed and haphazard. Charges are cramped and squeezed into the foot of the shield, or

▲ *The arms of O'Neill, with "internal supporters", the sacred salmon and the famous red hand.*

◄ *The arms of the Fitzgeralds show the simplicity of early heraldry, which arrived in Ireland with the Norman/English aristocracy.*

▼ *A knight of the Butler family looks out upon his fiefdom from 12th-century Jerpoint Abbey, in County Kilkenny. His heraldic shield is perfectly preserved.*

◄ *A knight of the Cantwell family, wearing the dress of a well-to-do military man of northern Europe in the second half of the 13th century.*

▲ *Symbols of piety are often found in the arms of Irish Catholic families, such as those of O'Donnell.*

propped up against other main charges. A particularly Irish phenomenon is the use of animals on shields to support another charge (such as the red hand). These "internal supporters" probably started life supporting the shield in the normal way but were shifted on to the shield through a mistake on the part of the stonemason or woodcarver reproducing the arms.

Among the symbols with mystic origins favoured by the Gaelic Irish was the sacred tree, usually the oak, that grew near the entrance to a chief's home. Its divine status was shared by the salmon. Both symbols were regarded as the insignia of royalty, and the most telling gesture a victor could make was to destroy the oak tree and despoil the salmon ponds of his defeated foe.

The salmon is closely associated with the heraldry of the O'Neills, medieval kings of Ulster who also made much use of the famous red hand, a charge found in the heraldry of many Northern Irish families. The origin of the red hand has been the cause of much speculation among Gaelic historians, but many believe it to be a symbol indicative of the bloodline of a royal house. In England the red hand of Ulster, for long associated with the province of Ulster, has gained a certain notoriety through misunderstanding of its significance, especially where it appears in the arms of baronets. Tourist guides are likely to refer to it as a mark given to families who have produced an infamous murderer.

The great beasts of the chase, the stag and the boar, were also considered noble attributes worthy to be included in the heraldry of the Irish clans. Charges commonly seen in Scottish heraldry, such as ancient ships, or religious symbols coupled to war-like symbols, can often also be found across the Irish Sea, indicating the common ancestry of many old Scottish and Irish families.

CLANS AND LINEAGE

As in Scotland and Wales, the Irish Celts placed great emphasis on a royal or noble past, especially through the medium of genealogy. But while the Welsh nobles tended to trace their lineage from many different ancestors, some legendary and others real, all Celtic Irish families traced their line back to one man, Milesius, who was believed to have brought the Celts to Ireland from Spain.

Milesius was said to have had eight sons, only three of whom produced offspring. Some of the Celtic symbols that found their way into heraldry as charges were associated with the bloodlines of Milesius' sons. For instance, it was from Eirehamon, the seventh son of Milesius,

▲ *A 19th-century copy of Charles Lynegar's genealogy of Bernard Maguire, originally drawn up in 1731.*

that the Northern Irish tribal groupings of the Ui Neill (O'Neill) and Ui Briuin sprang. While the former took the red hand as their symbol, the latter favoured the sacred oak tree.

ENGLISH RULE

Increasing English dominance over Ireland during the Tudor period meant that heraldry was increasingly adopted by the native Irish aristocracy. Having been forced by the Crown to surrender their ancient titles and territory, the Irish nobility had their lands re-granted and new English-style titles bestowed upon them. Not everyone was prepared to take advantage

of this manifestation of foreign dominance. The London government encouraged an influx of English and Scots settlers who, as they were often drawn from the ranks of the gentry, wished to have heraldic recognition of their new local status. This led in 1552 to the establishment of a heraldic office in Dublin, housed for many years in Dublin Castle, the seat of the English government of Ireland. Ulster King of Arms, with his deputy, Athlone Pursuivant, headed the office.

Many Irishmen of Celtic stock saw the "Ulster Office" as yet another example of English arrogance. In time, native Irish historians with a particular interest in heraldry set themselves up as heralds in open opposition to it. One such, Cathal O'Luinnín (anglicized as Charles Lynegar), issued heraldic certificates and pedigrees to Irishmen who did not recognize the jurisdiction of the English-appointed Ulster King of Arms. To make his point more forcefully to the English, O'Luinnín styled himself King of Arms of Ulster. Whereas a patent of arms issued by the Ulster Office bore the English royal arms, the patents issued by O'Luinnín bore the arms of the head of the House of O'Neill, the ancient Kings of Ulster.

O'Luinnín's certificated pedigrees are interesting in that they were written not only in English, but also in French and Latin. This reflected the nature of many of his clients who, disaffected with English rule, had fled abroad to Catholic countries, notably France, Spain and Austria, where many acquired the aristocratic titles of those nations.

The drain of the native Irish aristocracy became more pronounced after the Battle of the Boyne in 1691, at which the Catholic monarch, James II, was defeated by the Protestant prince, William of Orange. The departure into exile of a new wave of Irish Catholics was known ever after as "The Flight of the Wild Geese". Many of them ended up at the court of the exiled James II at St Germain-en-Laye.

At the Stuart court in exile, heraldic matters were at first taken care of by James Terry, Athlone Pursuivant, who fled to Paris

▲ A modern grant of arms by the Office of the Chief Herald of Ireland for a Fitzgerald, based on the ancient arms of the family.

▼ Confirmation of arms of Daniel O'Donnell by James Terry, Athlone Herald at the Jacobite Court in exile, St Germain-en-Laye, 5 April 1709.

taking with him not only many documents but also the seal of the herald's office from Dublin. Many well-born Irishmen sought employment within the armed forces and government services of the Catholic monarchies of Europe, for which some proof of their nobility was required. This, together with armorial certificates, was provided by the exiled Athlone. One such patent, confirming arms from Terry to Daniel O'Donnell, is now housed in the Irish Genealogical Office in Dublin.

HERALDRY IN THE IRISH REPUBLIC

In 1921 the Republic of Ireland was born. Today it consists of the whole island except for the six counties of the northern province of Ulster, still under British rule.

In an agreement between the Irish and British governments, all heraldic records relating to Ireland remained under the control of Ulster King of Arms until 1943, when the Office of the Chief Herald of Ireland was established. Heraldic matters relating to British-controlled Ulster were then transferred to London, and the office

▲ *The arms recently granted to Leixlip Town by the Office of the Chief Herald. The charges on the shield reflect the complex history of the town: a Gaelic motto, a viking ship and the rose of a 16th-century English resident of Leixlip Castle.*

of Ulster King of Arms was merged with that of Norroy King of Arms, thus becoming Norroy and Ulster King of Arms.

The Office of the Chief Herald of Ireland is empowered to grant patents of arms and record pedigrees for all citizens of Ireland, others normally resident in Ireland, persons living abroad who have strong links with Ireland, ancestral or otherwise, and public authorities and other corporate bodies. The Genealogical Office (Office of the Chief Herald) is headed by the Chief Herald of Ireland, who also holds the office of Chief Librarian. Although he has the final say on heraldic matters at all levels, the day-to-day running of the office rests with the Deputy Chief Herald and the consulting heralds. Although the Irish heralds have no official uniform they do have insignia of office of the "paper" variety, with crossed batons depending on their degree placed behind a shield of their family arms.

Because of the nature of the relationship between Ireland and England, it may be that those with strong republican sympathies resident in the six counties of British Ulster will, if they aspire to arms, tend to apply to the Chief Herald's Office in Dublin. However, many organizations and individuals in Northern Ireland, Protestant

as well as Catholic, have also applied to Dublin for patents of arms. Whatever their interest or religion, all are made equally welcome by the Irish heralds, who have their offices in Kildare Street in Dublin. The Irish Heraldry Museum is housed in the same building, and has a fine collection of heraldic artefacts. From the walls hang the banners of the chiefs of the main Irish families as recognized.

In common with other national heraldic authorities, the Office of the Chief Herald has certain rules with regard to difference marks. Those of the English type are used, although this may change. Cadency marks are used by all children of the name. For example, if the eldest child is a daughter, she bears a label, the second child bears a mullet, and so on. Illegitimacy has no status in Irish law, so no marks of difference exist for it. Women may apply for a full grant of arms, including helm and crest.

That most Irish of symbols, the harp, is not often granted as a charge because it is associated with national institutions. Badges and standards are rarely given,

except to those with a "following". Similarly, supporters are reserved for special uses, such as in the personal arms of the State President.

DUBLIN CASTLE

As well as Irish family arms, Dublin Castle contains many reminders of the days of British rule, when the viceroys made it their home. It houses the banners of the former Knights of the Order of St Patrick, whose stall plates, together with a further set of banners, are displayed in the choir of St Patrick's Cathedral. Dublin Castle also houses a set of the coats of arms of the Irish presidents since independence, and the former Chapel Royal in the castle precincts has a fine display of armorial glass and wooden heraldic panels relating to the former viceroys and lord lieutenants.

▼ *A window in the Chapel Royal, Dublin Castle, bearing the arms of the viceroys of Ireland appointed from Westminster – the last viceroy's arms just happened to coincide with the last available panel.*

FRANCE

The French nobility were of course at the forefront of the heraldic story – heraldry itself is presumed to have had its origins in the area that today comprises northern France and Flanders. It is not surprising, therefore, to learn that, in common with other courtly culture, the French model of heraldry influenced that of other nations. The very language used to this day by heralds in the English-speaking world is predominantly medieval French. However, whereas in England the kings of arms were not only trusted by their monarch to set down and oversee most matters armorial, but were also entitled to grant arms on behalf of the sovereign, their French counterparts never had such a right. The granting of arms in France (as in other European powers) was the exclusive right of the monarch.

In 1616 the power of the heralds was further eroded through the appointment by the king of a judge of matters heraldic, the Juge Général d'Arms de France. The judge was expected to rule over heraldic disputes and to ensure that those persons made newly armigerous by the monarch would bear arms that conformed to the principle of the noble science. The appointment soon took on a hereditary nature, and from 1641–96 it was held by a member of the d'Hozier family.

As with the heraldry of other nations, French achievements, while keeping to a certain uniformity of rule and practice,

▲ *The complete achievement of arms of the French monarchs, used at times from the reigns of Henry IV (1589–1610) to Louis XIV (1643–1715). The French fleur de lis are impaled with the arms of Navarre.*

▼ *A 19th-century illustration of the arms of the leading families of France includes variants of the French royal arms, showing a variety of bends, borders and labels.*

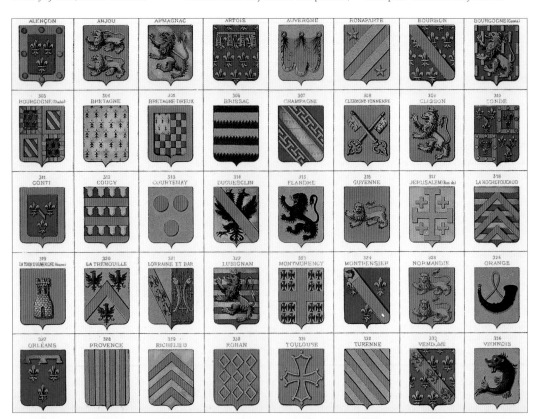

ALENÇON	ANJOU	ARMAGNAC	ARTOIS	AUVERGNE	BONAPARTE	BOURBON	BOURGOGNE (Comte)
303 BOURGOGNE (Duché)	304 BRETAGNE	305 BRETAGNE-DREUX	306 BRISSAC	307 CHAMPAGNE	308 CLERMONT-TONNERRE	309 CLISSON	310 CONDE
311 CONTI	312 COUCY	313 COURTENAY	314 DUGUESCLIN	315 FLANDRE	316 GUYENNE	317 JERUSALEM (Roi de)	318 LA ROCHEFOUCAUD
319 LA TOUR D'AUVERGNE (Ducs)	320 LA TRÉMOUILLE	321 LORRAINE ET BAR	322 LUSIGNAN	323 MONTMORENCY	324 MONTPENSIER	325 NORMANDIE	326 ORANGE
327 ORLÉANS	328 PROVENCE	329 RICHELIEU	330 ROHAN	331 TOULOUSE	332 TURENNE	333 VENDOME	334 VIENNOIS

▲ *An illustration from the second half of the 15th century showing King Louis XI at a chapter of the Order of St Michael. The arms of France modern are depicted at the foot of the page.*

developed a distinctive national style. For example, during the medieval period crests were borne only by knights of "tournament rank" – those who actually participated in tournaments – and they are rarely found in later French heraldry. In most cases, when a helmet is shown above the shield it is topped by ostrich feathers – a convention that spilled over France's southern border into Spain.

Coronets of rank existed for each tier of the nobility, a unique addition to which was the title of "Vidame". Its holder acted as commander-in-chief to the military forces of a bishop, and was therefore responsible in time of war for the defence of a diocese. The coronet of a Vidame consisted of a jewelled circlet bearing four crosses, which is depicted in heraldry with one full and two half crosses.

Certain nobles, whatever their rank, bore the additional title of "Pair de France", for which they were entitled to place behind their shield a robe referred to as a *manteau* or robe of estate. This robe was at first depicted as being charged with the arms (including quarterings) of the bearer, but in later times it was coloured blue and edged in gold.

FRENCH ROYAL HERALDRY

No other emblem has had such a lasting and turbulent career as the French lily, or fleur de lis. The love affair between French royalty and its fleur de lis predated heraldry, and the flower's adaptability and obvious beauty has ensured its survival despite the fall of its latter propagator, the royal house of Bourbon. It has managed to weather revolutions and republics, flowering again after each, and may still be seen in one form or another in many French civic arms.

From the early 13th to the end of the 14th century the golden lilies were liberally strewn over a blue field (France ancient). During the Hundred Years War between England and France the number of lilies on the French shield was reduced to just three (France modern), when the English kings promptly reduced the lilies on their shield to the same number.

The many offshoots of the dynasties of Valois and Bourbon made use of both versions of the royal arms differenced in a number of ways, usually by bends, borders and labels. All these could be further dif-ferenced from a more senior branch by the addition of smaller charges. Today, many variants of the royal arms are still in use by the departments from which the branches of the royal family took their titles.

The French nobility viewed the lower classes with a certain suspicion and believed them always wanting "to emulate what hitherto they admired", from fine furs to armorial bearings. The bourgeoisie and even the peasantry did indeed start to adopt arms, and if originally this was frowned on by nobility and monarch alike, the latter took the somewhat pragmatic view that it might bring the throne some increased revenue. So it was that in 1696 Louis XIV enforced an edict whereby those of armigerous status would pay a tax on their arms. All newly granted arms had to be entered into an enormous register, the *Armorial Général*.

▼ *The elaborate arms of Napoleon I, Emperor of the French. A beautiful example of the heraldic artwork that was inspired by Napoleon's lavish court – in this case on the door of the imperial coach.*

THE *ARMORIAL GENERAL*

In November 1696, King Louis XIV called for the implementation of a French general armorial, an inventory of all blazons and coats of arms used in the kingdom. Anyone who failed to submit their declaration of rank and honours was to be fined 300 livres, and have their properties seized.

The real aims of this edict were financial rather than heraldic. A long period of warfare had emptied the state coffers and the heraldic census was one way of refilling them. Apart from threatening fines for failure to declare arms, the order also imposed charges for the registration of arms, with rates fixed according to status. So an archbishopric was expected to pay 100 livres, an abbey 50 livres, a parish 25 livres and an individual 20 livres.

The first results of the edict were disappointing, with most declarations coming only from nobles and parishes. Thus in 1697 a second edict was passed. This went further than the first, particularly in the power it gave to the Judge of Arms to identify any who had not declared themselves.

▼ *The Napoleonic system of heraldry laid down a large number of symbols to show rank and profession. This oval denoted a countess, and the sword in pale showed that she was the widow of a military officer.*

In heraldic terms, these laws were of mixed value. The armorials do remain a useful source of documentation on the French heraldic landscape of the 17th century. However, the official lists include large numbers of coats of arms that were never

▼ *Examples of Napoleon's shields denoting rank (from left to right): eagle on a chief (sovereign prince); chief semy of bees (prince grand dignitary); semy of stars (duke); quarter Azure in chief dexter (count), charged for an officer in the imperial household; quarter Gules in chief sinister (baron), charged for a mayor.*

▲ *Heraldry has long been thought a suitable medium by cartoonists – here a British caricature of Napoleon's arms incorporates the Devil and his emblems.*

actually displayed, either because their bearers did not use a coat of arms at all or because they used a different one.

From 1699, in response to issues raised by the recording of arms, particularly the complaints of those forced to pay sums higher than were justified by the revenue from their estates, many exemptions were allowed and by 1709 declarations had become little more than optional.

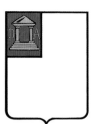

▲ *Under Napoleon, towns were divided into three degrees, identified by the style of their arms and mounts. This is the pattern for the 36 major cities ("bonnes villes").*

▲ *The designated pattern for a town of the second degree, whose mayor was appointed by the emperor.*

▲ *The designated pattern for a town of the third degree, whose mayor was appointed by the local prefect.*

THE NAPOLEONIC SYSTEM

By 1790 the French Revolution had swept away the notions of nobility and chivalric order, yet by 1802, Napoleon, who had already declared himself Life Consul if not yet emperor, had created a new chivalric order, the Legion of Honour. Once emperor, he went further. In 1806 he granted to his most loyal generals dukedoms of the lands conquered in Italy, and in 1808 he created a new nobility in France with six categories:

1 Sovereign prince (for those awarded sovereignty of a foreign principality)
2 Prince grand dignitary (for princes without sovereign power)
3 Duke
4 Count
5 Baron
6 Knight (with the Legion of Honour)

These six titles were hereditary, except for knights who were unable to prove an annual income of at least 3,000 francs.

Such was Napoleon's liking for control that a new set of heraldic rules was necessary for his brand new imperial nobility. Shields borne by the Napoleonic aristocracy showed the bearer's degree through a system of chiefs and cantons. Chiefs of rank were used for princes and dukes. Counts bore blue cantons in the dexter chief, barons bore red cantons in the sinister chief. Additional symbols borne on these cantons indicated the profession of the bearer. The arms of towns and cities of the empire were also designed according

▼ *Under Napoleon, coronets of rank for the aristocracy were replaced by embellished caps, the detail of which signified rank. Left to right, caps for: knight, baron, count, duke and prince grand dignitary.*

to set patterns indicating their size and importance. Coronets of rank were abolished and replaced by caps of dignity, called *toques*, of various degrees. This range of heraldic headgear bore no similarity to anything that had appeared before. The *toques* were not popular and were quickly forgotten after the return of the Bourbons in 1814, who promptly resurrected the pomp and ceremony of their ancestors.

Today, there is no national heraldic authority in France. The arms of towns and other municipalities are controlled and registered by the Ministry of Justice. Although no organization grants arms to individuals, this does not mean that personal arms are free to be exploited by anyone. As in other nations, there is protection of arms in French law. Anyone who finds that their arms are being used by another is entitled to seek legal redress against the usurper.

ITALY

Italian heraldry is rich with many curiosities not found in other national heraldries, making the country an armorial explorer's paradise. Many of these curiosities have their origins in the complex political and cultural history of modern Italy, a polyglot nation of former city republics and ancient family principalities and kingdoms. The separate states have been bonded together as a unified country under one ruler or government only in the last 150 years.

Since medieval times, Italian heraldry has made use of two characteristic shield shapes seldom seen in the heraldic styles of other nations: these are the teardrop shield and the horse's head shield or "chamfron". Sometimes these distinctive shapes were incorporated into the highest of art forms by the leading artists of the Renaissance in Italy, such as Brunelleschi and Donatello.

By commissioning men of such high artistic standing to execute their shields of arms, both on paper and sculpted on to the façades of their palaces and other monuments, great patrician families such as the Medicis and the Pazzis sought to outshine their rivals in heraldic statements of their wealth and power.

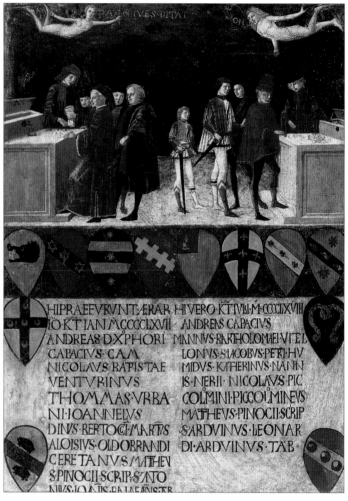

▲ A seal of one of Florence's political factions, the Ghibelline party, shows the eagle of the empire stamping on a monstrous serpent that symbolizes their political opponents, the Guelfs.

POLITICAL RIVALRIES

A further statement might be made by placing a symbol associated with a political faction in the arms, normally on the *capo*, or chief (the band occupying the upper third of the shield). The two most famous examples were the *capo d'Angio* (chief of Anjou) and the *capo dell'impero* (chief of the empire).

From the 12th to the 15th centuries, with the German-based rule of the Holy Roman Empire extending into northern Italy, the territory was prey to the intense

▲ *The teardrop shield is popular in Italian heraldry, as seen in this display of the arms of leading figures in the city state of Siena.*

rivalries of two factions known as the Guelfs, who bore the *capo d'Angio*, and the Ghibellines, identified by the *capo dell' impero*. The Guelfs, supported by the papacy, advocated the independence of the powerful city states of Lombardy. The Ghibellines were the supporters of the imperial house of Hohenstaufen, most famously of Frederick I (known as

Frederick Barbarossa) who was Holy Roman Emperor from 1152–90, and his grandson Frederick II (1212–50). Both emperors struggled to consolidate their imperial power in Italy.

The *capo d'Angio* was formed by using a red label over three gold fleurs de lis on a blue chief – a simplified variation of the arms of the House of Anjou. (Sometimes the chief was "semy de lis", or scattered with small fleurs de lis). The *capo dell' impero* was gold charged with a black eagle, single- or double-headed.

This rivalry did not only express itself heraldically. It was also possible to tell the political persuasion of townspeople and ruling families from the architectural style of the upper storeys of their houses,

▲ *The fleur de lis and red label in the chief, known as the* capo d'Angio, *proclaim the Counts Guidi as Guelf supporters.*

▲ *The imperial eagle in the arms of the Venosta family, on the* capo dell'impero, *shows them to be of the Ghibelline faction.*

ITALIAN CORONETS

One peculiarity worth seeking out within the polyglot world of Italian heraldry is the usage by noblemen who bear a lesser title than the head of a family. Two coronets of rank appear in their achievement: the one that surmounts the shield is for the bearer of the achievement, while the other is placed on the helm and is for the head of the house, as shown here in this bookplate for the family of Borio de Tigliole.

churches, castles and town halls. The battlements on those erected by the Guelfs were given horizontal tops, while the Ghibellines preferred an M-shaped edge. The latter device also appeared as a charge in the arms of Ghibelline supporters.

The political nature of the chief in Italian heraldry persisted into the 20th century. Under the fascist government of Benito Mussolini (in power from 1922 to 1943), all municipal authorities were supposed to sport the *capo del littorio* in their arms. This chief included the symbol of the Fascist party, the Roman "*fasces*" – an axe surrounded by a bundle of rods – within a wreath. In fact, however, few of the authorities took up the device.

The *capo* was also used to augment the arms of supporters of the House of Savoy. The *capo di Savoia* was Gules a cross Argent. Other variants bore the dynasty's badge, the Savoy knot.

THE DUCAL CAP

In Venice the elected ruler was known as the doge (a word meaning leader that shares its derivation with the word "duke"). The doge assigned his arms with the red ducal cap or *corno dogale*. This started life as the simple conical cap of Venetian fisherfolk, but in time became a

gorgeous object, ornamented with pearls and cloth of gold. Members of families who had at some time provided a doge were also entitled to include the ducal cap in their arms. It appeared either on the shield or, more often, as a crest, combining the two forms of headgear – the cap and the helmet – in one.

▼ *Even the shape of a castle's battlements could say something about the politics of its owner. The dovetailed crenellations in the arms of the Vismara family are typical of a Ghibelline fortress.*

▲ *The capo del littorio,* seen here in the *arms of the province of Genoa, indicated allegiance to the Fascist party. It disappeared in 1945.*

ECCLESIASTICAL HONOURS

Much Italian heraldic practice devolved from the heraldry of the Roman Catholic Church. Italian families were proud to place in their arms one or more armorial devices signifying some high ecclesiastical honour bestowed on one or more of their ancestors or relatives. The noblest of these was the coupling of the crossed keys of the papacy and the pavilion or *ombrellino*

▼ *The arms of Prince Boncompagni Ludovisi and his wife Angela Maria, Duchess Altemps: within the princely robe the* ombrellino, *or pavilion, and keys show that members of the family have been Pope.*

(umbrella). This was placed either above the shield or on a chief, and indicated that a member or members of the family had been Pope. An example can be seen in the bookplate of Prince Boncompagni Ludovisi. The arms are a combination of the Boncompagni dragon (for the family of which Pope Gregory XIII was a member) and the bends of Ludovisi (the family of Pope Gregory XV).

Other great families, who had provided "gonfaloniers", or standard-bearers, to the papacy, were entitled to charge their shield with a pale – or vertical band – of the Church, which resembled in simplified form the banner or gonfalone itself. Originally the pale was red, charged with the crossed keys, one gold, the other silver, surmounted by the papal tiara or (later) the pavilion.

▲ *The horse's head shield typical of Italian heraldry is here engraved on a plate of 15th-century Murano glass. Above the shield is the distinctive red fisherman's cap of the doge of Venice.*

DEFACED ARMS

In northern Italy (and over the border into southern Switzerland) some evidence of the turbulent times that followed in the wake of the French Revolution is still apparent. In the area that was created the Cisalpine Republic for example, the zeal for reform was strong, and the urge to break the back of the old order was taken to such extremes that orders were sent out from the people's committees to the citizens to tear down and deface the heraldry of the former aristocracy. In many places through the new republic the order was ignored, but in others the order was taken seriously. Even though the republic did not survive, still visible in the region today are the stippled stonework and rough plaster-work scars that mark the walls that once bore carved and coloured shields.

REGULATION OF HERALDRY

In Italy today (in common with many other modern European nations) there is no official procedure for registering or granting arms to private individuals, although heraldic designers will provide arms for clients for a fee. The Italian government does still maintain a heraldic office of arms, the Ufficio Araldico, which approves arms for civic, district and regional authorities, and maintains certain rules specific to Italy. For instance, in the medieval period the gonfalone was held in special regard by Italian communities, and

▼ *The façade of a building in Brescia in northern Italy: the empty plaques originally bore the arms of the town's mayors and captains, which were defaced during the period of the Cisalpine Republic.*

◄ *The recently designed gonfalone of the province of Milan.*

still is to this day; the Ufficio Araldico monitors regulations regarding the colours and trappings of any new gonfalones, which may be gold in colour for a province and silver for a community.

Sadly, the grants of arms issued by the office today take the form of printed documents without any pictorial depiction of the actual arms. This has been the norm since the late 19th century, although before World War II the grants made under the rule of the house of Savoy did have finely coloured borders decorated with the badges and orders of the Kingdom of Italy and its ruling dynasty.

The pattern for armorial bearings is carefully regulated by the Ufficio Araldico. Submissions must be of a uniform style that should not suggest any local influence. Marco Foppoli, a heraldic artist from the northern city of Brescia, had his work rejected by the office as being too northern in style, in that it suggested Swiss and German influences.

SPAIN AND PORTUGAL

Many of the characteristics of early Spanish and Portuguese heraldry were shaped by the centuries of warfare known as the *reconquista*, or reconquest. The Iberian peninsula had been invaded from the south in 711 by the Moors, Muslim forces from North Africa, whose civilization lasted nearly eight centuries. Moorish power reached its height under the caliphs of Cordoba in the 10th and 11th centuries, but the Christian rulers of northern Spain gradually reconquered the peninsula as the Moorish empire broke up in the 13th century, and Granada alone remained Moorish. Meanwhile, the Christian rulers were unifying, a process that culminated in the marriage of Isabella of Castile and Ferdinand of Aragon in 1469. When Granada fell to the Christians in 1492, Ferdinand and Isabella became rulers of all Spain.

The presence and activity of the great military-monastic orders, such as those of Santiago, Calatrava and Alcántara, in reconquering and eventually unifying the

▲ *A fine stone achievement for the Pinto da Mesquito family in Vila Real, Portugal.*

whole of the Iberian peninsula, and the chivalric ideals that these knightly orders represented, must have facilitated the development and use of heraldic symbols in the late 12th century. The continual border conflict between the Moorish and Christian kingdoms in medieval Iberia helped to reinforce a sense of ethnic identity in the Christian forces. This was described as *limpieza de sangre*, or "purity of blood", and heraldry was just one outlet for this form of national expression.

There were attempts to make arms distinctive of class as well as ethnicity. In Portugal, King Afonso V (1438–81) restricted burgher arms to the use of colours only, while King Manuel I (1495–1521) forbade the use of arms to all but the titled classes. The Castilian sovereigns followed suit and the right to arms was restricted to members of the nobility.

QUARTERING
The need for social identification found a creative outlet in the marshalling of arms. The heraldic principle of quartering had its origins in Iberia: the Portuguese system aimed at representing every one of an armiger's ancestors, both heraldic heiresses and others. Moreover, since quarterings could be shown in any order, a system of differencings, or *briça*, was instituted by Manuel I to identify an armiger's grandparents. The quarters of paternal and

maternal grandfathers were identified with small charges and cantons (also sometimes charged) respectively; the quarters of paternal and maternal grandmothers were shown respectively with half cantons (*meia briça*) and cushions.

THE REGULATION OF ARMS
Spanish pursuivants, heralds and kings of arms were appointed directly by the sovereign. The junior officers had to be at least 20 years old and to be nominated by two heralds. They underwent a ceremony in which the king baptized them with water and wine, and after at least seven years they could be promoted, provided they had the blessings of two kings of arms and four heralds. New heralds and kings of arms had to take an oath of office and the latter were appointed only with the consent of every officer of arms.

Heralds, or *cronistas de armas*, were usually named after provinces and non-capital cities, such as Bethune and Cataluña, while kings of arms were named after the

▼ *King João II of Portugal (1481–95) holds his shield of arms. The bordure of castles was added by King Afonso III (1248–79).*

▼ *The quartered arms of Castile and León cover the robe of King Alfonso X of Spain in this 13th-century illustration.*

Spanish kingdoms, including Toledo (who bore Azure an imperial crown Or) and Granada (created in 1496 to honour the reunification of Spain). While these appointments were not hereditary, at least 15 Spanish families have produced more than one herald each in the past 500 years (compared to about the same number for England, Scotland and Ireland together).

The Portuguese King João I followed the Spanish lead in the early 15th century by appointing kings of arms, including the Englishman Arriet. The Portuguese armorial law of 1495 requiring armorial registration stimulated the production of two famous armorials, the *Livro do Rei d'Armas* and the *Livro do Armeiro-mor*.

Spanish heralds served in both palatine and private capacities, the former including diplomatic and ceremonial roles. The 17th century even saw the heralds engaged in *vistas de armas*, or visitations to the provinces and overseas colonies of Spain to locate, inspect and correct heraldic irregularities. Their regulatory powers were such that none but the most powerful royal officials could interfere in their tours. In 1649 they castigated the Archbishop of Mexico, for irregular use of arms in the Cathedral of Los Angeles, New Spain.

The beginning of the 20th century saw many changes. The establishment of the Portuguese Republic in 1910 abolished the body of heralds in Portugal. Meanwhile, a royal decree of 1915 reformed the practice of appointing heralds in Spain. After this, heralds had to possess a degree in law or philosophy and be examined by a board of historians, notaries and archivists, while their armorial certificates were valid only if they were authorized by the Ministry of Grace and Justice.

The proclamation of the Second Spanish Republic in 1931 was soon followed by a ministerial edict abolishing the Corps of Chronicler Kings of Arms, stripping the heralds of their pensions and depositing their archives in the National Library. In Portugal, the heralds' situation improved with the founding of the Council of

▲ *Many town walls in Spain bear the imperial arms of the Habsburg monarchs, as here on a bridge in Toledo.*

Nobility by the Duke of Bragança in 1945, but in Spain it was not until 1947 that the Spanish Ministry of Justice re-established the position of the *cronista*. By ministerial decree of 1951, the heralds were allowed to apply for recognition as private professionals (the corporate body of heralds remained dormant) and four *cronistas* were permitted to continue certifying arms for the following 30 years.

A post-republican herald, Don Vicente de Cadenas y Vicent (who also served as King of Arms to Archduke Charles of Austria-Tuscany, the Carlist pretender to the Spanish throne) was appointed in 1951. In 1992 the provincial government of Castile-León appointed Don Alfonso Ceballos-Escalera y Gila, Marqués de la Floresta, Chronicler of Arms of Castile and León. Today, these Spanish heralds, along with the heraldic commission of the Associaçao dos Arqueálogos Portugueses and the Instituto Portuguese de Heraldica, continue the history of Iberian heraldry.

◀ *The Duke of Alva, governor of the Spanish Netherlands, with his family arms. Around the shield are banners taken in battle, usually from the Moors, often found in the achievements of Spanish nobles.*

GRANTS OF PERSONAL ARMS

As the Spanish heralds' palatine activities decreased, their private functions – namely the issuing of armorial certificates – grew in significance. Their monopoly on armorial certificates was confirmed in a royal order of 16 June 1802, which recapitulated an earlier order of 17 November 1749, and in the early part of the 20th century, kings of arms had their right recognized to certify the new armorial bearings of nobles in the name of the king.

On 17 July 1907, a royal order of the War Ministry authorized the Army Corps to solicit the kings of arms for armorial certificates with respect to their military units. The Spanish Ministry of Justice recognized the heralds' certificates and made the *cronistas* solely responsible for their accuracy in the reforms of 1915 and 1951, while at the same time organizing the different types of certificates into seven categories dealing with nobility, arms and genealogy. Citizens of South American republics and other countries that were formerly claimed by Spain have the same rights as Spaniards with respect to this legislation.

The practice of certifying and conferring armorial bearings to foreigners began with certificates issued to residents of the Spanish Netherlands in the 17th century. By the 18th century, Spanish kings of arms were certifying the arms of citizens of other countries, including France, Ireland and England. This practice was extended to the Americas in the 19th and 20th centuries. Even though the Spanish sovereigns reserve the right to grant new arms, and

▲ *The use of charges in the form of words and phrases from prayers is characteristic of Iberian heraldry, as here in the arms of the Mendoza family.*

◄ *The achievement of arms of King Juan Carlos I of Spain on the cover of a modern armorial certificate.*

▶ *The arms of Pedro Fernandez de Andrada, c1580, include a bend engoulé (being swallowed). Such a charge being devoured by wolves or dragons is a typical feature of Spanish heraldry.*

the certification of armorial bearings does not in itself constitute a new coat of arms, burgher arms (sometimes designed for a client by the *cronista*) certified by a herald are protected under Spanish law.

Today, the recipients of new Spanish titles may have armorial certificates countersigned by the king, and supporters may also be certified for those who can demonstrate a direct descent from an ennobled ancestor, or those who hold the rank of knight commander or higher in one of the dynastic or Catholic orders of chivalry.

NATIONAL HERALDIC FEATURES

Although Spanish and Portuguese arms follow rules common to all heraldry, national traits still emerge, as in the heraldry of many other European nations. Roman Catholicism is manifest through the frequent inclusion of exhortations to the saints or the Virgin Mary: often these words of prayer appear as charges on a bordure, a sub-ordinary that is much used throughout Iberian heraldry. Alternatively it may be charged with small saltires – said to be indicative of a particular battle that features in the family history.

▼ *An 18th-century viceroy of Peru, Manuel Amat de Junget, with his arms; by his time even Aztec nobility would know heraldry.*

In Spain the bordure is sometimes charged with castles and lions (for Castile and León), suggesting descent or special honours from those royal families. In Portugal the *quintas*, or escutcheon, charged with five plates taken from the royal arms, performs a similar function. Another charge peculiar to Iberian heraldry is the cauldron. In ancient times this was the sign of an *hombre rico* (rich man), who was meant to keep his cooking pot filled as a duty to the poor in times of hardship.

Grandees of Spain hold a title that is set above all others within the aristocracy, and is afforded special prerogatives at court. Heraldically, the title is suggested in an achievement of arms by a robe of estate, and a coronet of rank is placed directly upon the shield, without the helmet.

▲ *The ceiling of the Palace of Sintra bears the arms of the Portuguese aristocracy.*

▲ *In the arms of the former Portuguese overseas province of São Tome, the dexter side bears the arms of Portugal, the sinister side the provincial arms. The waves in the base signify an overseas location.*

GERMAN-SPEAKING LANDS

Through much of the period in which heraldry was in use, the German-speaking nations were loosely united under the Holy Roman Empire. Although the relationships between the emperor and the various princes, kings and other city governments were often turbulent, it was the emperor who was ultimately the fount of all honours, including arms.

The emperors delegated the granting of arms to other high-ranking personages, but they often took a keen interest in heraldic design, and kept certain honours, such as augmentation of part of the imperial arms, very much under their personal control.

Under the emperors of the house of Hohenstaufen (1138–1254), the eagle became the accepted symbol of the rulers of Germany, and through a series of embellishments was turned from a simple one-headed bird (black on a gold shield) into the glorious two-headed creature that became the symbol of the Holy Roman Emperor. From 1437 until the end of the Holy Roman Empire in 1806, the title of Emperor was held by the head of the Austrian house of Habsburg, except for the brief reign of Charles VII of Bavaria (1742–5), who placed the arms of his own family, Wittelsbach, on the eagle's breast.

▲ *The Holy Roman Emperor (centre top) and the seven electors, each shown with his arms, from the Hausekopiar, 1484, Cologne.*

◀ *Part of the heraldic frieze in Lauf Castle, near Nuremberg, which contains an early example of an armorial hall painted in 1360.*

THE ELECTORS

For centuries it was the practice for certain great princes to elect the Holy Roman Emperor, and for much of the period the number of electors was limited to seven. They were the Archbishops of Mainz, Trier, and Cologne (who were respectively the Arch-Chancellors of Germany, Gaul and Italy) and four lay dynasts, who each enjoyed certain offices during the coronation: the King of Bohemia (Imperial Cupbearer), the Duke of Saxony (Imperial Marshal), the Count Palatine of the Rhine (Imperial Steward), and the Margrave of Brandenburg (Imperial Chamberlain). The arms of the lay electors each tended to include the symbol of their imperial offices.

Therefore the Dukes of Saxony bore an escutcheon (sometimes shown as a quarter) bearing the crossed swords of the marshalcy. The Duke-electors of Bavaria bore an escutcheon with the orb of the empire, and the Margraves of Brandenburg charged their arms with an escutcheon bearing the emperor's sceptre.

These officers of the Holy Roman Empire often delegated some of their duties, and with them the right to their insignia, to lesser members of their families. This is why the Swabian branch of the Hohenzollerns (the family of the Margraves of Brandenburg) placed in the centre of their quarters a blue escutcheon charged with crossed sceptres.

IMPERIAL DIGNITIES

In the Holy Roman Empire, the granting of arms usually went hand in hand with an act of ennoblement. Families, and even prelates of the Church, who came to hold high office within the empire, were quick to include in their shields a compartment or escutcheon devoted to their regalian rights. Among these is the splendid achievement of Franz Georg von Schönborn (1729–56), Archbishop of Trier, Prince-Bishop of Worms, Prince-Provost of Ellwangen and Prince-Abbot of Prüm, who also happened to bear the glorious title of Oberst-Erblandtruchsess (Hereditary High Steward) of Austria, a fact indicated in his shield by the imperial eagle and a crowned escutcheon of the arms of Austria. Lion supporters also held high his banners of office. In common with many other high-ranking prelates of the time, his achievement includes no sign indicating ecclesiastical rank, unless, almost as an afterthought, it is by way of the cross on his princely bonnet.

Another unusual item that has found its way on to an achievement of arms is the horse's comb borne by the (now extinct) Princes of Schwarzburg-Sondershausen, who were hereditary Masters of the Imperial Stables. Also included in their achievement is a curious device like a pitchfork, which could be mistaken for an implement used to muck out the imperial horses; in fact it is associated with other rights connected with the mining of silver in the Harz Mountains.

▼ *A show of heraldic pomp for Archbishop Franz Georg von Schönborn on the entrance to the monastery of Prüm.*

▲ *The complex quarterings of the princes of Schwarzburg-Sondershausen, complete with a comb to groom the imperial horses.*

▼ *The device on the shield of Andreas Gassman of Basel, c1583, has its origins in a Swiss merchant's or house mark.*

The Princes of Schwarzburg also made use of a unique crest, an allegory of a very special dignity, that of the "greater *Komitiv*", which conferred the right to grant arms, to ennoble commoners, and to install barristers. Such a right was associated with the title of Hofpfalzgraf (Count Palatine of the Imperial Court). While the right to grant arms in the Holy Roman Empire rested with the emperor, some secular and ecclesiastical princes, certain universities and persons of high standing, were granted the right of *Komitiv*. The "lesser *Komitiv*" was limited to legitimizing children and granting arms to commoners. The Counts of Schwarzburg-Sondershausen were created Hofpfalzgrafen by Leopold I on 22 December 1691. On 3 September 1697, they were raised to the degree of princes, and were then granted augmented arms that included the crest denoting the greater *Komitiv*: a knight with a sword.

CHARGES IN GERMAN ARMS

Germanic heraldic style combines conventional geometric charges, or ordinaries, with charges of particular charm and curiosity not found in British or southern European heraldry.

The horse head gable ends of the local houses were a favourite in the arms of communities in northern Germany, together with an even older charge – a wolf's claw – based on an implement used in German forests to drag logs (of which a variant is still used).

In Switzerland and southern Germany, burgher families made use of "house marks". These took the form of various geometric figures, often appearing as a series of lines resembling numbers, and

▲ *Emperor Frederick III states his control over 95 lordships in the armorial display on the façade of the Cathedral Church of Wiener Neustadt in Austria.*

they were used on property as well as market goods, often stamped alone without heraldic accoutrements. Similar marks were used by merchants on their wares. At a later date the user of such devices might place them on his shield and helmet, aping the aristocracy.

THE *WAPPENSAAL*

German-speaking nobles, perhaps more conscious of their lineage than any of their class elsewhere in Europe, often set aside a room in a mansion or castle as a *Wappensaal*, or armorial hall. Usually the shields were formally lined in a frieze around the walls in order of precedence, with the local rulers given prime position.

In Austria a popular theme was a family tree of the imperial family, often with figures depicting individual members accompanied by their shield of arms. Sometimes the scenes depicted were all too graphic, as in Tratzberg Castle in the Tyrol. Here, a frieze shows Albrecht of Habsburg, the King of the Romans, being stabbed to death by his nephew Johan "the Patricide" in 1308. The evil nature of the deed is expressed by showing Archduke Johan accompanied by a snake.

The Habsburgs themselves were keen to claim descent through heraldry, not only from the former ruling dynasty of Austria, the house of Babenburg, but also from legendary rulers of Austria. This theme is played out in its fullest form on the front

▼ *A family tree in Tratzberg Castle, Austria, showing the murder in 1308 of King Albrecht I by his nephew Johan.*

▼ *The arms of Albrecht Dürer and his wife. Placing the helm between the two shields accolee (side by side) is typical of German marital arms.*

of the Cathedral Church of St George, in Wiener Neustadt, where the coronation of Emperor Frederick III was commemorated in 1453 through the *Wappenwand*, a heraldic frieze representing a fantastical genealogical tree of the House of Austria through 95 lordships.

The theme of maintaining the *status quo* through heraldry is awesomely expressed in the Provincial Council House of Carinthia, Klagenfurt, where each noble family, abbey and town is represented through a baroque cartouche of arms. Not content with one *Wappensaal*, the heraldic scheme, which includes nearly 700 shields in all, also finds its way into a second, smaller chamber.

GERMAN TITLES
In the Holy Roman Empire it was usual for a family's arms to be augmented with quarters as it advanced up the social scale. The original arms were usually kept as a *Herzschild* ("heart shield"). Coronets of rank were used but often a simplified variant of the arms with a crest coronet, or the family shield and crest displayed in simple medieval style, was preferred.

One unusual form of heraldic headgear worth looking out for is the cap or bonnet of the electors of the Holy Roman Empire, a scarlet cap with a large (often scalloped) ermine brim. Such a cap can be seen in the arms borne by the Hanoverian King George III of Britain, as Prince-Elector of the Holy Roman Empire.

There is some confusion outside German-speaking lands about the prefixes attached to the title of *Graf* ("count"), such as *Burggraf*, *Pfatzgraf* or *Markgraf*. These simply designate a particular territorial responsibility and were not heraldically distinguished. A *Burggraf* ruled over a *Burg* or fortress; a *Pfatz* was a palatinate and a *Mark* was a marcher, or border, land.

The prefix *von* in a name corresponds to the French *de*, both simply meaning "of". In both German and French names, the word is followed by the place name of the family home, although as an adjunct of nobility it was common practice to add the *von* and place name to a surname after ennoblement. Families of ancient nobility

▲ *A panel depicting the complete achievement of arms of the Hungarian Dukes Batthyany, Counts Strattman.*

took their surnames from their estates. No family name was required, they were simply *von...* For those families of ancient origin still in possession of their estate, *von* was replaced by *zu* ("to"), or even *von und zu*, although this style was not so commonly used. In later centuries the use of *von* in front of a name became debased, becoming almost as common as the *van* in Dutch surnames.

Since World War I, the position of the armiger, whether a private individual or a civic authority, has proved complex and curious in German-speaking lands. Before that time, a noble title was inherited by all the legitimate children of a noble father, not just the eldest son, as is the case in the British nobility. After 1919, the bearing of noble titles was banned altogether in Austria, while in Germany the title was allowed in effect to become affixed to the family's surname. Therefore, in name if not in fact, the German aristocracy may survive long after the demise of the nobility of other nations.

This change meant that for the first time the adopted children of noble fathers, who could previously use the family name but could not inherit the noble title, were now able to call themselves, for example, "Hugo Graf von..." or "Gisela Freifrau von..." and pass the name on to their own children.

THE REGULATION OF ARMS
World War I swept away not only the German and Austrian Empires, but also various other German monarchies (those of Baden, Württemberg and Bavaria), which had each maintained their own heraldic authorities. Where once the German heralds granted arms on behalf of monarchs, their place has now been taken by a number of heraldic societies (for private individuals) and state government (for local authorities), although in both cases the certification of arms is purely a registration process, without any formal authority to grant armorial bearings.

Each federal state follows its own course with regard to the registration of arms for local authorities within its boundaries. While some, such as the administration of Lower Saxony, maintain a formal register of arms deposited within their archives and are happy to advise on good heraldic practice, others demonstrate little or no interest in such matters. This has led to the adoption of quasi-heraldic symbols or even non-heraldic logos by some municipal councils in Germany.

▼ *The arms of the Counts von Zeppelin, depicted in simple medieval style with a single charge and crest.*

NAZI HERALDRY

▲ *The ancient arms of Coburg on the left, replaced with the National Socialist-approved symbol on the right.*

National Socialist authorities so much that in 1934 they changed the arms completely. The new shield was Per pale Sable and Or, a sword issuant from base point downwards, the pommel charged with a swastika counterchanged. In 1945 the Morenkopf of St Maurice was restored.

Even in relatively modern times, the power of heraldry has been acknowledged, as evidenced by the interest taken in this unlikely and archaic subject by the Nazi regime in 1930s Germany. The need to manipulate and adapt heraldry to suit the ideological ideals of Hitler and his henchmen was spelt out in a decree from the Interior Ministry dated 15 December 1937. Marked "Confidential", it gave the following direction to local Nazi party leaders with regard to the approval of arms of district authorities:

▲ *The swastika, an ancient symbol taken by the Nazis as their own, dominates a rally at Nuremberg, 1933.*

In accordance with the deputy/representative of the Fuhrer, I therefore request in future, that instead of overtly ecclesiastical emblems (saints, croziers, mitres, etc) other emblems be chosen for district arms which relate to other historical events, or express the particular characters of the community at present and the current state of affairs.

TEUTONIC PRIDE

Between the late 1920s and the outbreak of World War II, Germany experienced a resurgence of interest in personal heraldry. It was yet another manifestation of the Teutonic pride expounded by all members of the Nazi hierarchy, none more so than the leader of the SS, Heinrich Himmler. Though far from Aryan perfection himself, Himmler was obsessed with the cult of Germanism, and was encouraged in his

▼ *The state of Thüringia saw the need to show approval and support of the new order by adding the swastika to the traditional arms of Hesse.*

The decree stated that the cross and other symbols of the confessional aroused anger in 100 per cent of National Socialists, and local leaders were encouraged to extend their control over such institutions as community centres, once dominated by the elders of the Church.

In fact, few German councils paid much notice, and most tended to favour keeping their often ancient symbols. The government of Thüringia did, however, place a swastika between the paws of the Hessian lion in its state arms, although it was almost too small to notice. At least one town council felt bound to toe the party line. Coburg had for centuries borne a Moor's head, representing St Maurice, but such an un-Aryan character rattled the

▼ *SS Brigadefuhrer Karl Maria Weisthor's Nazi arms, each part of which he endowed with its own mystic meaning.*

fantasies by such men as Karl Maria Wiligut (1866–1946) and Guido von List (1848–1919), a leader of the Ariosophy movement, which was an amalgam of nationalism and occultism. Both men claimed that the origins of heraldry were more remote than is usually agreed. In their view, it began in the world of the Teutonic gods – above all Wotan, the god of war, whom dead heroes met in Valhalla, and who knew the secrets of the runes.

RUNES AND MYSTICISM

The origin and meaning of runes obsessed many Nazi "theologians", and List and Wiligut, as the most famous exponents of this secret heraldry, saw to it that runes became the basis for the Nazis' own heraldry. It was no coincidence that the colours of the SS were also those of the

▶ *The apotheosis of Nazi heraldry, the arms of a new Teutonic Knight such as would have decorated the Knights' Chamber at Wewelsburg Castle.*

▼ *The bookplate of a Nazi party member – the eagle, which faced left for the state, faces right for the party.*

Teutonic Knights. At Schloss Wewelsburg, Himmler sought to combine the ideals of the Teutonic Knights and Teutonic mythology, together with the court of King Arthur, complete with round table, into a new "noble fraternity", who were to meet in a newly synthesized complex of rooms decorated with runic motifs.

Around the round table of solid oak would sit Himmler and his 12 senior SS commanders (the successors, so he believed, to the Teutonic Knights). Behind each officer would hang his own coat of arms, especially designed, as most of the 12 – including Himmler himself – lacked family arms. New arms were devised by the Ahnenerbe, the institution attached to the SS that dealt with racial purity and Teutonic history, using designs influenced by the runic translations of Karl Maria Weisthor (Wiligut had changed his name to what he believed was his ancient family name).

Among other odd outpourings, Weisthor/Wiligut claimed the power of "ancestral memory", which allowed him to trace his own unbroken family history back to the Teutonic peoples in the year 228,000 BC, his family springing from a coupling of the gods of water and air. He was also able to see the time when the earth was inhabited by mythological beings, including dwarves, giants and races such as the Lemurians – giant brown-skinned hermaphrodites with four arms. (Not surprisingly, after threatening to kill his wife, he was confined in a mental asylum.) Weisthor/Wiligut claimed to know the secret spells and meanings of the runes and used them in charges designed for his own family arms. He brought several of them together in one of the most fascinating objects associated with SS ritual (much of which he conceived): the Totenkopfring der SS, or SS death's head ring, which included both the swastika and the double sigrune of the SS.

The swastika was a mystical symbol of good fortune, used from ancient times by peoples from Tibet to northern Europe. In

▲ *The bookplate of Hans Raven, typical of the Nazi period, with the swastika much in evidence and bearing a crest straight out of the age of the Teutonic Knights.*

Europe it was associated with Donner (or Thor), god of adventurers, and became popular in 19th-century Germany as a symbol of racial and national unity. The latter would seem to have been the main reason for Hitler's love of the swastika, which he used as a heraldic device coupled with the German eagle.

The sigrunes of the SS symbolized victory and were first drawn side by side in 1931 by SS member Walter Heck, a graphic designer employed by the badge-manufacturing firm of Ferdinand Hoffstatter in Bonn. Both the swastika and the SS runes were among many devices chosen to decorate the new shields of arms in Wewelsburg Castle, although the outbreak of war seems to have placed the heraldic scheme there on hold. The only case of such arms being created would appear to be for SS Obergruppenfuhrer Pohl, as they appear on a ring given to him by his son in 1938.

As a postscript to this account of extraordinary quasi-heraldry, it is worth looking out for signs of "human attention" on a mountainside near Schloss Wewelsburg, for it is known that in 1945, on Himmler's orders, all the remaining Totenkopfrings (which incidentally were treated as awards, and had to be returned on the death of each recipient) were blast-sealed into a mountain, and as yet they have never been found.

RUSSIA

Heraldry came relatively late to Russia, in comparison with much of western Europe. It is generally accepted that its flowering owed much to Tsar Peter I ("the Great", 1682–1725) who during his travels in Europe saw the splendour that could be achieved by its use in such media as stained glass, carved stone and furniture. The first Vice-Master of Heraldry, appointed by Peter the Great, was an Italian who saw to it that Russian heraldic practice followed that of contemporary European nations. Not that heraldic symbolism was unknown in Russia before Peter's reign: Russian cities, such as Astrakhan with its crown and sabre, and Novgorod, with its throne and flanking bears, had used pictorial devices since the early 16th century. Some civic symbols were even older, and the most famous Russian royal devices, the double-headed eagle and the horseman slaying a dragon, had appeared on the seals of the Grand Prince of Moscow, Ivan III, in 1497.

▼ *A Russian herald at the coronation in 1896 of the last tsar of Russia, Nicholas II.*

▲ *The small state seal of Tsar Ivan IV. One side bears the imperial double-headed eagle, the other a unicorn.*

EARLY HERALDRY IN RUSSIA

During his reign, Ivan IV ("the Terrible", 1547–84) required that a register of nobility was to be maintained, known – because of its cover – as the Velvet Book. At this time the Russian nobility had no titles of rank except for that of *kniaz* (prince), which was used in the main for those descended from the reigning house of Rurik. The maintenance of the Velvet Book, together with the other formal heraldic registers, was later overseen by the Heraldry Office, which was established in 1722 by Peter the Great under the control of a Master of Heraldry.

Despite Peter the Great's enthusiasm for European heraldry, Russian arms did not ape western styles and customs to the point of exactness. Indeed, Russian heraldry, like its other art forms, is a distinctive mixture of western European style and the exotic. This blend can often be observed in the official armorials of the Russian Empire, the *Obshii Gerbovnik Dvorianskikh Rodov Vserossiiskoi Imperii* (*Obschii Gerbovnik* for short) published in ten volumes between 1797 and 1840.

Peter the Great introduced the ranks of baron and count, and in 1722 decreed that all officers of the army and navy, and functionaries of the civil service above a certain rank (major in the army), were automatically entitled to enter the ranks of the aristocracy (untitled), and were thereby of armigerous status. Russian barons and counts were entitled to coronets of their degree, in European style, while princes of Russia were entitled to bear a princely crown as well as their robe of estate. The greater part of the Russian untitled nobility were entitled to bear a crest coronet from which issued three ostrich feathers.

CHARGES AND AUGMENTATIONS

The shields of the Russian nobility are often divided into several fields, each bearing one or more charges that reflect the family history. These often refer to acts of valour and may be accompanied by a citation appearing in place of a motto, such as that of the Counts Plavtov: *For fidelity, courage and indefatigable labours.* Tartar, Cossack and Polish emblems often appear in Russian heraldry, suggesting the diverse mix of nations that made up the empire.

Many Russian arms bear some direct reference to the monarch in whose reign the family was ennobled. Often the imperial eagle appears, charged on its breast with a particular emperor's cypher, and sometimes with part of one of the orders of chivalry. A distinctive heraldic honour

▼ *A variant of the arms of a Leibgardets family, with the augmentation of honour appearing in the chief.*

▲ *The arms of Count Alexander Suvurov-Rymninsky (1730–1800) before his advancement to the rank of Prince; already heavily augmented, the later arms even included a map of Italy.*

was created in 1741 for soldiers who had led the *coup d'etat* that placed Elizabeth Petrovna on the Russian throne. They were created *leibgardets* ("life guards") to the empress, automatically raised to the rank of nobility and given an augmentation to their arms in the form of a new coat, Sable on a chevron Or between three mullets Argent as many fire bombs or grenades Proper. The augmentation was usually borne per pale with the family arms – the augmentation on the dexter side, the family coat on the sinister. Each life guard (and his descendants) was also entitled to bear a crest of a grenadier's cap with wings and

▼ *The arms, probably from a coach door, of Prince Michael Golenishchev-Kutuzov, Russian commander-in-chief in the country's campaign against Napoleon, 1812.*

ostrich feathers, and the motto (in Russian), *For loyalty and zeal.*

An extraordinary example of heraldic distinction for bravery must be the shield of arms borne by one Dmitry Chuvash Narbekov who, during fighting against Kazan in the 16th century, was badly injured by a spear in the back. He was then hit in an eye by an arrow, and as if this were not unfortunate enough, as he tried to extract the arrow he had his arm blown away by a cannon ball. Amazingly,

▶ *The arms of the Grand Duchy of Finland while it was under Russian rule. The Finnish lion replaces the usual warrior and dragon, and the shields on the eagle's wings are of Finnish provinces.*

he survived. Among the honours he received from his grateful monarch was a grant of arms, showing in graphic detail his various acts of heroism.

IMPERIAL ARMS

By the late 19th century, the Russian heralds had formulated rules, on the orders of the emperors, regarding armorial achievements of members of the imperial family itself. Each royal personage was entitled to bear two variants of arms, greater and lesser, and their proximity to the throne was generally designated by their heraldic supporters. The immediate family – the tsar, the tsarina, the tsarevich (the heir apparent) and his eldest son – bore as

▼ *The arms of Dmitry Chuvash Narbekov show in lurid detail the various wounds he received at Kazan.*

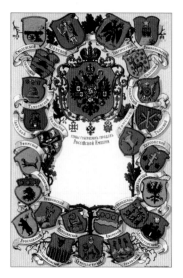

▲ *A postcard of the early 20th century shows the arms of the principal cities of the Russian Empire.*

supporters the Archangels Michael and Gabriel. The younger sons of the tsar had two Varangian guards as their supporters; the grandchildren by younger sons bore two unicorns Or, and so on, down to the great-great-grandsons of the tsar, who bore two griffins Sable armed Or and langued Gules. Female descendants when unmarried were entitled to the same arms and supporters as their brothers, but on a lozenge instead of a shield. There were also marks of difference other than supporters: they mainly consisted of a lessening of the number of territorial shields that accompanied the imperial arms, and the helmets, coronets and crests that were part of the territorial achievements.

CIVIC ARMS

Between the late 18th and late 19th centuries, the authorities laid down a complex series of exterior ornaments to be borne in the arms of towns and provinces. For a lesser authority the coronet might take a simple mural form, while townships of some importance had a red mural coronet with just two crenellations. The cap of Monomakh (an ancient form of jewelled fur cap) was granted to former capitals of the ancient Russian grand dukes. There were specific crowns for Kazan, Astrakhan, Poland, Finland and Georgia.

Most of these heraldic coronets date from an imperial decree of 1857, which also stipulated other ornaments to be placed on either side of the shield, such as crossed hammers for industrial cities, ears of wheat for cities in agricultural areas and vine leaves for those in wine-producing regions. Baron von Kōehne, who invented the system, had intended that maritime municipalities should display crossed oars, but this was changed to anchors.

A special set of attributes was provided for "fortress cities", which were entitled not only to a special combination of coronet and imperial eagle, but also crossed flags. Those that had withstood a siege had the crossed flags charged with the cypher of the monarch in whose reign the siege had been conducted. Ribbons of the Russian orders of chivalry helped to complete these splendid achievements. By the same decree, civic shields were charged with a canton of the arms of the *guberniya*, or province, in which the city lay. Prior to 1857, the arms of the latter had been charged in chief of a shield per fess, the arms in the base being of the city itself.

POST-REVOLUTIONARY ARMS

After the revolution of 1917, heraldry was still required. A commission was set up by the temporary government to look into the matter of the national arms. It suggested that although crowns, sceptres and other symbols of monarchy should be abolished, the double-headed eagle could stay, although it vied for a time with the swastika (another popular symbol signifying eternity and prosperity). The crown was replaced by a soldier's cap.

The eagle was for a short time accompanied by soldiers and peasants, although

▼ *The arms of the town of Mohyliv-Podilsky, Ukraine as borne in the late 19th century. The grapes signify its position in a wine-producing region; the moon and cross on the canton show that the town was in the guberniya (or province) of Podillya.*

▲ *The star of communism replaced the old tsarist emblems after the fall of Emperor Nicholas II in 1918.*

by spring 1918 it was felt that the imperial bird was too symbolic of pre-revolutionary Russia, and an entirely new coat of arms was needed. The hammer and sickle were selected for use on the state seal of the Russian Federation, symbolizing the alliance between the industrial workers and the peasantry. The new arms kept the old heraldic colours of red and gold, but placed the hammer and sickle in front of the rising sun of socialism.

The first regional arms, those of the Moscow regional government (*guberniya*), were approved by the praesidium of the Moscow Soviet in September 1924. They included a five-pointed star, the Statue of Freedom erected in 1918, and the hammer and sickle. On either side were blades of cereals and at the base were the attributes of labour, including anvils, shuttles and an electric motor. The Moscow arms never had a full official description and although they were supposed to set an example to be followed by other Soviet *guberny*, the idea never really took off.

The various republics of the Soviet Union took the state arms of the USSR as their model. In these a shield was not employed; a garland of wheat instead surrounded a rising sun above which was a globe charged with the hammer and sickle. The wheat blades were bound together by a red ribbon bearing the legend *Workers of*

▶ *The star of communism in the arms proposed for Volgograd when it was declared a "hero city" in honour of its citizens' bravery during World War II.*

the world unite in the various languages of the individual republics. Above the entire design shone the red star of communism. While the arms of most of the republics were devoid of any national character, some managed to achieve a localized flavour. Kirghizia had the rising sun over a local landscape, and Azerbaijan placed an oil-well against a backdrop of the rising sun. Each was dominated by the red star.

Curiously, the pre-revolutionary civic arms granted by the tsars were not abolished by the Bolsheviks; they had meant to do so but the order was never signed. In the 1960s, when many new towns and cities were created in the Soviet Union, interest in civic arms was aroused, and this was harnessed by the authorities to encourage civic pride. Soviet deputies would instigate competitions to find new designs. The arms had to include a symbol unique to the place, encapsulating a "small motherland" that exuded its own patriotic zeal. Several hundred new civic arms were designed between the 1960s and the 1980s. The designs could be quite striking, such as that of Novokusnetsk, which had a block of coal heating the furnace of a steel works.

This arousal of interest in heraldry was not welcomed throughout the Soviet Union. In the occupied Baltic States it was seen by local communist officials as a catalyst for nationalistic fervour, and was firmly curtailed.

HERALDRY AFTER COMMUNISM
Since the collapse of the communist regime and the demise of the Soviet Union at the end of 1991, many symbols that are

▲ *The new state arms of Russia were established by a presidential decree in 1993. The traditional symbols of eagle, rider and dragon have been re-established after nearly a century.*

reminiscent of tsarist times have re-emerged, particularly the double-headed eagle, regally crowned. The crown of Peter the Great appears between the eagle's heads, and it is charged on its breast with the horseman slaying a dragon. The eagle is gold (as opposed to the imperial kind, which was black) and the horseman points to the sinister, as opposed to the dexter in the later imperial arms. The figure is simply described as a rider, and before the heraldic reform of Peter I it was thought of not so much as St George but more as an allegorical representative of the sovereign overcoming his enemies.

In today's Russia, the President as head of state executes his heraldic duties through the State Heraldic Office. The office keeps a register of all state and civic arms, flags and official insignia. It does not, however, grant arms, and at the time of writing, no legal body in Russia is entitled to do so, either for personal or civic use, although various societies and heraldic colleges exist that will advise on new heraldic designs for their members. These organizations often ally themselves to one or other member of the former imperial family, which is supposed to give them some form of quasi-official status, although the State Heraldic Office does not recognize the connection.

COMMUNIST HERALDRY

Though a leveller of class, communism still saw the need for heraldry, and understood its potential power. Therefore coats of arms could be tolerated as long as their content bore no symbols that went against the cause. For the most part this meant a ban on religious or nationalistic (other than state) motifs.

▲ *In early post-tsarist Russia the old symbols of the eagle and rider remained in favour, but were soon to be swept away.*

▼ *Workers and peasants unite around the hammer and sickle of the new Soviet Union.*

In this, as in other aspects of communism, Russia led the way. The hammer and sickle, the symbols favoured by the workers' collectives in March and April of 1918, paved the way for the designs of the arms of the Russian Federation and the various Soviet Republics.

NATIONAL TRADITIONS

At the end of World War II, nations with heraldic traditions that were centuries old came under Soviet control and influence. Most symbols associated with the old order were soon banned by the increasingly hard-line regimes installed by the Soviets in Poland, Hungary, Bulgaria and Czechoslovakia, and the red star of socialism loomed large in the rhetoric of the new order. However, certain symbols were of such an emotive nature to the individual nations that even the party apparatchiks were loathe to tamper with them, although in the German Democratic Republic, the Soviet leaders' most loyal and dependent satellite, the leadership followed Soviet symbolism to the letter.

The new national arms of the GDR were an almost exact replica of the Soviet arms, except that the sickle was replaced by a pair of compasses and the ribbon that bound the ears of corn was in the German national colours of red, gold and black. These were derived from the ancient arms of the German nation: the black eagle with its red claws and beak on a gold field.

Other nations, which did not have so much reason to forget their recent past, found that their own communist bosses approved of the most curious of heraldic alliances between the past and the post-war period, even if that past was bound up with royalty. Therefore, the twin-tailed lion of the Bohemian kings continued to appear beneath the red star, as also did that most enduring of national emblems, the white eagle of the Piast dynasty that ruled medieval Poland; in the latter case the red star that replaced the royal crown was so insignificant that it looked like a crest on the noble bird's head.

▲ *The arms of the Republic of Azerbaijan in the Soviet era show the red star of socialism set high above a Soviet dawn.*

PERSONAL ARMS

The traditional users of arms – the nobility – were now taboo, and most of those who had not fled or died languished in dingy prisons or windswept gulags. Others who had dared to follow the noble science of heraldry were viewed with suspicion by the Soviet authorities. While heraldists are today usually perceived by non-heraldists as harmless cranks hankering after a romantic and improbable past, to the hard-line Marxist-Leninists of the late 1940s and 50s, anyone who professed an interest in the plaything of the nobility was probably a supporter of the old order, who wished to see the return of feudal repression. Those who enthused about heraldry were harassed by the secret police and even thrown into prison for involvement in activities "contrary to the interests of the proletariat". Personal arms were very much a thing of the past.

CIVIC ARMS

With civic heraldry the position was not nearly so clear cut. Civic pride was allowed to exist and often nurtured, since it helped citizens to focus their thoughts firmly on the immediate locality rather than further afield. The ancient arms of Prague and Pelhrimov were retained, for example, with the addition of the republic's arms on

leadership, it had to be replaced altogether. The ancient shield of the Lithuanian city of Joniskis, which bore St Michael killing a dragon, was replaced during Soviet rule by a red shield bearing a straightened scythe, the weapon of the local peasantry, between 28 pointed golden suns.

Elsewhere in Lithuania, the city of Marijampole, which bore in its ancient arms the figure of St George and the dragon, acquired not only new arms, but a new name (Kapsunkas). The new design included a canton of revolutionary red and the flame of learning.

Even these new approved designs were banned by the Lithuanian communists after a song festival in 1970, when the participants made too much show of their city arms. From then on until the fall of the Soviet regime, in Lithuania at least, city arms, and of course the old state arms, were banned.

NEW SYSTEMS OF HERALDRY
Of all the nations that had fallen under the spell of socialism, Romania was the only one that actually developed any formal system for its civic and regional arms. The arms designed by the state committee on

▲ *The arms of Baja in Hungary, designed in the 1970s, conform to the style set by the community heraldry of the Soviet era.*

▲ *The arms of the cities of Marijampole (left) and Joniskis (right) in Lithuania; both shields were banned in the 1970s by the Soviet authorities because of their religious content, and replaced with new designs.*

shield or crest. Despite the treatment that was meted out to the aristocrats themselves, the arms of many ancient lords, complete with their coronets of rank, were permitted to remain on the civic shields of their old domains.

In the German Democratic Republic, civic arms were not entirely banned, but they were not permitted to be used for official purposes. Instead, the local council was to use the state arms enclosed by an inscription stating the name of the town, city, or district.

In the Soviet Union, saints and other overtly religious symbols in civic heraldry were replaced by figures representing heroism or patriotic workers. Even the heavenly eye of providence was replaced by a golden sun. If a coat of arms was so religious as to be totally offensive to the

▼ *During the Soviet era, new arms were devised for Krasnoznamensk in the Moscow region. The USSR's supremacy in the space race made a most suitable subject for a modern Soviet town.*

▲ *The arms of the municipality of Hunedoara, Romania, are typical of the pattern of Romanian civic arms during the years of the Ceausescu regime.*

heraldry cannot be considered beautiful. Traditional heraldic symbols long associated with the ancient rulers of Wallachia (an eagle) and Moldavia (an auroch's head), found themselves sharing a shield with images of the modern industrial world, such as petro-chemical plants, blast furnaces and weavers' shuttles. Each new shield was also charged with an escutcheon bearing the symbols and colours of the Romanian state.

In 1974, Romania's neighbour, Hungary, also attempted to impose a heraldic scheme in keeping with the new way forward, replacing the ancient arms of 83 towns and cities with those with a new socialist flavour. Whereas in communist Romania, some vestige of the heraldry of the old order had often been retained, the Hungarian regime required a clean sweep on the model of the Soviet Union, with simple, stylized figures of people reaching out towards the rising sun of a socialist dawn. Parents and toddlers replaced the symbols of the nobility, with the red star triumphant over all.

It was not heraldry as we know it, but it was heraldry, sometimes innovative though usually bland. When communism collapsed, so did most of the "heraldry" that had paid it lip service for the past 50 or more years, unloved and unlamented.

POLAND

Mᵒ ore than any other nation, Poland has maintained a heraldic "apartness", which stems mainly from the nature of its lesser nobility, or *szlachta*. This social group may be thought of broadly in the same way as the English gentry.

Those who fell into the group were members of an affiliation of noble families, known as a *ród*. Before the arrival of heraldry, each *ród* had its own standard in the form of a staff bearing a unique emblem. The devices were simple figures that cannot be described in heraldic terms: most consisted of sets of lines, curves, X- and V-shapes, which have led to the popular belief that they were adapted from Viking runes. The Vikings were just one of many peoples with whom the Poles came into contact, for the Polish area of influence was a thoroughfare for traders on their way eastwards into what is now Russia.

From the east came more warlike peoples, the Tartars and later the Turks. These roving bands had their own totemic standards – staves bearing streamers, horsetails and horns. Something similar can be seen

▼ *Herb Woroniecki, showing Christian symbols defeating the Turkish crescent. These charges would have originated as simple lines and curves that were later adapted to heraldry.*

▲ *This pedigree shows tribal arms typical of Polish heraldry. Such a document was required as proof of nobility for Poles wishing to become officers in the imperial Austrian army in the late 19th century.*

today in the Turkish crescent or "jingling Johnny", a musical instrument used by German military bands, which resembles a standard hung with silver bells and horsetails. Perhaps the eastern standards and the Viking runes were married together by the Poles to make their own distinct tribal insignia.

ADAPTATIONS TO HERALDRY

In the second half of the 10th century, Poland's first ruler, Mieszko, brought Christianity to his people, and many tribal standards had their extremities made into crosses. When heraldry eventually reached Poland, other changes were made to the symbols to produce acceptable heraldic charges, such as arrowheads and crescents. The original emblem had usually been cut out of metal, so in Polish heraldry it is very rare to find a charge that is not gold or silver. The fields of shields are almost always red or blue; green and purple are virtually unknown, and heraldic furs are not used.

Each *ród* had its own rallying cry, such as *Dolega*, *Dabrowa*, or *Pilawa*, and the tribal device came to be identified by it. In effect the war cry and the device were the same entity. When, by the late 13th century, Polish *ród* started to place their old totemic emblems on shields, the practice of identifying the arms by the relevant war

cry persisted, and for this reason there has never been a need for a system of heraldic blazon in Polish heraldry.

A single coat of arms, or *herb*, was used by all members of the *ród*, no matter their position, for in effect all members were equal. However, arms were sometimes adapted through marriage. In the case of Herb Slepowron ("blind crow"), the original arms were varied after an important marriage to a lady of the Pobog clan, by placing the black crow of Herb Slepowron on the Herb Pobog, which bore a horseshoe topped by a cross.

It is rare to find more than one charge on the shield of a Polish *ród*. Ordinaries are rare, as are quarters and supporters. Some shields were credited with legendary origins: for example, that of Ogonczyk, an arrowhead issuing from a semicircle, is said to relate to an occasion when a maiden was being abducted by Tartars, and members of the tribe pursued the Tartars at the speed of an arrow. Crests are usually ostrich plumes or peacock's feathers issuing from a crest coronet. There is no set pattern for the helmet, although the barred tourney helm is mostly used.

SOCIAL ORGANIZATION

Titles such as count or baron were forbidden to Poles. Only after the partition of Poland by its neighbours in the 18th and 19th centuries did Poles take foreign titles, although this was considered unpatriotic.

A *ród* could be any size, and could number hundreds of separate families. In theory they were all related but, as with Scottish clans, other families could sometimes be taken under their wing. If a king wished to favour a subject he might ask a *ród* to take him under its name and arms.

In later centuries when members of the *szlachta* settled in towns, villages, or on their own estates, they adopted surnames by placing Z in front of the place name, in the manner of the French *de* or the German *von*. In time the Z tended to be replaced by adding *ski* or *cki* to the end of the name, and the connection with the *ród*

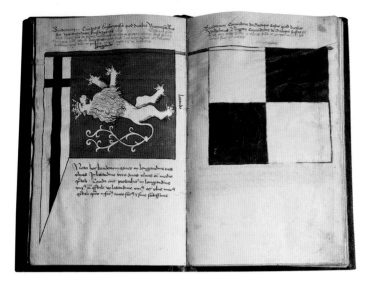

rider in pursuit of his enemy. Part of this device, the rider's armoured arm holding a sword, known to the Poles as the *pogonia*, was used as a kind of augmentation under the Polish–Lithuanian commonwealth, giving rise another *ród*; Pogon. The rider's shield was often charged with the double-armed cross of the Jagiello dynasty. Later, the dynastic arms of the Polish sovereigns were placed on an escutcheon on the quartered shield of Poland–Lithuania.

The last of the Jagiello line, Sigismund II Augustus, died in 1572. From then on, monarchs were elected by a general assembly of the nobility. Kings' powers were severely curtailed and they were closely watched by the nobility in this "royal republic". Elections were one of the great sights of Europe, with the *szlachta* making their way in groupings of *ród* to the Electoral Fields outside Warsaw. In 1573, no less than 50,000 nobles came to vote.

Many of the elected monarchs were chosen through the connivance of various factions allied to the interests of Poland's enemies and neighbours. In 1772 the first partition of Poland between its neighbours was instituted, and the kingdom of Poland–Lithuania disappeared. Both nations regained their independence following World War I.

was kept alive by placing the tribal name before the surname, as in Sas-Tarnawski or Jastrzebiec-Marikowski.

ROYAL HERALDRY

Polish culture, art and learning were greatly admired and coveted by its larger neighbours, notably Prussia, Russia and Austria. All these powers saw the Polish state as an obstacle to their territorial ambitions, but Poland had ambitions of its own.

In 1386, Jadwiga, the daughter and heiress of the Polish–Hungarian monarch, Louis of Anjou, took as her husband Grand Duke Wladyslaw Jagiello of neigh-

▲ *At the Battle of Grunwald (Tannenberg), on 15 July 1410, a Polish–Lithuanian army decisively defeated the Teutonic knights, capturing many of the Order's standards, all of which were beautifully painted in 1448 for the Royal Archives in Krakow.*

bouring Lithuania, setting the scene for a period of great expansion. In 1413 the Union of Horodlo between Poland and Lithuania saw the adoption of many members of the Lithuanian nobility into the names and arms of the Polish tribes. The alliance was reflected heraldically in the arms of the Polish–Lithuanian sovereigns. The white eagle of the Poles had been borne on seals since the reign of Boleslaw V (1227–79), and is one of the most famous and enduring symbols in Europe. During the medieval period the eagle was often charged on its breast with a half moon device ending in stylized clover leaves or crosses, and from the late medieval period the eagle was crowned.

The arms of Lithuania were every bit as fascinating. They consisted of an armed

▼ *The arms of Wroclaw (Breslau), bearing the lion of Bohemia, the eagle of Silesia and the city's patron saint, John the Baptist.*

◄ *An illustration from the early 16th century shows the eagle of the Polish monarchs below the mounted horseman of the Grand Duchy of Lithuania; the top right shield bears the arms of the Lithuanian Gediminas dynasty.*

THE AMERICAS

The development of heraldry by British settlers in North America was slow, and was curtailed by the Revolution. However, the colonization of the central and western areas by the Spanish and French, in the 16th and 17th centuries, gave rise to a parallel, separate heraldic development (to say nothing of the Russian presence in the state of Alaska and the native monarchy in the state of Hawaii). The division of the continent between the major European powers fragmented the exercise of heraldic authority in what would become the United States. A comparison of the heraldic regulation exercised by the British in eastern North America, and by the Spanish in the western territories, suggests some of the differences in the colonizing methods of the two powers.

COLONIAL HERALDRY

Between Columbus's voyage in 1492 and the Declaration of American Independence in 1776, both England and Spain attempted to introduce and regulate heraldic activities in their respective

▲ The arms of the descendants of the Aztec Emperor Montezuma II, attributed by the Spanish heralds, are a mixture of European heraldic charges and native symbols.

▲ The first, rejected, design for the arms of the new United States included a rose for England, a thistle for Scotland, a harp for Ireland, a fleur de lis for France, a lion for Holland and an eagle for Germany.

spheres of authority. Among the symbols and regalia at the marriage of Philip of Habsburg and Joanna of Spain, celebrated in 1496, was a banner bearing arms for the West Indies, or the Kingdom of the Fifteen Islands. The first English grant of arms in the New World was made in 1586 to the city, governor and assistant governors of Ralegh in Virginia, while Newfoundland would receive a grant of arms about 50 years later.

These early grants made use of native scenes, wildlife and peoples, the last of which seems to have played most strongly on the heraldic imagination. Writing in 1682, Bluemantle Persuivant John Gibbon remarked on the quasi-heraldic body paint worn by Virginian natives during war-dances: "The Dancers were painted some Party per pale Gu[les] and Sab[le] from forehead to foot…at which I exceedingly wondered, and concluded that Heraldry was ingrafted naturally into the sense of the humane Race."

Meanwhile, the Spanish colonizers granted titles and arms to the native aristocracy and royalty they had conquered,

as a way of excusing them from the *encomienda* system of forced labour imposed by the Spanish rulers during the 16th century. Native American leaders could avoid this if they could successfully claim the privileges of the Spanish nobility. One remarkable instance is the case of the descendants of the Aztec emperor Montezuma II, who ruled central Mexico from 1480 to 1520. Philip II of Spain granted the title of count to Don Pedro Tesifon Moctezuma de la Cueva in 1627, and Isabel II granted the titles of marquess and duke to other descendants in 1864 and 1865. The family bore arms blazoned Vert within an orle of five roses Argent a falcon and tiger Or in pale a bordure Gules charged with thirty coronets Or, or alternately, Azure an imperial crown Or and a falcon and tiger Argent all in pale a bordure Vert charged with thirty coronets Or.

In 1984, a claimant to the Aztec throne, Don Guillermo de Grau-Moctezuma, appointed a personal herald, the Cronista Rey de Armas de la Casa Imperial Azteca.

English and Spanish heralds attempted to establish heraldic regulation in North America during the 17th and 18th centuries. In 1705, Laurence Cromp, York Herald, also became Carolina Herald, although the office expired on his death ten years later, without any grants of arms having been made. Spanish heraldic jurisdiction in the New World was more effective: in 1649, the visiting Spanish heralds censured the Archbishop of Mexico for the inaccurate display of the Spanish royal arms in the Cathedral of Los Angeles.

AFTER INDEPENDENCE

The early leaders of the independent United States and Mexico were not opposed to the principle of bearing arms. Mexico freed itself from Spanish control not as a republic but as a short-lived empire, under the rule of the armigerous cavalry officer-cum-monarch Agustín de Itúrbide. Heraldry was also esteemed by George Washington, who wrote: "It is far from my design to intimate an opinion, that Heraldry, Coat-Armor, etc. might not be rendered conducive to public and private use with us; or that they can have any tendency unfriendly to the purest spirit of Republicanism. On the contrary, a differ-

▼ In a splendid return to medieval heraldic design, the flag of Maryland uses the arms of its founder, George, 1st Lord Baltimore.

▲ The great seal of the US presidents, the main design of which dates from 1782.

ent conclusion is deducible from the practice of Congress, and the states; all of which have established some kind of Armorial Devices, to authenticate their official instruments."

Congress set Benjamin Franklin, John Adams and Thomas Jefferson to the task of designing the arms of the new republic on 4 July 1776. In the first sketch, the shield was blazoned Quarterly of six: 1 Or a double rose Gules and Argent (for England), 2 Argent a thistle proper (for Scotland), 3 Vert a harp Or (for Ireland), 4 Azure a fleur de lis Or (for France), 5 Or an imperial eagle Sable (for the German Empire) and 6 Or a lion rampant Gules (for Holland). Fortunately, perhaps, this cluttered design did not meet with approval, and the famous arms Argent six pallets Gules a chief Azure were designed in part by Charles Thompson, Secretary of Congress, in 1782.

THE REGULATION OF ARMS

Civic heraldry prospered in the independent republic, and today such symbols are protected from misuse by legislation, but personal heraldry in the USA remains unregulated. Interest is high, however, as witnessed by the success of "bucket-shop" heraldry, and both private agencies and official bodies have sought to address the current state of affairs.

In 1928 the New England Heraldry and Historic Genealogical Society of Boston's heraldic committee began to publish the inherited and adopted arms of Americans, and in 1972 the American College of Heraldry was founded. This body has been very effective in drafting and publishing arms of adoption, with a dedication to the principles of heraldic design, while the setting up of the College of Arms Foundation in the 1980s has set a good precedent.

On an official level, several European heraldic agencies have in the 20th century begun to grant and register American arms. The Office of the Chief Herald in Dublin and the Court of Lord Lyon in Edinburgh both grant arms to eminent Americans of, respectively, Irish and Scottish descent. The College of Arms in London has granted honorary armorial bearings to eminent Americans of English descent since the early 20th century, though the practice began without a general warrant from the Earl Marshal, and these documents go unrecognized by the Irish and Scottish authorities. The English College also issues devisals of arms to American corporations with the approval of their respective state governors. The Spanish Corps of Chronicler Kings of Arms issues armorial certificates recognizing the arms of citizens of American republics once claimed by the Spanish crown, including most of the USA (such certificates protect these arms under Spanish law).

These different organizations and avenues are made use of by many Americans, testifying to their heraldic interest. While there are many drawbacks to the USA's lack of a native central heraldic authority, the present unregulated situation at least allows America's plurality of heraldic traditions to develop organically.

SCANDINAVIA

The migration of heraldry from its historic centre in northern France and Flanders was rapid, and by the 13th century arms were being used by the nobility of Denmark, Sweden and Norway. Just as the nobles of Spain, Italy and England felt themselves to belong to a social group sharing a common goal that knew no borders, towns and cities throughout Scandinavia showed a common pride, taking up seals whose central motifs, such as town walls, castles and saints, could be found all over Europe.

The noble families of Finland were mainly of Swedish origin. Few were of local Finnish stock, and the indigenous families usually changed their names as they moved from estate to estate, so that sons might have different surnames from their fathers. Just one Finnish family, the Princes Menshikov, attained princely rank, a reminder of the period from 1809–1917 when the Grand Duchy of Finland was part of the Russian Empire.

The Menshikovs also reflect the polyglot nature of Scandinavian nobility in general, which assimilated into its ranks Scots, English, French and German families. Not surprisingly, the nobility of

▼ *The arms of Baron Örnsköld have the two helmets and crests accorded to a Swedish baron. The quarterings are divided by a cross throughout, in a style characteristic of Swedish heraldry.*

Scandinavia adapted the heraldic style of northern Germany, including the use of peacock feathers in crests, and arms that became increasingly augmented with quarterings as families rose to higher rank. But gradually Scandinavian heraldry took on its own flavours, and some of its charges have few equivalents elsewhere in Europe. In Denmark and Sweden, for instance, a cross throughout may divide various quarterings, and this is a practice seldom met with elsewhere, except in Scotland.

HERALDIC FUNERALS

A practice dating from the late 16th century, peculiar to Sweden, Finland and much of the Baltic coast, was the carrying of heraldic shields on poles in the funeral procession. A large achievement of the defunct's own arms, known in Sweden as the *hufvudbaner*, was carried at the head of the coffin, with smaller shields (*anvapen*) belonging to the paternal and maternal ancestors on either side.

The *anvapen* were borne separately at first, sometimes by as many as 16 bearers, but in about 1660 Queen Hedvig Eleonora decreed that such a show of pomp should be confined to the royal family. From then on just two *anvapen* were carried, but these were, if anything, more splendid: each developed into the form of a heraldic family tree, with its branches adorned with many separate shields. Both the *hufvudbaner* and the *anvapen* were carved from wood, bright with gold and silver leaf and fully coloured.

ARMORIAL COLLECTIONS

Both Sweden and Finland maintain Houses of the Nobility, in Stockholm and Helsinki respectively. Although now much reduced

▲ *A plaque for President Eisenhower of the United States, made a Danish knight of the Order of the Elephant.*

in power, they still enjoy a certain kudos and maintain splendid collections of family arms. In both cases, the arms of the nobility are grouped together through rank and chronology. Because the Finnish House of Nobility was established while Finland was under Swedish rule, it followed the Swedish system.

The Swedish Riddarhuset (the "house of nobility") contains a total of 2,320 armorial plaques, which are numbered in order of seniority. Among them is the achievement of the Counts of Wasalborg (No 5) with the curious punning charge of two crowned fish. The family was descended from Gustav Gustafsson, illegitimate son of Gustavus Adolphus, and a merchant's daughter from Gothenburg called Margareta Kabiljau (*kabelju* means "dried

▲ *The armorial plaque of the noble family of Stöltenhielm in the Riddarhuset in Stockholm. The progenitor's wooden leg appears as one of the charges.*

cod" in Swedish). The achievement includes the arms of the house of Vasa, with a bendlet sinister to show illegitimacy.

Many families have punning arms, including a troll in the arms of Trolle, and a wooden leg, or stilt, in the Stöltenhielm arms. Coats of arms of the Swedish aristocracy sometimes feature a scarlet hat, which was worn by members of the monarch's council of state. They may also include the arms of a province, if a member or members of the family had been the monarch's representative there.

ORDERS OF CHIVALRY
Many noble families of foreign extraction originated with high-ranking military officers who staffed the armies of northern Europe during the expansionist wars of the 17th and 18th centuries. They also swelled the ranks of the ancient orders of chivalry in both Denmark and Sweden.

The chapel in the Castle of Frederiksborg at Hillerød, to the north of Copenhagen, contains the armorial plaques for knights of two Danish orders: the Order of the Elephant (believed to have been founded in 1464) and the Order of the Dannebrog. The Order of the Elephant

is the senior order, and its foreign knights include Sir Winston Churchill and President Eisenhower. Its badge is a white enamelled elephant charged with a cross of five plate diamonds, guided by a mahout and bearing a golden tower. The collar of the order is charged with elephants and towers. Churchill was once seen wearing the insignia of the Elephant and when asked if it happened to be an "Order Day", he replied in the negative. He was in fact in mourning for an elephant that had just died at London Zoo.

Before 1975, Sweden maintained four orders of chivalry. The Order of the Seraphim, founded in 1748 by Fredrik I, was the highest. Each order had its own room in the royal palace in Stockholm, the wall decorations of which were taken from the collars of the orders. Today only two survive, the Order of the Seraphim and the Order of the Polar Star, but neither can be conferred on Swedish citizens other than the royal family. The Order of the Seraphim is most often conferred on foreign heads of state. Notable among non-royal knights is Nelson Mandela, whose shield bears the South African flag.

The insignia include golden seraphs, the monogram of Christ – IHS – and three nails from the Cross. Ladies of the Order and prelates have their arms within a pale

▲ *The hufvudbaner and anvapen (arms of alliance) for Diedrich Kagg (d1671) in Linköping Cathedral, Sweden.*

blue ribbon, from which the badge is suspended. Female sovereigns, like male knights, have the collar. The arms of all female members are placed on an oval. Since 1748 the Seraphim has been conferred on nearly 800 men and women, and of those over 600 have their achievements

▼ *For the memorial service of a newly deceased knight of the Order of the Seraphim, the heraldic plaque is displayed on an easel before the altar of the Riddarholmskyrka in Stockholm.*

on plaques hung, three-deep, on the walls of the Riddarholmskyrka ("Church on the Knights' Island") in Stockholm.

PERSONAL ARMS

In general the Scandinavian heraldic authorities are concerned with national, royal and military matters, rather than personal arms. Personal heraldry is usually treated like a trade mark and can be registered as such for protection, although state authorities will give advice on corporate and personal arms, especially in regard to correct blazon. Guidance can also be gained from heraldic societies and foundations. Some of the foremost heraldic experts in northern Europe collaborate under the aegis of the Societas Heraldica Scandinavica in bringing out the twice-yearly magazine *Heraldisk Tidskrift*.

Those living in Scandinavia can register their arms through the *Skandinavisk Vapenrulla*, the Scandinavian roll of arms. It has its own heraldic artists and consultants to ensure that every coat of arms is correctly treated.

CLARITY AND SIMPLICITY

While each of the Scandinavian nations enjoys its own heraldic customs and styles, during the 20th century there was a noted interaction between heraldic designers and authorities within the northern states, which provided some of the liveliest discourse and debate in the heraldic world. The most distinctive styles emanated from a handful of heraldic craftsmen and designers, notably Hallvard

Trætteberg in Norway and Gustav von Numers, Ahti Hammar and Olof Eriksson, all from Finland. Trætteberg's ideas had a profound effect not only on the civic and municipal heraldry of his own country, but also on that in neighbouring Sweden.

Norway has no state herald (the duties being undertaken by the National Archives), but Trætteberg, who worked in the Archives, may be regarded as the nearest thing to it. Between 1920 and his death in 1987, he was very much the influence behind Norwegian heraldry. His controversial stand on the matters of tincture and charges still strongly influences Norwegian military and civic heraldry.

Trætteberg advocated a number of heraldic rules, the most notable being that no more than two tinctures, one colour and one metal, should be used on a shield. He also liked the idea of one charge being used, in a singular or multiple fashion, and suggested that no shading or shadow should be applied to the charge. His theories have made modern Norwegian heraldic style the starkest and most uncompromising in use today. Those used to British arms may regard his shields as too plain, yet a Scandinavian heraldist might characterize English civic heraldry as cluttered and lacking in style.

CIVIC HERALDRY

In Finland, meanwhile, von Numers, Hammar and Eriksson were revolutionizing their nation's civic and municipal arms with a series of shields unparalleled in their symbolism and simple beauty. Taking into

▲ *Possibly the most influential of modern styles is that of Finnish municipal heraldry, with its unusual divisions of the field and combinations of charges, seen here in the arms of Liminka commune.*

account the local dialect, geographical curiosities and folklore of each place for which they devised arms, these three visionaries produced new heraldic designs that were often daring in their simplicity. Their ideas gave food for thought to the then new heraldic authorities of South Africa and Canada.

Among their innovations, ordinaries were offset in unusual fashion, sometimes combined with other charges, at other times standing alone. Among the former, the shield of the municipality of Kuivaniemi, with its single wavy flanche and seal embowed, suggests Kuivaniemi's position on the coast of the Gulf of Bothnia. Other fascinating designs include those of the municipality of Pielavesi, which features the local musical instrument – a horn made of birch bark.

Native flora and fauna are often depicted in the most unconventional forms, as in the arms of Simo in Lapland, which is one of the oldest parishes in the

◀ *Two civic arms exemplify the simplicity of modern Norwegian heraldry: the shield of Målselv (left) includes the district's river; for Bardu (right) a wolverine represents the area's forests.*

province, and is also famed for its salmon fishing: its twin distinctions are neatly married in a cross composed of fish tails.

Lines of partition were drawn anew by Trætteberg and the Finnish designers, with the fir trees that cover so much of the country as a favourite motif. In much modern Scandinavian heraldry, the charges, trees especially, are stylized in a simple form. This can make for a refreshing clarity, as in the arms of the Swedish border town of Haparanda: these include in their design a border post between two trees, surmounted by the midnight sun, which is enjoyed by the community for several months each year.

Inevitably, the point was eventually reached when nearly all communities, of whatever size, had had arms designed for them, and the steam went out of the innovative phase of Finnish civic heraldry. Now even this heraldic nation has started to embrace the logo. But in general Scandinavia enjoys its civic heraldry and uses it to the full. It is usual for communities to place their arms not only on buildings but also on local transport and on the boundary signs on the approaches to cities, towns and villages. In Finland, fans of civic heraldry can find plenty to spot, and are often rewarded with a two-in-one "prize", for the community arms may well be twinned with those of the local province. The latter date in the main from the 16th century, when Finland formed part of the kingdom of Sweden. Many of the provincial arms appeared on banners carried in the funeral procession of King Gustav I in 1560.

▲ *Four salmon tails in the arms of Simo in Lapland form a cross for the see of Uppsala.*

▲ *The arms of Pielavesi commune, Finland, with its birch bark horns.*

▲ *A wonderful example of a heraldic hybrid species representing forests and lakes, in the arms of the city of Zarasai in Lithuania, created in 1969.*

▲ *The arms of the Finnish municipality of Inari include an extraordinary marriage of two species raised on local farms.*

▲ *The approach to many Scandinavian towns and villages is clearly marked with heraldry, as in Haparanda in Sweden.*

▶ *The sublimely simple punning arms of the Finnish community of Sumiainen – sumu means "foggy" in Finnish.*

AFRICA

While it belongs first and foremost to the nobility of western Europe, heraldry has such an attractive character that it was bound to be taken by Europeans to the lands they invaded, subdued and settled, not the least of which were the colonial territories of Africa.

SOUTH AFRICA

Heraldry was first taken to South Africa in 1488, with the Portuguese adventurer, Bartholomew Diaz, who had stone crosses erected bearing the arms of Portugal. Although the Portuguese did not actually colonize South Africa, what was probably the first grant of arms to an indigenous armiger in this area, the Emperor Monomatapa, was made by the King of Portugal in 1569. The blazon was Gules, between two arrows Argent an African hoe barwise bladed Argent handled Or, the shield surmounted by an Eastern crown.

The Dutch ruled the land that now forms the Republic of South Africa between 1652 and 1806. They were followed by the British, who brought with them their own heraldic tradition. For much of the period of British rule, South African arms were typical of the lacklustre heraldry the British heralds of the time were foisting on the colonies, in the fussy overladen style of the late Georgian and Victorian eras.

In 1961 the Republic of South Africa broke its ties with the British Commonwealth, incidentally cutting itself off from the authority of the British heralds. Some two years later the South African Bureau of Heraldry was established in Pretoria. The Bureau has at its head a State Herald to whom any person or corporate body may apply for grant and registration of armorial bearings. When granted, these are officially published in the Government Gazette. (Many armigers in the United Kingdom have asked for their heraldic authorities to publish such a record.)

SCANDINAVIAN INFLUENCE

The new authority looked to the Scandinavians, notably the Finnish heraldic artists, Gustav von Numers and Ahti Hammar, for inspiration. In recent years it has come up with some of the simplest and most splendid designs in modern heraldry, taking its themes from the modern Scandinavian style. In 1974 the State Herald of the time, Mr Hartman, visited Finland to meet the Finnish heraldic experts and gain insight into their local styles and design techniques. Some five years later, Hartman's successor, Frederick Brownell, followed his example.

From their time spent with their Finnish colleagues, the South African heralds decided on a fresh approach to heraldic design. Simplicity was to be the first principle, followed by new lines of partition based on the local architecture, flora and fauna. Elements of innovative Finnish design were to be incorporated into the heraldry of South Africa, where these were considered appropriate.

The marriage of the two national styles produced some strikingly simple designs. New partition lines were based on the gable ends of the Dutch-style farmhouses in the Cape and the national flower, *Protea cynaroides*, the stylized petals of which were used to create a striking new motif reminiscent of the fir twig partition line found in Finnish and Swedish arms.

The indigenous tribes of South Africa had long marked their oval shields with a system of colour and symbol, which was not so much heraldry as armory. Such symbols were part of a "regimental" identification system, rather than a personal or family one. The South African Bureau of Heraldry has made much use of traditional native shields in the designs of arms of black townships.

HERALDRY AFTER APARTHEID

The future status of the South African Bureau of Heraldry can only be guessed at, although it is of necessity not of the first importance to the post-apartheid government. State Herald Brownell has done much to ensure that heraldry can be enjoyed by people of all creeds and colours, for in his own words, heraldry is "colourful, but colour blind".

Frederick Brownell and his fellow heralds have sought to combine English, Afrikaans and Portuguese heraldic traditions with the symbols of the indigenous African tribes. However, despite his good intentions, heraldry is bound to be viewed

▲ *The arms granted to South Africa's Emperor Monomatapa by the Portuguese king in 1569.*

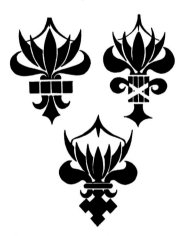

▲ *Three different designs by the South African State Bureau of Heraldry based on the national flower, the protea.*

▲ *The arms of the Republic of Zimbabwe include in the crest the star of socialism and behind the shield an automatic rifle.*

▼ *In the arms of Harare, capital of Zimbabwe, heraldry finds its way on to a shield of traditional African shape.*

▲ *The arms of Soweto, a mixture of traditional African symbols and classical medieval European heraldry.*

by the vast majority of the population as yet another toy of the old European oppressors, fit to die a natural and unlamented death.

For the new national arms for the Republic of South Africa, the Bureau of Heraldry was bypassed and a design commissioned from a non-heraldic artist. The achievement was adopted in April 2000. The motto is in the now extinct Khoisan language spoken by the oldest known inhabitants of the land, and it means *Diverse people unite.* The shield is enclosed within elephants' tusks, symbolizing wisdom and strength, and ears of wheat to represent fertility and growth. The human figures are shown in an attitude of unity.

ZIMBABWE

In the neighbouring republic of Zimbabwe, the state arms have a traditional British flavour to them, and use the heater-shaped shield of medieval European heraldry.

However, this traditional shape has been married to typical Marxist-style militancy, with symbols of the workers and peasants side by side. An AK47 assault rifle, the weapon that armed many revolutionary struggles of the late 20th century, takes its place against the red star of socialism. In the arms of the capital city, Harare, the great Zimbabwe bird is used as a traditional charge, but has been placed on an African-style shield.

HERALDIC SURVIVALS

While some ex-colonial territories, such as the former Portuguese provinces of Angola and Mozambique, have wished to throw off heraldry, seeing it as an uninvited import of their former white rulers, others have taken it to their hearts. The former French territory of Gabon, for example, has employed a French heraldic designer to create (with local assistance) arms for its regions, districts and communities. In these, typically European heraldic practices are twinned with the most striking of local African fauna, flora, customs and art, creating fine examples of good heraldry.

▲ *The new coat of arms of the Republic of South Africa, a modern application of heraldry fit for the second millennium.*

CANADA

The newest of all national heraldic authorities, that of Canada, came into being in 1988 after Queen Elizabeth II, acting in her capacity as Sovereign of Canada, authorized the Governor General to exercise in Canada one of her Royal prerogatives, the right to grant arms.

The Canadian Heraldic Authority, unlike its Scottish and English counterparts, does not have a king of arms as its chief officer. That office is exercised by the Chief Herald of Canada. However, there are heralds and pursuivants, as would be found in any of the more ancient state heraldic offices.

INDIGENOUS STYLE

The Authority grants arms to Canadian nationals and corporate institutions after receiving a formal petition, presented in the same way that any English or Scots person or corporation would do to their own heraldic authority. But the arms

▼ *A splendid stained glass window showing the insignia and badges of the Canadian Heraldic Authority and its officers of arms set against a background of the arms of the Canadian provinces. Made by Christopher Wallis in 1990.*

▲ *Some years ago the College of Arms in London granted a pilot's helmet in lieu of the traditional medieval warriors' helmet – a theme taken up and expanded by the Canadian Heraldic Authority. The crests of* granted by the CHA, though they keep to the age-old tenets of European heraldic tradition, often have a very distinct flavour. Right from its beginning, as well as employing artists and historians belonging to the European tradition in Canada (notably French, English and Scots), the CHA has sought out those of the indigenous peoples. All the West Coast Indians and Inuit tribes have fascinating histories, symbols and folklore that can be drawn from and adapted to serve the heraldic achievement of arms.

Nowhere does this happy mixture of native and imported traditions become more manifest than in the achievement of arms of the Canadian Heraldic Authority itself. Its shield bears a maple leaf charged with an escutcheon, the like of which could be found on any Scots, English or Scandinavian shield of arms, conventional

these three arms are, clockwise from top left, an Indian Shaman's headdress for Mr Norquay, a Maccabean warrior's helmet for a synagogue, and a fur parka hood for Helen Maksagak, former commissioner of the Northwest Territories.

but efficient in its effect. The supporters, however, are wonderfully aboriginal in their execution and content. They are two fantastic creatures, half polar bear, half raven, dancing energetically and resembling figures that might be found at a West Coast Indian tribal gathering or on one of its totem poles.

This combination of "first nation" and European symbolism allows the Canadian heralds a wealth of charges open to no other heraldic organization, except the South African Bureau of Heraldry, which has a similar blend of colonial and indigenous symbols at its disposal. Two more creatures straight from a totem pole support a shield charged with traditional European heraldic charges – bezants and a pallet wavy – in the arms of the Honourable Judy Gingell, Commissioner of the Yukon Territory. Elsewhere, in the arms of the city of White Rock, an iceberg can be seen along with an aboriginal representation of a killer whale.

Jewish communities are unusually well represented in Canada. While individual Jewish people have long been commemorated in the heraldry of certain European nations (notably Italy), few Jewish communities are heraldically recognized.

ACCESSIBILITY AND EQUALITY

A combination of cultures is not limited to the pictorial display of arms. In the patents issued by the Canadian Heraldic Authority, the blazon and formal declaration of the grant are written in both French and English – a legal requirement for all official Canadian documents.

The requirement to make arms known to "all and singular", whatever the reader's origin, has been taken even further by the CHA. When granting arms to the new

▲ *Cadency marks for two children of James Robson: on the left a label for an eldest son, and on the right the ermine spots in the top corners that are the mark for a second daughter in the Canadian cadency system.*

Territory of Nunavut, established on 1 April 1999, the text and motto were fully translated on the patent into the native language of the local Inuit people of that region, and the wording was first approved by local linguistic experts.

Although it may be only a babe in arms in comparison with the English College of Arms and Lord Lyon's Office in Scotland, the CHA is very much the new star of the heraldic world. It has already produced its own marks of difference for women, and

it does not discriminate between men and women in respect of helms and crests: Canadian grantees of either sex are entitled to them. Women may also use the heater-shaped shield or lozenge without any mark to differentiate their arms. As sexual equality is enshrined in Canadian law, it is considered illegal for the Heraldic Authority to treat women differently.

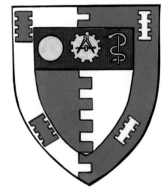

▲ *The shield of arms for the British Columbia Institute of Technology is charged with computer symbols.*

▼ *The patents of arms for Canadian institutions and individuals are usually worded in English and French, but native languages may also be included.*

TO ALL TO WHOM these Presents shall come or whom the same may in any way concern, GREETING: By Robert Douglas Watt, Chief Herald of Canada: WHEREAS the Very Reverend Peter Gordon Elliott, Rector of Trinity of the Episcopal Divinity School in Cambridge, Massachusetts, United States of America, Dean and Rector of Christ Church Anglican Cathedral, Vancouver, Province of British Columbia, in the Church of the Anglican Church of Canada, has represented to the Chief Herald of Canada that the Parish of Christ Church, Vancouver, was established on the 12th day of November 1888 (the day the first Rector was appointed) with the present church building having been opened for divine worship on the 6th day of October 1889, the church being designated as the Cathedral Church of the Diocese on the 12th day of February 1929, the structure being designated as a heritage building by the City of Vancouver on the 17th day of December 1974 and further, that it is his wish, expressed for and on behalf of the Rector, wardens, council and laity of the parish, supported by the Bishop of New Westminster, the Right Reverend Michael Ingham and by the Chapter of Christ Church Cathedral, that the aforesaid Cathedral Church be granted armorial bearings by lawful authority; AND WHEREAS a Warrant dated the 28th day of May 1897 has been issued by Lieutenant-General James Cyrille Gervais, Chancellor and Commander of the Order of Military Merit, Deputy Herald, Chancellor of the Canadian Heraldic Authority, authorizing the Chief Herald of Canada to grant armorial bearings to CHRIST CHURCH CATHEDRAL, VANCOUVER, such armorial bearings as are deemed fitting and appropriate; NOW KNOW YOU that pursuant to the authority vested in His Excellency the Right Honourable Roméo-Adrien LeBlanc, a Member of the Queen's Privy Council for Canada, Chancellor and Principal Companion of the Order of Canada, Chancellor and Commander of the Order of Military Merit, Governor General and Commander-in-Chief of Canada, to devise the armorial prerogative of Her Majesty Queen Elizabeth II as Queen of Canada, by Letters Patent dated the 4th day of June 1988, and the terms of my Commission of Office, I, the Chief Herald of Canada do by these Presents grant and assign to CHRIST CHURCH CATHEDRAL, VANCOUVER, the following Arms: Argent in base two bars wavy Azure surmounted by a Celtic cross throughout Gules charged at the centre with a Salish spindle whorl Argent bearing a Cha Blia Azure enclosing by three salmon in Salish style interlaced Gules; and for a Motto: I-HOLD-BEFORE-YOU-AN-OPEN-DOOR; And I do further grant and assign as a Supporter: A representation of a cathedra prayer set as apex an escutcheon of the Arms of the Diocese of New Westminster of the Anglican Church of Canada; And for a Flag: A banner of the Arms; And for a Badge: A heart surmounted by a Celtic

À TOUS CEUX QUI verront les présentes ou que les présentes concernent, SALUT : DE la part de Robert Douglas Watt, Héraut d'armes du Canada : CONSIDÉRANT QUE Peter Gordon Elliott, Recteur auditeur, maître et théologue de la Episcopal Divinity School de Cambridge aux Massachusetts, États-Unis d'Amérique, Doyen et Recteur de Christ Church, Anglican Cathedral à Vancouver, province de la Colombie-Britannique, dans le diocèse de New Westminster de l'Église anglicane du Canada, a avisé le Héraut d'armes du Canada que la paroisse de Christ Church, Vancouver, a été fondée le 12e jour de novembre 1888 (jour où le premier pasteur fut nommé), que l'église actuelle ouverte au culte le 6e jour d'octobre 1889, fut désignée cathédrale du diocèse le 12e jour de février 1929 et classifiée édifice d'intérêt patrimonial par la ville de Vancouver, le 17e jour de décembre 1974 et, qu'en outre, le pasteur Elliott a exprimé, au nom des marguilliers et marguillières du conseil et des fidèles de la paroisse, avec l'appui de l'Monseigneur Michael Ingham, Évêque de New Westminster, et du chapitre de Christ Church, Cathedral, le souhait que des emblèmes soient officiellement conférés à ladite cathédrale; ET CONSIDÉRANT QUE le Lieutenant-général, James Cyrille Gervais, Chancelier et Commandeur de l'Ordre du mérite militaire, Vice-chancelier d'armes de l'Autorité héraldique du Canada, a émis un mandat daté du 28e jour de mai 1897 autorisant le Héraut d'armes du Canada à concéder à CHRIST CHURCH CATHEDRAL, VANCOUVER, des emblèmes jugés convenables et appropriés; SACHEZ QUE conformément à l'autorité dont se vaut Son Excellence le très honorable Roméo-Adrien LeBlanc, membre du Conseil privé de la Reine pour le Canada, Chancelier et Compagnon principal de l'Ordre du Canada, Chancelier et Commandeur de l'Ordre du mérite militaire, Gouverneur général et Commandant en chef du Canada, d'exercer la prérogative en matière d'armoiries que Sa Majesté la Reine Élizabeth II, à titre de Reine du Canada, lui a conciliée par lettres patentes datées du 4e jour de juin 1988, et conformément aux dispositions de mon commission d'office, moi, le Héraut d'armes du Canada, par les présentes, concédons et assignons à CHRIST CHURCH CATHEDRAL, VANCOUVER, les armes suivantes : D'argent à une croix celtic non alésée de gueules, chargée en abîme du volant d'un fuseau salish d'argent inscrit du chrisme d'azur entouré de trois saumons de style salish entrelacés de gueules, brochante en pointe sur deux burelés ondés d'azur; et pour devise : I HOLD-BEFORE-YOU-AN-OPEN-DOOR; Et nous consentons et assignons comme support : Une cathèdre au naturel, ornée sur le dossier supérieur d'un écu aux armes du diocèse de New Westminster de l'Église anglicane du Canada; Et pour drapeau : une bannière aux armes; Et pour insigne : Une croix celtic de gueules liserée d'or ajourée d'azur et chargée en abîme du volant d'un fuseau salish d'argent

JAPAN: THE OTHER HERALDRY

Few nations and societies outside Europe have ever maintained any system of recognition comparable with heraldry in length of service and application. There is one extraordinary exception: the crests or badges used for many centuries by the Japanese courtiers and military elite. Such devices are called *mon*.

THE *MON*

To understand the precise meaning of the word *mon* it is necessary to decipher the two Japanese characters that make it up: they mean "thread" and "markings". In other words, the badges originated as embroidered costume decorations. Often, as with heraldry, they employ as symbols the simplest household objects, such as fans or kitchen implements.

Various heraldic writers have been intrigued by the similarity in usage between Japanese *mon* and European heraldry, for the former were used by Japanese warriors on their armour and battle flags, and on the clothing they wore for formal occasions. Even so, throughout the periods during which warfare raged in both

Japan and Europe, neither system can have had any influence on the other. In modern times, along with the importation into the West of so much that is Japanese, has come the triumph over heraldry of the western equivalent of the *mon* – the logo. Very often in recent years, corporations that previously sported full achievements of arms have shelved them in favour of a corporate emblem that in style would not have looked out of place on the battle banners of a 15th-century shogun.

As early as the 8th century, the emperors of Japan were using specific emblems associated with their dynasty. It followed that what the ruler did was aped by those who served him and formed his social circle: the courtiers and court officials. The early *mon* were often Chinese in flavour, with symbols such as the phoenix, cloud formations, peacocks and dragons reflecting the influence and respect felt by the Japanese court for the powerful T'ang dynasty and its court across the water.

MILITARY USE

Although in its early life the *mon* was primarily a feature kept firmly within the walls of the imperial court, its use was watched with envy by the other leading group in Japanese feudal society: the military, or warrior, class. As this group grew in strength it made inroads into the formal life of the court and adopted much courtly style as its own. Yet often the two classes viewed each other with mutual suspicion. The court saw the warrior caste as brutal and barbaric, while the warriors regarded the courtiers as effete and weak-willed.

Having started as a symbol that identified the courtier's possessions and costume, the *mon* became associated with the trappings of the military man. The three main platforms for its display were the standards or battle flags (*hata*), tall, narrow banners up to 3m (10ft) in length; cloth curtains (*tobari*) used in the military camp to partition the commander's formal enclosure; and the formal garment (*hitare*), made of silk brocade, which, although worn

▲ *The marriage of two distant and distinctive symbolic traditions: a recent grant of arms to a gentleman of Japanese origin now living in Canada has placed the family* mon *on a European warrior's shield.*

▼ *Just as in Europe heralds and heraldic writers drew up rolls of armorial bearings, in Japan the history and characters of* mon *were studied in great detail, especially by artists. This is a page from a Japanese artist's book of* mon.

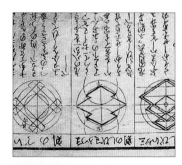

▲ *The* jimbaori, *the Japanese nobleman's equivalent to the tabard or jupon. This example bears the* mon *of the Honda clan.*

beneath armour, was visible through sleeves and leg coverings. Small flags bearing mon were also attached to helmets.

In time, European influence did make its presence felt in Japan and the clothes worn by Portuguese and Spanish adventurers led to the development of a Japanese version of a coat of arms. The *jimbaori* was a sleeveless garment worn over armour and often decorated with the bearer's *kaemon*, a substitute, or lesser form of, *mon*. The garment was much favoured by the *daimyo*, or feudal lords, who controlled much of Japan between 1400 and 1416. The essential difference between the *jimbaori* and the medieval western warrior's "jupon", or tabard, was that the former was removed before battle commenced.

From the late 17th century onwards, the *mon*, which had up to then been thought of as the prerogative of the courtiers and warrior classes, began to be adopted by anyone, of any status, who was in some way associated with them – such as the kabuki actors and courtesans who helped the samurai or the palace official to forget his heavy day. As in Europe, where inroads

were made into heraldry by the merchant classes, Japanese commentators of the period bemoaned the usurpation of noble dress and insignia by those of less ancient and less honourable status.

MON MOTIFS

The *mon* of the military elite were often adapted from those of the courtiers in a way that emphasized the former's martial nature. Flowers, which were associated with a more gentle way of life, therefore had their petals interspersed with sword blades; instead of butterflies or birds, the warriors might choose axe blades and a spirited representation of the helmet horns (*kuwagata*) favoured as an adornment by Japanese warriors.

The design of the *mon* is usually very simple. Multiples of motifs are rare, as are combinations of more than two different objects. The device may be left by itself or fitted into a frame formed by a ring, square, diamond, or several-sided border (as opposed to the shield shape that is essential to heraldry).

Mon are seldom of more than one colour, and the choice of this depends on the background. Black lacquer, for example, used in Japan for many articles from furniture to armour, tends to be decorated with the family *mon* in gold. Battle flags might be of white cloth charged with the

commander's *mon* in either red or black, though if the flag was black the *mon* would probably be in white.

Whatever the nature of the motif – whether it was a bird, flower, geometric pattern or ideograph (written character) – the *mon* was designed to fill the frame in which it was used. So much of Japanese life was dominated by the symbolism of superstition that, unlike European heraldry, the *mon* might consist of a character representing an auspicious meaning, such as "good luck" or "longevity".

Many a Japanese *mon* could be translated heraldically, bars and pallets being just two devices that heraldists would recognize as directly comparable with heraldic ordinaries. But there the similarity ends, for far from being simple geometric shapes, in Japan much that is simple carries a hidden meaning through symbolism that is sometimes several millennia old.

Although formal systems of difference marks for children or branches of a family do not exist as they do in European heraldry, junior branches of a Japanese family grouping often adopted modified versions of the *mon* of the senior branch or leader. In addition to their formal mark (*jomon*), families also had several substitute symbols (*kaemon*), which might, through common practice, be granted to another family related by marriage.

▼ *A 17th-century battle scene shows in vivid colour and detail the use of the* mon *by the Japanese clans (in this case the Minamoto and the Taira); battle flags and standards are much in evidence.*

THE HERALDRY OF CONFLICT

From its earliest days, heraldry has been seen as an adjunct to conflict. Just as one person's freedom fighter is another's terrorist, so also the signs and symbols of either side can promote inspiration or hatred. Heraldry grew up during a period of conflict between Christian Europe and the Islamic East, and there is some evidence that it may have had its origins in Islamic emblems. Many shields bearing crosses or crescents are said to have their origins in the Crusades, but such symbols pale beside the heraldic imagery of Hungary, whose noble families saw themselves as the last bastion of Christendom against the Turks. At least a third of all Hungarian arms bear Turkish body parts.

The clash of ideologies spilled over into the arms of other noble families of the Holy Roman Empire. The Princes of Schwarzburg, for their part in defeating a Turkish army at Raab in Hungary, were given an augmentation consisting of a Turk's head having its eye pecked out by a crow. Another augmentation, granted to the Barons Hochpied, shows the hand of a Christian freed from Turkish fetters. But heraldry can be a witness to all parties, whoever the oppressor. In the arms of the Gabonaise district of Ogooué-Lolo, broken fetters represent the countless people who were forced into slavery by Europeans.

▲ *Heralds of the Holy Roman Empire and Hungary point to the freeing of Christian slaves in the arms of the Barons Hochpied.*

▼ *An arm patch of a Croatian Special Forces unit during the conflict in Yugoslavia. The Sahovnica, the chequered shield of Croatia, appears in the background.*

EUROPEAN CONFLICTS

More recent struggles have been commemorated on the shields of arms of many towns, from Sweden to Serbia. The struggle for freedom from Russia by the Lithuanian townspeople of Pandorys was recorded by a rising hawk blooded in one wing, while the infamy of the Nazi concentration camp at Flossenburg in Czechoslovakia is recorded in the arms of the nearby town of Holysov, featuring a red rose rising from behind barbed wire. The division of Germany between East and West was recorded with more barbed wire in the arms of Wennerode in Lower Saxony, where the watchtowers and trip mines of the East German border zone actually passed along the edge of the parish: the heraldic Saxon stallion easily leapt the manmade absurdity.

The manipulation of symbols by men of war is of course far older than heraldry itself, but recent conflicts provide vivid examples of this use of heraldic emblems.

▲ *The rose of freedom throws its head above the wire of the concentration camp in the arms of Holysov.*

▼ *The Saxon horse leaps to freedom over the Iron Curtain in the arms of Wennerode.*

The break-up of the former Yugoslav Federation saw heraldry that had remained dormant for many years revived with fervour. Slovenia adopted entirely new arms, despite having a national identity many centuries old. Other states such as Bosnia-Herzegovina, Serbia and Croatia, re-adopted heraldry that each associated with a glorious past, real or imaginary.

To the Croats, the Sahovnica – their shield of white and red chequers – was a symbol of pride worn since the medieval period, but during World War II it was banned by Tito for 45 years. After 1991 it re-appeared everywhere, on flags, badges,

▲ A Serbian military official denounces NATO bombing against a backdrop of the arms of the Yugoslav Federation, Serbia and Montenegro, Belgrade 1999.

key rings and car stickers, and was viewed with horror by Serbs. In turn, the Serbs replaced the red star on the Serbian flag with their ancient coat of arms – a cross between four Cyrillic letter Cs – in a direct challenge to the hated Croatian chequerboard. The Cs stand for *Samo slago Srbina spasava* ("Only unity saves the Serbs").

▼ In Northern Ireland both sides of the political divide make their presence known through heraldry. This display by a Loyalist group mixes conventional heraldic charges with local symbols such as unit numbers.

NORTHERN IRELAND

The tempestuous twinning of symbol and sensibility has nowhere been more manifest than in Northern Ireland. Both Republicans and Ulster Unionists know equally well the power of symbols. From the 1960s to the 1990s, the most vivid by-product of the Troubles has been the development of "house art", or murals. Each side has seen this as a means of displaying the essential episodes of its history.

Heraldry has played a large part in the mural movement. The Republicans' desire to see Ireland united has often been manifested by presenting the arms of the country's four provinces – Leinster, Connacht, Munster and Ulster – on a single shield. In these cases the arms of Ulster are those of the Republic's province of that

name: a field of gold with a red cross (the arms of the de Burgh family), its centre charged with the bloody hand of the O'Neills. The British province of Ulster places the red cross on a white field, with the red hand surmounted by a crown.

Many tales are told of the origins of the red hand. It is not, as some would have it, a sign used by those who fought on the Protestant side at the Battle of the Boyne in 1690, but a charge borne in the arms of the O'Neill family. They were kings of Ireland, and the hand is said to commemorate the legend that their ancestor was part of a Viking raiding force. The Vikings had decided that whoever was first to place his hand on Irish soil would be its rightful ruler. The O'Neill ancestor, seeing that the ship of a rival would ground before his, cut off his hand and threw it on to the shore.

The hero of Protestant Loyalists is William of Orange, king of Britain 1689–1702. The Union Jack and its colours are used to decorate lampposts and kerbstones in Loyalist areas, and each Loyalist faction displays its badge combining the red hand and the crown. In murals, these may be placed beside the arms of Derry or Belfast, accompanying the portrait of a "local hero". In Republican areas, paintings of masked gunmen may be seen against a backdrop of the arms of the Republican provinces, and also of other national groups around the world.

▼ In Republican Belfast the arms of the city of Valencia are used to express solidarity with the freedom fighters of Catalonia.

THE CONTINUITY OF HERALDRY

The heraldic tradition stretches back at least eight centuries, but for most of
that time no knight in armour has carried a coloured shield or worn a
helmet decorated with a crest to identify him in the thick of battle.
Heraldry has long outlived its original function on the battlefield, because it
has also served other purposes: the assertion of noble status, the declaration
of allegiance and the rallying of loyalty. Its vivid imagery and venerable
traditions still have persuasive power today, when even though few heraldic
authorities remain, coats of arms still lend grace and authority to many
products of the modern world, from cigarette packets to submarines.
Displays of the heraldry of earlier centuries are vivid reminders of our
cultural history and stability, and there are many who are proud to continue
heraldry's long tradition.

◀ *The achievement of arms of Robert Harrison,*
painted by Dan Escott.

HERALDRY'S PAST AND FUTURE

As the world enters the third millennium of Christian history, heraldry will soon be able to celebrate its first thousand years of being. Although the exact date of its birth is, of course, unknown, perhaps 2150 might be a good time to celebrate its first millennium. Certainly by 1150 the main tenets of heraldry – as a hereditary system of colour and symbol based on the shield – were already in place. What then will heraldry look like in 2150? How might it have progressed, and will it be used in any way that resembles its original function?

Is heraldry still the preserve of the aristocracy? Britain is now possibly the only nation that continues to renew its aristocracy, by the creation of life peers. Of those who take up their seats in the House of Lords, about two thirds still apply to the English College of Arms for a grant of arms and supporters. However, the number of peers that do not bother to take up their entitlement is growing. Their attitude may be best summed up in the words of Baroness Ryder of Warsaw, better known through her charity work as Sue Ryder, who firmly rejected armigerous status:

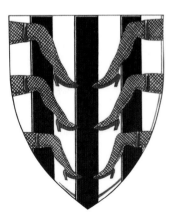

▲ *In past centuries many arms featured body parts, and even a wooden leg was used as a charge. In the modern age, prison bars and six female legs grace the arms posthumously granted to a judge who often presided over cases involving prostitutes.*

Those funny fellows the heralds asked me if I wanted a coat of arms. I saw how much they were asking for it and thought of how many food parcels I could send with the money. I cannot think what type of person would go for such an absurd anachronism.

Well, there are such people: they do still approach the College of Arms and feel a certain pride in a grant of armorial bearings. They may number in their hundreds in a single year, though this is unusual.

CHARGES OLD AND NEW

Those who do wish to become armigerous are taking part in a centuries' old tradition that has served and been adapted and fuelled by the fashion of the age. In heraldry's heyday, heralds compiled rolls of arms known as "ordinaries", which were catalogued according to the charges they bore. If an updated ordinary of arms were to be compiled by today's heralds, it would reflect the whole span of the history of heraldry, setting "then" alongside "now" on the same sheet.

It would be possible, for instance, to see medieval dress sense mixed with that of modern times, starting with the maunch, a medieval lady's sleeve that still graces the shields of the English families of Hastings and Cowper, just as it did in the days when such an item was actually worn some 700 years ago, and the Dutch family of van Abbenbroek still use their punning arms of a pair of breeches, in the style worn by the men of the family four centuries ago.

Beside the shields of those families might be placed that of an English judge from the late 20th century, who often had to pass sentence on the local prostitutes: he is commemorated in arms – granted (posthumously) by the English heralds – charged with pallets (representing prison bars) and six ladies' legs clad in fishnet stockings and garters.

Heraldry has shown itself to be a survivor, and will probably long continue to survive. Whereas once achievements of

▲ *Trinity House, the corporation that administers English and Welsh lighthouses, had its arms granted in the Tudor period and now uses them on its helicopters.*

arms could be seen on the coach panels of the aristocracy, today they are more likely to be painted on a lorry belonging to a supermarket chain, or a municipal garbage truck. Where once shields of arms were used to decorate the dinner services on noblemen's tables, today you are more likely to see a coat of arms on a china teacup on sale in a seaside souvenir shop, or on a pewter plate decorated with the arms of a German district.

SOCIAL STATUS

The longing for social recognition shows itself in many ways. The obtaining of a grant of arms is perhaps just the most blatant expression of such a need, and is not confined to the nobility.

In 17th-century France the middle classes, and even the peasantry, were encouraged to take up arms (though many of the latter were forced to accept such an honour, and were then taxed for the privilege). In Switzerland, heraldry of a domestic nature was commonly adopted by the townsfolk: builders, decorators, and even funeral directors were keen to curry favour with the middle classes. The gable ends of their houses might bear heraldic charges such as crosses, or even shields, and if the owner could make no claim to arms, his initials or the date of the house's construction could fill the space, which on

▲ *Imitation is the highest degree of flattery, and the use of heraldry always confers a certain respectability, even when it appears in a condom advertisement.*

the nobleman's house would bear his heraldic achievement. In death, the coffin fittings of the middle classes were shaped like shields or cartouches to lend an air of nobility to the funeral observances.

It is a theme carried on into our own age. Many companies associated with the leisure and pleasure industry, from playing card manufacturers to condom makers, look to an achievement of arms, real or

▼ *Arms designed by the English heralds for the Maharajahs of Jaipur appear on a plaque in Elveden Church, Suffolk, England. It commemorates the son of Duleep Singh, the Maharajah from whom Queen Victoria obtained the Koh-i-noor diamond.*

assumed, to give them a respectability associated with the traditional users of heraldry. Cigarette manufacturers notoriously commandeer coats of arms for their own ends – almost half of all popular cigarette brands are stamped with quasi-heraldic bearings in an attempt to distract attention from the message of the government health warnings prominently printed alongside.

The notion of conferring nobility through arms was behind the urge to bestow splendid achievements on those of royal or noble status who came from nations where heraldry was not known. One recipient of a regal achievement, whether he wanted it or not, was a young ward of the British Raj in India, the Maharajah Duleep Singh of Jaipur. Duly shipped off to Britain, in 1849 the Maharajah was persuaded to "present" Queen Victoria with the principal jewel of his treasury, the magnificent diamond known as the Koh-i-noor, now part of the British crown jewels. The grateful Queen, who treated the young Maharajah as one of her own family, saw to it that the coat of arms drawn up for him by the English heralds included an escutcheon of the Cross of St George – an allusion to his nominal conversion to Christianity. The Maharajah eventually moved to France, disillusioned with British control of his former realm.

LIVERIES AND SYMBOLS

Once upon a time men in armour watched over the land, bearing their personal devices on breastplates and shields. Today

▲ *In the medieval melée – the part of a tournament in which all the combatants took part together – heraldry was often the only way to identify the contestants.*

the armorial bearings they display are more likely to belong to a police force: the armoured man still exists, no longer a knight in shining armour but a member of a police anti-riot squad. Yesterday's war horse is today's battle tank or fighter bomber, though the modern German armed forces still bear the iron cross, the famed sign of the Teutonic Knights.

The medieval melée, or staged battle, with its milling knights and liveried troops,

▼ *The modern equivalent of a tournament melée can be seen on the crowded floor of the Chicago Board of Trade, where the traders identify themselves by wearing jackets in the liveries of their companies.*

▲ *The collapse of communism is vividly depicted in a Hungarian political party poster. The ancient shield of the kingdom of Hungary smashes through the arms of the communist state.*

▲ *The coat of arms of the Princes of Schwarzenberg, constructed by Franticek Rint in 1870 from human bones. It hangs in the remarkable ossuary at the monastery of Sedlec in the Czech Republic.*

has been replaced by the financial market floor, where groups of traders in coloured jackets jostle and gesticulate in a scene worthy of King René's tourney book or a painting by Uccello. A similar scene is played out in modern-day horse racing, with the jockeys wearing the liveries of the racehorses' owners, much as any household retainer might have done in the medieval period.

In Italy the great horse race of Siena, known as the Palio, takes the viewer back to medieval times. Not only does each rider wear the colour of his *contrada* (ward) but the whole day is one of medieval splendour, with each *contrada* represented by banner-bearers wearing the dress of the 15th century.

HERALDRY AS A WEAPON

While those of a certain degree have long been afforded armorial bearings, the very exclusivity of armory meant that it could be harnessed by those who wished to pour scorn on its noble and royal patrons – and this has been the case from the medieval period until the present day. Cartoonists and more formal artists have had fun with

the heraldic beast, turning even the most ferocious monsters into cuddly figures of fun at the expense of the armiger.

The political satirist has frequently turned the statement "Know by arms" on its head, poking fun at the pompous, the proud and the unpopular through their heraldic bearings, but cartoonists and poets have at times needed to tread a careful line between acceptability and prosecution, or even worse. In England in the late 15th century, the work of William Collingborne

of Bradfield Manor, Wiltshire, who chose to pen a satire on the rule of Richard III and his cronies, was just too much for the last Plantagenet monarch. Collingborne's political satire included the famous rhyme, "The Cat, the Rat, and Lovel our Dog, Rule all England under the Hog". Each name represented one of Richard's chief officials: Sir William Catesby, Sir Richard Ratcliffe, and Francis, Viscount Lovel. Sir William's crest was a cat, Lord Lovel's a dog and the King's badge was the white boar, or "hog". The author of the rhyme was seized and executed for his temerity in 1484.

ADAPTABILITY

Heraldry lends itself to a whole world of application, from the conservative to the crazy. An outstanding example of the latter can be found in the ossuary (or bonehouse) of the former Cistercian monastery at Sedlec, near Kutna Hora in the Czech Republic. Faced with a mound of up to 40,000 complete sets of human bones, the local authorities commissioned a local woodcarver, Franticek Rint, to put them in some kind of order.

Rint's original solution was to arrange them into the most bizarre decorations for the chapel, including an altarpiece and a chandelier. He started work in 1870 and,

▼ *The colours of heraldry are vibrantly rendered in a massive stained glass window displaying the arms of the Princes of Schwarzenberg in Prague Cathedral, Czech Republic.*

▲ A magnificent collection of heraldry on the ceiling and walls of the chamber of the land registry court, Prague Castle, in the Czech Republic.

▲ Heraldry in miniature is a popular motif in jewellery. This diamond and ruby brooch, c1550, is in the shape of the imperial double eagle, the arms of Austria.

▲ The eagle and child crest of the Stanleys appears in Liverpool's Anglican Cathedral on the monument to the 16th Earl of Derby, d1906, designed by Sir Giles Gilbert Scott.

wishing to commemorate the new owner of the chapel, the Prince of Schwarzenberg, he used some of the bones to construct the heraldic achievement of the Prince. The eeriest part of this composition must be the augmentation granted to the family for its part in the Battle of Raab in Hungary, in which the Turkish army had been defeated. In the Sedlec ossuary, the Turk's head of the augmentation, with its eye being pecked out by a crow, is represented by a real human skull.

The Schwarzenberg arms are more traditionally depicted in stained glass in the Cathedral of St Vitus in Prague. This depiction, almost 6m (20ft) high, is kaleidoscopic in its colour, and the viewer needs to know his or her heraldry well to understand the composition.

In nearby Prague Castle, the Schwarzenberg arms also appear with many other shields of the Bohemian nobility. One of the smallest of the castle

▲ Heraldry has been adapted to every period of its history. In this design for an IT company, the British royal arms are suggested through computer parts.

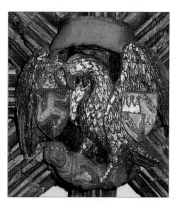

▲ The crest of the Stanleys, Earls of Derby: the eagle and child in its medieval form.

▶ A modern British heraldic standard, for Anthony Ryan of Bath, England. The arms are placed on the hoist (the area nearest the flag pole) and the other segments are charged with the crest (twice) and badge.

chambers contains the finest collection of heraldry. The court of the land registry met here to decide matters relating to the estates of the nobility. Its high officials, the judges and their deputies, all from the aristocracy, are represented by their shields. Each term of the court's life is depicted by arranging the shields of arms of its members in hierarchical order, with the shield of the king at the head of the display, the senior judges below it and the arms of the deputies below them.

Stained glass, murals and human bones: these three examples of the ways in which it has been depicted illustrate the varied appeal of heraldry. Its adaptability and ability to evolve has been its strength.

This book shows how heraldry has used medieval fashion, the paraphernalia of war, animals, imaginary beasts, sputniks, meat hooks, mine workings and musical instruments. All are bound together and held within the world of "belonging", which is what heraldry is all about. In recent years this power to adapt has meant that it has

even taken its place in outer space. In 1992, six copies of the coat of arms of the Canadian Space Agency accompanied Dr Roberta Bondar, the Canadian astronaut, on her voyage in the space shuttle *Discovery*. Back on earth, space travel itself has featured as a motif in the arms of several Russian municipalities, reflecting the pride felt in the USSR over its lead in the 1960s space race.

The use of modern media of all kinds has also helped with heraldry's adaptation into the 21st century. A particularly striking and unusual example was to be found at the former British headquarters of the construction toy company Lego, in Wrexham, North Wales. The building's foyer was dominated by the coat of arms of the Borough of Wrexham Maelor – constructed in Lego, of course.

There was a time, not so very long ago, when the study of heraldry was considered to be the preserve of those who made most use of it – the well-to-do. Now, however, it is open to all, and heraldry societies, both national and local and all less than half a century old, are proliferating. In the age of the internet, genealogical hits on the web are said to be second in number only to pornographic sites.

USING THE FAMILY ARMS

The creativity of modern heraldic artists begs the question, how in the 21st century can one best serve heraldry while using it?

▲ *The heraldic maxim that the charge should fully fit its field was observed by A.W. Pugin when he incorporated the arms of the Talbots in his design for the doors of the Catholic church in Cheadle, England.*

There is a thin line between good and bad taste. Many people of ancient lineage would probably never be seen dead in anything as vulgar as a blazer bearing the family arms or crest; that would be associated with "new money". A discreet signet ring engraved with the family crest might be thought to be acceptable anywhere, yet, confusingly, a recently published guide to job interviews suggested leaving such a ring behind, claiming that it would suggest the wearer was attempting to show their social superiority over the other candidates for the post.

A flag bearing arms would be fine if you had a stately home to fly it from, but is not so appropriate on the average suburban house. But the hard-up owners of British stately homes, who are forced to open their crumbling piles to the public to make a living, may feel that they might as well flaunt the family escutcheon on everything from the guide book to the souvenir china mugs. In view of the declining family fortunes,

▲ *Lego bricks were used to build the local borough's coat of arms, in the foyer of the former Lego offices at Wrexham in North Wales.*

▶ *The heady delights of Amsterdam are advertised in this version of the city arms, with the traditional saltires replaced by objects reflecting the motto.*

▲ *Heraldry can be adapted to suit most needs, and most creeds. Here the coat of arms of the Jewish family of Mocatta makes use of the texts of Hebrew prayers, whose letters make up the entire heraldic design.*

their noble ancestors – victorious commanders at the Battle of Agincourt or, more probably, the owners of a sugar plantation in Barbados – are probably already turning in their crested coffins within the family vault.

▼ *The helm, crest and mantling of medieval times are here adapted to the modern needs of an English football club. Southampton's halo crest reflects the team's nickname – "the Saints".*

BUCKET-SHOP HERALDRY

From the time that heraldry became established in Europe in the Middle Ages there was a constant battle between those who had a right to it and those who had not. There were many complaints from members of the aristocracy about those, such as merchants, who assumed armigerous status for themselves. In every age there have been artists ready to design and execute armorial bearings for any client, or to supply them with coats of arms that really belonged to some other family who happened to have the same surname.

The practice is still alive and well today and is usually known as "bucket-shop" heraldry. It may be as much as some people want. However, "a coat of arms for your name" will almost certainly not have the slightest connection with anyone related to you, and although it might make a pleasant decoration it would certainly be fraudulent to start using the arms on your letter heading, or in any other way that suggests it is your personal property.

For those who have a need to be noticed, there are plenty of institutions that will take their money to help them achieve this, especially bogus orders of chivalry. Such organizations offer their members the chance to take part in curious ceremonies, dress up in cloaks and funny hats and don sparkling badges and stars. They will relieve their credulous clients of even more money as they rise in rank in the "order".

Some of these bodies may be harmless, and some may even contribute to charity. Some may boast a member of an exiled royal family as their "Grand Master". Most are simply money-making enterprises, and the area is a minefield for the innocent subscriber, especially prevalent in those countries that no longer have any legitimate orders of chivalry.

In Britain, there is also the matter of lordships of the manor, which increasingly become available for sale. A lordship of the manor is a feudal title that simply concerns the ownership of land. The property in question may be perhaps no more than a small patch of turf upon which once stood an actual manor house, now long gone. Such a title gives the owner no seat in

Parliament, no peerage and no automatic right to a coat of arms (though, like anyone else, he or she can apply to the College of Arms for a grant). If you are the lord of a manor you could put the title on your letter heading, but you would risk derision from those in the know, and to call yourself "Lord..." or "Lady..." would be considered decidedly beyond the pale.

▲ ▼ *In recent years the logo has often replaced the coat of arms as a more apt device, yet it needs to be designed just as carefully. In this logo for a restaurant chain the hand of the little man, seen in the original version (above) was later removed after members of the public pointed out an unfortunate interpretation – it looked as if he was trying to make himself throw up.*

A MODERN GRANT

Few nations today still retain formal heraldic authorities that grant arms to individuals. If they have heraldic institutions at all, these tend to concern themselves with matters relating to the regulation of civic and military heraldry, though those of Canada, the Republic of Ireland and Scotland often grant arms to individuals as well as to corporations. Let us take a look at how the oldest heraldic authority in the world, the English College of Arms, approaches the matter.

THE PETITION

Before an achievement of arms can be granted to an individual, he or she must formally request the right to bear them. If an attempt to prove a right to arms through descent from an earlier grantee has failed – direct male descent from the grantee being necessary in England – or if no claim to existing arms is put forward, an individual of English or Welsh nationality, and (outside Canada) of English descent, must formally petition for a patent of arms from the Crown, which is the "fount of all honour".

Patents creating and conferring the right to display armorial bearings, and to transmit them to one's heirs, are granted by the Crown through its officers, commonly called the heralds (appointed by separate letters patent from the Crown) for the purpose, upon payment of certain fees. This is the system that has existed in England since the late medieval period.

Although anybody of English nationality or descent is entitled to petition the English heralds for arms, it is not an unquestioned right that arms should be granted to them. There are certain criteria that the heralds look for when deciding if the petitioner is worthy of bearing arms. Just what these criteria are is known only to the heralds themselves, although the publicity material issued by the College of Arms makes mention of persons "eminent" in certain fields. The matter of around £3,000 ($4,200), the cost of a patent of arms at the beginning of the 21st century,

▲ *The heraldic artist Andrew Jamieson works on the patent of Baz Manning.*

▼ *Baz Manning's patent seen in its resplendent finished state.*

▲ *The patent of arms granted by Ireland's Chief Herald to the Irish Genealogical Society in March 2001. The patent is worded in both Gaelic and English.*

may also inhibit some people who might otherwise have considered the possibility of making a petition.

The whole business of payment for the patent can raise the questions, "Can arms really be considered an honour? Are they just a purchasable conceit like any other status symbol?" Whatever the answer to this conundrum, for those who do eventually decide to press forward with their petition, the business will proceed along the following lines.

The petitioner may have a particular Officer of Arms in mind when approaching the College of Arms, but it is more likely that he or she will deal with whoever is the Officer in Waiting at the initial approach. Each of the heralds takes a turn at being duty officer and will meet any casual enquirer during the period of duty. Assuming that the officer believes the petitioner to be of good character and therefore likely to be granted arms, the process can begin in earnest.

THE MEMORIAL

First, the petitioner submits a quaintly worded "memorial" to the Earl Marshal of England, His Grace the Duke of Norfolk,

who on the advice of the officer of arms will officially endorse the petition. The memorial includes the following words:

The Memorial of…showeth, That your Memorialist being desirous of having Armorial Bearings duly established with lawful authority has the honour to request the favour of Your Grace's Warrant to the Kings of Arms for their granting and assigning such Arms and Crest as they may deem suitable to be borne and used by him and his descendants with due and proper difference according to the Law of Arms. And Your Grace's Memorialist will ever pray, etc."

A curriculum vitae (CV) also has to be submitted by the petitioner. All being well, once the petitioner has been found to be of good character and generally an asset to society, the business can proceed. Prompt payment of the fee helps to speed the process up, although it can still be several years before the petitioner has the finished patent in his or her hands.

The reason given by the College of Arms for the time taken from payment to patent is the number and complexity of the stages through which it passes before being signed, sealed and registered. The Officer of Arms (known as the "agent") who is assigned to the petitioner now discusses any ideas that he or she may have for a heraldic design. Before a suitable design can be finalized, the agent is required to check through the College's splendid collection of ordinaries of arms, or armorial rolls, showing all the arms already granted, to make sure the prospective design of the shield is truly unique – not only when it is displayed in full colour, but also in black and white.

The petitioner is kept fully informed about the progress of the patent, and is made welcome at the office of the agent should he or she wish to call personally

▼ *The patent of arms of the late George Messer of Bath, granted in 1992. The designs are unique, but keep to medieval simplicity and clarity.*

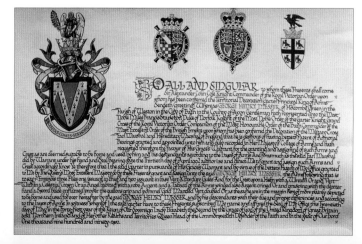

▲ *One of the innovative recent heraldic designs from the English College of Arms, sketched by Peter Gwynn-Jones, Garter King of Arms, for Prior's Court Foundation for autistic students. The jigsaw piece is the symbol of autism. The crest reflects the love of cats of the foundation's founder, Dame Stephanie Shirley, and the unicycle is a sport much enjoyed by the pupils.*

(with prior appointment) at the herald's private office in the College of Arms. The agent is always pleased to discuss the

client's personal requirements for an armorial design, and once this has been approved, the agent will commission an artist to paint the arms on the patent.

DESIGNING A COAT OF ARMS

Anyone desiring their own coat of arms would do well to have some idea of what is deemed good and not good in heraldic design. It is the duty of heralds (in those countries where they are still to be found), or heraldic designers, to educate their clients, whether they are individuals or district councils. It would be easy to include a multitude of charges representing an armiger's personal cares and conceits, but it is important to remember all the different ways in which the arms might be used after the achievement is approved.

One of the most popular ways of displaying a shield or crest is on a signet ring, and it can be awkward to place a very complex design on an area this size. Charges that point in a particular direction are another problem: usually they point towards the dexter and for a seal or signet application this has to be reversed if the impression is to be correct. A non-directional charge may be preferable.

A LESSON IN DESIGN

The heraldic author and designer, Arnold Rabbow of Brunswick, Germany, is often called upon to design new arms for district

or community councils in his own province of Lower Saxony. His approach to the subject of heraldic design – whether civic or individual – offers a lesson to both prospective armiger and herald.

Herr Rabbow first asks for a meeting with the client – usually a town or regional council at one of its regular sittings – during which he asks for details of the history of the community, together with any special points of interest, such as local customs, distinctive geographical features, flora, fauna and dialectic curiosities. The notes he makes on the information he is given may run to many pages, since everyone will want to have their say.

He then takes out three existing armorial designs, usually all shields of German provinces. One might be complex, such as the arms of Rheinland-Pfalz, in which four separate arms are quartered on one shield. He then shows a shield of middling complexity, with several charges, and finally a simple shield, perhaps that of his own province of Lower Saxony, which bears a single charge of a white rearing horse on a red field. Herr Rabbow takes away the three shields and asks the assembly which one they remember. The answer is usually the arms of Lower Saxony – in other words, the simplest shield.

At a subsequent meeting, Herr Rabbow's next step is to show three shields he has designed based on his discussions with the

▲ *The arms of the state of Rheinland-Pfalz. A complex design that says a great deal but is difficult to recall.*

▲ *A slightly less complex shield for Schleswig-Holstein, combining the lions of Schleswig and the nettle leaf of Holstein.*

▲ *The simplicity of the German state of Lower Saxony's arms makes it the most memorable of these three designs.*

assembly. The first includes all the ideas that were suggested as charges, the second features several of the most popular ideas, and the third is a simple design, often using one colour and one metal, and with very few charges, or even a single charge. After the lesson of the previous meeting, the clients choose the third design.

Herr Rabbow does not always hit the right note. Some years ago when he was asked by a community near Wolfsburg to design its arms, he came up with a shield charged with a single red water lily leaf, a design that, for several reasons, he thought appropriate to the place. However, when he showed it to the village elders it was received with a mixture of amusement and embarrassment. When he asked why, he was eventually told that the design bore an unmistakable similarity to the glowing red neon heart that hung over the entrance of the local brothel.

APPROPRIATE CHARGES

Whichever heraldic authority would-be armigers consult, they will be asked to present some form of curriculum vitae, detailing their hobbies, military service, family pedigree (if known), any knowledge of ancestors, professions, tales of bravery or, indeed, infamy. Personal paraphernalia, ranging from pets to puns on a surname – the more the merrier – all help to give the herald or heraldic artist a précis of the individual's life and likes. Yet too much knowledge can be a dangerous thing, especially on a shield of arms. It is good to remember the principle of early heraldry – that a shield of arms should be identifiable across a battlefield. Happily, most people today do not have to worry about being clubbed over the head by a knight on a charger, but the same rule can still be usefully applied. Any

▼ *The arms of the English heraldist Robert Harrison, interpreted in a medieval style by one of the greatest modern heraldic artists, the late Dan Escott.*

▲ *This lily leaf charge designed for Mörse by Arnold Rabbow caused raised eyebrows on the local council.*

▲ *The finalized arms for Mörse, reflecting its name, derived from the phrase meaning "a marshy place".*

art student knows that simplicity is the essence of good design.

Surprisingly, there are still many designs of a simple geometric nature available for a new coat of arms, and heraldic authorities are delighted to see innovations in partition lines, counterchanging and such like, so long as the designs are sufficiently different from other existing arms. Lions, unicorns, and other ancient heraldic beasts can still be made distinct through a variety of attitudes and attributes, especially when combined with other charges.

Counterchanging can lead to a refreshingly simple and unique design. The important thing is to think in medieval terms, and if possible restrict the design to two tinctures – one colour and one metal. This does not mean that modern objects cannot be included, but can a boiler flue, or a computer chip, be represented in a way appropriate to heraldry? Any charge should be recognizable to the layman and easily translated into blazon. If the charge is a creature, its characteristics should be reasonable. It might be able to hold something in its paws or claws, but would not like having another charge, such as a key or a star, pinned on its neck or wings.

A coat of arms does not stop at the shield. The crest needs to be designed in the round. The English heralds are now taught to do so, although some modern crests still appear too much like "paper heraldry" – they could never be worn on a real helmet. Real crests, as depicted in medieval scenes of the *Helmschau* ("display of helmets"), especially that in King René's tournament book, were full of imagination, and were designed to be seen from the back and front, not just from the side as in a standard heraldic painting.

In those nations that possess full heraldic authorities, the heralds are there to guide the would-be armiger in matters of design. The correspondence between herald and client is just one of the delights involved in the making of a new coat of arms. When the whole process is complete it can literally be said to be a splendid achievement, not only for the armigers themselves, but for their descendants, part of a tradition going back many centuries.

CHOOSING AN ARTIST

If you live in a country that has its own heraldic authority, you will have had your arms granted by a herald who will have a wide range of artists and craftsmen to call upon. He may put you in touch with the relevant people, or offer to organize all the work on your behalf. For the patent itself, an English herald might choose one of the herald painters at the College of Arms to execute the painting. These artists have their studios in the attic rooms at the top of the College building, reached by an ancient staircase of many flights. Many a famous name in heraldic artistry has had his studio, as befits a herald painter, in the cramped attics of the College of Arms. Once appointed they tend to stay for many years. Several have died up there, which can pose a problem as few people venture into the venerable chambers (there is no lift).

Often the herald painter is of such renown as to have a backlog of work, and the herald may decide to farm out the work to an out-of-house heraldic artist,

◀ *The arms of the Cornish heraldic artist, Dennis Endean Ivall, painted in Mr Ivall's own characteristic Celtic style.*

▲ *A bookplate by the Dutch artist Daniel de Bruin in which the lozenge of the armiger is portrayed in a surreal style.*

whom he knows to be capable of such a commission. Should the petitioner favour a particular heraldic artist, it is essential to make this preference clear at the outset. They are perfectly entitled to do so, although any delay in declaring such an interest might cause inconvenience and embarrassment if the agent has already approached an artist of his choice.

Part of the pleasure of applying for a new grant of arms, or adapting the re-discovered arms of a direct ancestor, is choosing for yourself ways in which your personal arms can be portrayed. If you live in a country without a heraldic authority you will have no option but to deal directly with an artist.

THE SOCIETY OF HERALDIC ARTS

The organization that exists as a shop window for heraldic artists in England is the Society of Heraldic Arts, based in Reigate, England. Its craft members are expected to meet a particularly high degree of craftsmanship to join, and range from stained glass artists to bookplate designers. Not only do they experiment in different media, they often have very different styles, ranging from the graphic style of the Dutch artist Daniel de Bruin, through the medievalism of Anthony Wood and Andrew Jamieson, to the swirling Celtic creations of Dennis Ivall. Associate membership, which is open to all, enables heraldists to receive the Society's journal and to rub shoulders with the artists. Clients receive a register of members whom they can contact direct, listing the items each produces and showing examples of their work.

There are very few heraldic artists in the world, so it is not surprising that a trawl through the telephone directory will not often produce a result, although a heading does exist for them in the British Yellow Pages. It is more productive to join a heraldry society, as their journals carry advertisements from a wide variety of artists, many of whom do not belong to the SHA and may only otherwise be found by word of mouth.

HERALDIC STYLES

The painting of a coat of arms on the patent is by no means the only way in which it can be portrayed. Heraldry is always open to interpretation, and the re-visualizing of a coat of arms by a number of different artists can be a stimulating and enjoyable experience.

No two artists will draw in the same way. The house style of the English College of Arms differs markedly from that of the Scottish Lyon Court, and the personal styles of British artists can be remarkably varied and often instantly recognizable, while bookplates executed by a Dutch artist and a Canadian one will be refreshingly different from each other. Artists as far apart as Russia, Sweden and Zimbabwe may all be keen to execute private commissions and all will produce distinctive interpretations of arms.

For every occasion a coat of arms is used, it can be rendered in a different way. Slaveish copies of the grant painting do not do justice to the creative skills of heraldic artists, and can look appalling in the wrong situation. A large colour painting to hang on a wall can have a great deal of detail added to it, while a small bookplate should be drawn quite differently. An engraver will want to draw a design suitable for cutting, while monochrome artwork for stationery will be rendered with clarity of line and small-scale printing in mind.

A large number of shield shapes have been used over the last 850 years of heraldry, and each will give a different feel to the arms. The charges and the crest may all have a variety of possible designs, all heraldically accurate yet each distinctive and often unusual.

▼ *The bookplate of the English heraldic author Stephen Friar shows the versatility of the modern artist, Andrew Jamieson.*

GLOSSARY

abatement: heraldic mark of dishonour

accolée: descriptive term for two coats of arms set side by side, to indicate marriage, with the charges on each facing each other

achievement: the complete display of armorial bearings

addorsed: of beasts, back to back

affronty: of a *charge*, facing the viewer

ailettes: "little wings", shoulder plates bearing the arms of the wearer

alwyte: bright steel armour from the late medieval period

Argent: silver

armed: of a human being, clothed in armour; of a beast, having teeth, beak or claws in a separate colour

armiger: a person who is entitled to bear arms

arming cap: a padded cap worn under a helmet

arming doublet: a long-sleeved, hip-length tunic worn as an undergarment for armour

armorial bearings: the symbols borne by an *armiger* to distinguish him or her from others

armorial: a roll or book listing *armorial bearings* arranged alphabetically by the names of the bearers

armory: the study of *coats of arms*, heraldry

at gaze: of deer, looking towards the viewer

attainder: the extinction of civil rights, including the right to bear arms or titles, following conviction for treason or felony

attitude: of a beast or human being, posture

attribute: of a beast or human being, a characteristic with which it is represented

attributed arms: arms devised posthumously for individuals who lived before the age of heraldry

augmentation: an addition to the arms that reflects the gratitude of the donor

aventail: a chain mail neck guard

Azure: blue

bachelor: a knight of the lower order

badge: a heraldic device belonging to an *armiger*, worn by retainers

banner: a square or oblong flag bearing a knight's arms

bar: a narrow horizontal stripe

baron: heraldic term for a husband; also the lowest rank of the peerage

bascinet: a lightweight, close-fitting domed helmet

Bath, Order of the: a British chivalric order

baton: a narrow diagonal band which does not reach the edges of the shield

bedesman: or beadsman, someone who was employed to pray for another person or group of people

bend: a diagonal stripe on a shield, from *dexter* chief to *sinister* base

bend sinister: a diagonal stripe on a shield, from *sinister* chief to *dexter* base, often used as a mark of illegitimacy

bendlet: a narrow *bend*

bezant: a gold *roundel*

billet: a small rectangular *charge*

billetty: covered all over with *billets*

blazon: the verbal description of *armorial bearings*

Bleu celeste: sky blue

bonacon: a mythical heraldic beast

bordure: a narrow band around the edge of the shield

boss: a circular protruding central knob on a shield

brizure: a difference mark used in *cadency*

cadency: a system of small alterations and additions to differentiate the arms of children in a family from those of its head

canting: of arms, with a design that alludes to the name of the bearer, also known as punning arms

canton: a square section, smaller than a *quarter*, in the top *dexter* or *sinister* corner of a shield

chamfron: a horse's head-guard

chapeau: a hat with a turned-up fur lining, symbolizing dignity

charge: a device on a shield or other item

chequey: covered all over with squares of equal size, in two alternating colours

chevron: an inverted V-shaped stripe on a shield

chevronel: a small *chevron*, or bent *bar*, on a shield

chief: the upper third of the shield

cinquefoil: a stylized flower with five petals

cipher: a monogram

coat armour: a quilted linen garment worn over armour and emblazoned with *armorial bearings*

coat of arms: the common term for the heraldic shield

cockatrice: a mythical heraldic monster, part serpent and part cockerel

cognizance: a distinguishing *badge*

compartment: the representation of the ground or other surface on which the *supporters*, shield and motto stand

coronel: blunted, crown-shaped lance tip used in jousting

couchant: of a beast, lying down with head erect

counterchanged: descriptive of a partitioned shield where the disposition of *tinctures* on one side of the partition line is reversed on the other side

counterermine: see *ermines*

couped: of a *charge*, such as an arm or branch, clean cut

couter: armour worn to protect the elbow

crest: a three-dimensional object adorning the top of the helmet

cross crosslet: a cross with the end of each limb itself crossed

cuir-bouilli: leather boiled in oil to make it malleable

cuirass: plate armour for the torso

cuisse: leg armour

cushion: a *charge* in the shape of a cushion with tassels at the corners

dancetty: "dancing", of a *line of partition*, a zigzag with large indentations

degradation: demotion from knighthood

delf: a square geometric *charge*

dexter: right (from the point of view of the shield bearer)

diaper: an all-over pattern resembling designs woven into damask fabric

difference mark: a *charge* added to a shield to differentiate a branch of a family

dimidiated: an early form of *marshalling* arms by halving them

dovetailed: of a *line of partition*, like a joint in carpentry

embattled: of a *line of partition*, like battlements

engrailed: of a *line of partition*, scalloped, with the points facing outwards

ensign: to place a crown, coronet, cap, helmet or cross above, and touching, a *charge*

erased: of a *charge* such as a limb, torn off

ermine: one of the *furs*, white with black tails (the stoat's winter coat)

ermines or counterermine: one of the *furs*, black with white tails

erminites: like *ermine*, with a red spot on each side of the black tail

erminois: one of the *furs*, gold with black tails

escarbuncle: a wheel-like device with spokes radiating from the centre of the shield

escutcheon: a small shield

escutcheon of pretence: a small shield bearing the wife's family arms set in the centre of her husband's shield

estoile: star with wavy points

femme: heraldic term for a wife

fess: a horizontal stripe across the middle of the shield

field: the background *tincture* of the shield

fimbriated: of a *charge*, edged with a narrow band of another *tincture*

fitched: usually of a cross, pointed at the foot

flanches or flaunches: a pair of curved segments on each side of the shield

fleur de lis: a stylized heraldic lily

formy: of a cross, having triangular limbs wide at the ends and narrow at the centre

fountain: a *roundel* bearing blue and white wavy bars

fraise: a white *cinquefoil* representing the strawberry flower

fret: a *voided lozenge* interlaced with a *bendlet* and a *bendlet sinister*

fretty: covered all over with a grid of diagonal lines

fur: a *tincture* representing an animal pelt

fusil: an elongated *lozenge*

gambeson: a quilted undergarment worn with chain mail

gambs: animals' paws

garb: a sheaf (usually of wheat)

Garter King of Arms: the most senior English herald

Garter, Order of the: the senior order of knighthood in England

golpe: a purple *roundel*

gonfalone: a large flag often hung from a cross-beam

gonfalonier: a standard-bearer of the Church

gore: a portion of the shield cut off by a curved line, like a *flanch*, but ending in a point

gouttes: small *roundels* or droplets

goutty: covered all over with *gouttes*

great helm: a helmet made with a

series of hammered plates rising to a gradual point

greaves: leg-guards

griffin or gryphon: a mythical monster with the forepart of an eagle and the hindquarters of a lion

guardant: of a beast or human being, looking out of the shield at the viewer

guidon: a long flag used in battle as a marker or standard

guige: a strap to hold a shield when not in use

Gules: red

gusset: a side portion of the shield, cut off at top and bottom by diagonal lines

gyron: a wedge-shaped *charge*

gyronny: covered with *gyrons*, arranged around the centre of the shield

harness: a suit of armour

hatchment: a diamond-shaped board painted with a *coat of arms* to indicate the death of the bearer

heater shield: shield shaped like the base of a flatiron

heraldic heiress: the daughter of an *armiger*, who inherits his arms in the absence of any sons

hoist: the area at the top of a flag near the pole

honour point: the upper middle point of a shield

hurt: a blue *roundel*

imbrued: bloodied

impalement: the placing of two *coats of arms* side by side on a single shield

impress or impresa: a personal *badge* incorporating a motto

in chase: of deer, running

indented: of a *line of partition*, with small saw-like points

inescutcheon: a small shield borne in the centre of another shield

invected: as *engrailed*, with points facing inwards

jupon: a short, close-fitting quilted coat, usually decorated with the bearer's arms

king of arms: a senior herald

knight banneret: 1 a high-ranking knight in command of a body of

men; 2 a square or oblong banner denoting his presence in battle

label: a difference mark across the *chief* of the shield applied to the arms of a son, usually the heir

langued: of a beast, with a tongue in a separate colour

line of partition: a line delineating a division of the shield

lists: a jousting enclosure at a tournament

livery: the uniform worn by a lord's retainers, made in his colours

livery collar: a chain of office indicating allegiance

lodged: of a deer, lying down

lozenge: 1 a diamond-shaped *charge*; 2 a diamond-shaped device used to display the arms of women

Lyon, Lord: the chief herald in Scotland

mantling: material protecting the back and sides of the helmet and the wearer's neck

marshal: to combine two or more coats of arms on one shield

mascle: a *lozenge* with its centre removed

matriculation of arms: the updating of family arms in Scotland

maunch: a medieval sleeve with a hanging pocket

melée: a battle staged as a tournament event

mullet: a five-pointed star

mural coronet: a circlet of stone with battlements or columns

Murrey: mulberry, a purplish-red

nebuly: of a *line of partition*, shaped like the edges of clouds

nombril or navel point: the lower middle point of a shield

officer of arms: a herald

ogress: a black *roundel*

Or: gold

ordinary: 1 a basic geometric *charge* on a shield; 2 a *roll of arms* in which *coats of arms* are catalogued according to the charges they bear

orle: a narrow band following, but set in from, the edge of the shield

pageant helmet: a helmet with ornamental bars across the face

pairle: a division of the *field* into three sections radiating from the centre

pale: a vertical band down the middle of the shield

pall: a Y-shaped band on a shield

panache: a feathered *crest*

paper heraldry: a derogatory description of accessories, such as *crests*, designed after heraldry ceased to have a practical function, which could not have been used for their ostensible purpose

partition lines: see *lines of partition*

passant: of a beast, walking across the shield

patty: of a cross, having triangular limbs which are wide at the ends and narrow at the centre

pean: one of the *furs*, black with gold tails

pellet: a black *roundel*

pencil: a small *pennon*

pennon: a personal flag, long and tapering, with a rounded or divided end

peytral: a horse's chest-plate

pheon: an arrowhead

pile: an *ordinary* consisting of a triangular wedge with one side along the top of the shield

plate: a silver *roundel*

point: the base of the shield cut off by a horizontal line

point champain: the base of the shield cut off by a shallow concave line

pomme: a green *roundel*

potent: in the shape of a crutch

proper: shown in natural colours or form

punning arms: see *canting*

Purpure: purple

pursuivant: a junior herald

quarter: 1 a *sub-ordinary* occupying the top *dexter* quarter of the shield; 2 to divide a shield into any number of divisions each bearing a different *coat of arms*

quatrefoil: a stylized four-petalled flower, similar to a clover leaf

queue fourchy: a forked tail

raguly: of a *line of partition*, like battlements but set obliquely

rampant: of a beast, rearing up to fight

recursant: usually of an eagle, displayed with its back towards the viewer

reguardant: looking backwards

respectant: of two beasts or human beings, looking at each other

reversed: upside-down

roll of arms: a herald's catalogue of *coats of arms*

roundel: a circular *charge*

rustre: a *charge* like a *lozenge* with a hole in the middle

Sable: black

saltire: a diagonal cross on a shield

Sanguine: blood red

segreant: of a *griffin*, rearing up to fight

sejant: of a beast, sitting upright facing *dexter*

semy: covered all over with small *charges*

sinister: left (from the point of view of the bearer of the shield)

springing: of a deer, leaping

stain: a heraldic colour that is not one of the primaries

standard: a long tapering flag in *livery* colours bearing the national emblem, usually placed at the commander's tent

statant: of a beast, standing facing *dexter*

sub-ordinary: one of the smaller, less frequently used geometric *charges*

supporters: figures supporting the shield of arms

surcoat: a quilted linen garment worn over armour and emblazoned with *coats of arms*

tabard: a short tunic emblazoned with *coats of arms* and worn by heralds

talbot: a large hunting hound, now extinct

targe: a shield

Tenny: tawny orange

Thistle, Order of the: the senior order of knighthood in Scotland

tierced in pairle: of a shield, divided in three in the form of a Y

tilt: a wooden jousting barrier

tincture: the generic term for heraldic colours, stains, metals and furs

torse: see *wreath*

tourney shield: a small rectangular shield, with a notch for a lance

tourteau: a red *roundel*

trapper: a development of the saddle-cloth which covered the horse entirely, decorated with *armorial bearings*

tressure: a narrow band following, but set in from, the edge of the shield, narrower than the *orle* but often doubled

tricking: a method of noting a *blazon* in shorthand

trippant: of deer, walking or trotting across a shield

vair: one of the *furs*, represented as a pattern of blue and white

Vert: green

visor: the opening front of a helmet

voided: of a *charge*, represented in outline only

vulned: of a beast, wounded and bleeding

wreath, torse: a twisted cord of material around the top of the helmet, below the crest

wyvern: a heraldic winged dragon with two feet and a serpentine tail

yale: a heraldic beast resembling an antelope with tusks and curved horns, always shown parted.

BIBLIOGRAPHY AND ACKNOWLEDGEMENTS

Barber, Richard and Barker, Juliet
Tournaments: Jousts, Chivalry and
Regents in the Middle Ages
(Boydell Press, Woodbridge,
1989)

Bascape, G.C. and Del Piazzo, M.
Insegne e simboli (Ministero per i
beni culturali e ambientali,
Rome, 1983)

Bedingfield, Henry and Gwynn-
Jones, Peter Heraldry (Magna
Books, Leicester, 1993)

Campbell, Una Robes of the Realm,
300 years of Ceremonial Dress
(Michael O'Mara, London, 1989)

Carek, Jiri Mestské Znaky v Cesk'ych
Zemich (Academia, Prague, 1985)

Casas, R. D. Arte y Etiqueta do los
Reyes Catolicos (Editorial
Alpuerto, Madrid, 1993)

Cascante, Ignacio Vincente
Heraldica General y Fuestes de las
Armas de Espana (Barcelona,
1956)

Ceballos-Escalera y Gila de, A
Heraldos y Reyas de Armas en la
Corte de España (Prensa y
Ediciones Iberoamericanas,
Madrid, 1993)

Collectible Stamps of the Arms of
German Districts and Towns
(Kaffee Hag, 1900–1930s)

Corswant-Naumburg, Inga von
Huvudbaner och anvapen under
stormaktstiden (Ödin,
Stockholm, 1999)

Coss, Peter The Knight in Medieval
England 1000-1400 (Alan Sutton
Ltd, 1993)

Crouch, David William Marshal
(Longman, Harlow, 1990)

Csáky, Imre A Magyar királyság
vármegyéinek címerei a
XVIII–XIX (Corvina, Budapest,
1995)

D'Acosta, Lino Chaparro Heraldica
de los Apellidos Canarios (Estudios
Tecnicos del Blason, 1979)

De-la-Noy, Michael The Honours

System (Allison & Busby,
London, 1985)

Dennis, Mark D. Scottish Heralds:
An Invitation (Heraldry Society of
Scotland, 1999)

Dower, John W. and Kawamoto,
Kiyoshi The Elements of Japanese
Design (Walker/Weatherhill, New
York, 1971, revised 1979)

Foppoli, Marco Gli stemmi dei
comuni di Valtellina e
Valchiavenna (Alpinia Editrice,
1999)

Foss, Michael Chivalry (Michael
Joseph, London, 1975)

Friar, Stephen A New Dictionary of
Heraldry (Alphabooks,
Sherborne, 1987)

Friar, Stephen and Ferguson, John,
Basic Heraldry (Herbert Press,
London, [1993])

Gittings, Clare Death, Burial and the
Individual in Early Modern
England (Croom Helm, London,
1984)

Given-Wilson, Chris and Curteis,
Alice The Royal Bastards of
Medieval England (Routledge &
Kegan Paul, London, 1984)

Godlo i Barwa Polski
Samorzadowej (Instytut
Wzornictwa Przemyslowego,
1998)

Gonzalez-Doria, Fernando
Diccionario Heraldico y Nobiliaria
de los Reinos de España (Bitacora,
Madrid, 1987)

Guerra y Villegas, J. A. de Discurso
Histórico Politico Sobre el
Origen y Preheminencias de el
Oficio de Heraldos, Reyes de
Armas, Feciales y Caduceadores
(Mateo de Llanos y Guzmán,
Madrid, 1693)

Heim, Bruno Heraldry in the
Catholic Church (Van Duren,
Gerrards Cross, 1978, revised
1981)

Hildebrandt, Adolf M.

Wappenfibel, Handbuch der
Heraldik (Degener, Berlin, 1967)

Hopkins, Andrea Knights (Collins &
Brown, London, 1990)

Hupp, Otto Deutscher
Wappenkalender (1900s–1930s)

Innes of Learney, Sir Thomas Scots
Heraldry (Oliver & Boyd,
Edinburgh, 1934, revised 1956)

Janácek, Josef and Louda, Jiri Ceské
erby (Albatros, Prague, 1974,
revised 1988)

Kissane, Noel, ed. Treasures from the
National Library of Ireland (Boyne
Valley Honey Co, 1994)

Laars, T. van der Wapens, Vlaggen
en Zegels van Nederland (van
Campen, Amsterdam, 1913)

Leaf, William and Purcell, Sally
Heraldic Symbols: Islamic Insignia
and Western Heraldry (Victoria &
Albert Museum, London, 1986)

Litten, Julian The English Way of
Death: the Common Funeral since
1450 (Robert Hale, 1991)

Mandich, Donald R. and Placek,
Joseph A. Russian Heraldry and
Nobility (Dramco Publishers,
Florida, 1991)

NAF Veibok 2001 (NAF, Oslo,
2001)

Niesobski, Mariusz Popularny
herbarz rodzin i radów polskich

(Tychy, Kadem, [1991])

Nordenvall, Per Kungliga
Serafimerorden (Armorial Plaques
of the Knights of the Seraphim),
1748–1998 (Swedish Royal
Orders, Stockholm, 1998)

Nyulásziné Straub, Eva Öt évszázad
címerei a Magyar Országos
Levéltár címereslevelein
(Budapest, Corvina, 1987)

Pastoureau, Michel Heraldry: An
Introduction to a Noble Tradition
(Abrams, New York, 1997)

Pinches, J. H. European Nobility and
Heraldry (Heraldry Today,
Ramsbury, 1994)

Platts, Beryl Origins of Heraldry
(Procter Press, London, 1980)

Rietstap, J. B. Armorial General.
Originally published in the 19th
century, reprinted several times
since, and can be obtained
through the services of Heraldry
Today, Ramsbury, England.

Rothero, Christopher Medieval
Military Dress, 1066–1500
(Blandford Press, Poole, 1983)

Scheffer, C.G.U. Svensk vapenbok
för landskap, län och städer
(Generalstabens litografiska
anstalt, Stockholm, 1967)

Uden, Grant A Dictionary of
Chivalry (Harmondsworth,
Kestrel, 1977)

Urquhart, R.M. Scottish Burgh and
County Heraldry (Heraldry Today,
Ramsbury, 1973)

Urquhart, R.M. Scottish Civic
Heraldry (Heraldry Today,
Ramsbury, 1979)

Woodcock, Thomas and Robinson,
John Martin The Oxford Guide to
Heraldry (Oxford, OUP, 1988)

Zieber, Eugene Heraldry in America,
1895 (New York, Greenwhich
House, 1984)

AUTHOR'S ACKNOWLEDGEMENTS

For making this book possible and
for the hospitality always shown to
me, Steve and Kate Friar. For the
inspiration to follow the project
through, Arnold Rabbow of
Braunschweig. To Arnaud Bunel,
Sebastian Nelson and Peter Taylor
for help with parts of the text.
Thanks to William and Mrs Sybil
O'Neill for the kindness in allowing
me at all times to make use of Terry's
library. Joan Robertson, Karen and

John Say, and Margaret Smith for
their companionship in the many
hours I have bored them silly over
escutcheons and hatchments. Baz
Manning, without whose help and
kindness I would have been unable
to complete such a project. Mikhail
Medvedev of St. Petersburg for his
answering my many questions on
Russian heraldry. Alice Hall for her
translating letters to foreign
locations. Roland Symons for his

delightful and unfailing assistance.
Sr Marco and Sra Lia Foppoli for
their long and happy friendship.
James and Mrs Cathy Constant for
the refuge they so often afford me.
Robert Harrison for his unstinting
encouragement. Sebastian Nelson, a
true friend of heraldry from the
United States. The Officers of Arms,
College of Arms, London for their
kindness and expertise in answering
many a curious and obscure

question. David Hubber with many
thanks for his kindness and his
artwork. The staff at QinetiQ
Larkhill, most especially Andy Pike
for his patience and understanding.
Joanne Rippin of Anness Publishing,
whose patience and tenacity have
largely been responsible for making
sure this work became a reality and
Beverley Jollands for her excellent
copy editing. Russ Fletcher for the
use of his library. Mrs Manning for

her excellent deciphering of my scatty notes. Daniel de Bruin for his kindness in giving me access to his splendid collection of grants/patents of arms. Veneta Bullen for finding some of the more obscure pictures.

Thanks also to the following people and organizations for help with information or images: Peter Trier of Warpool Court Hotel, St David's; Lt Colonel Herbert A. Lippert (Retd); Mrs Malina Sieczkowska; Michael Messer;

Anthony Ryan; the Staff of HM Security Service; The Central Intelligence Agency of the United States, John Uncles; HH the Prince of Oettingen; Herr Willem Jorg; Herr Gunter Mattern; Anthony Jones; Colonel Carnero, Military Attache, Spanish Embassy, London; Risto Pyykko; Keith Lovell; Gordon and Jean Ashton; Bruce Patterson, Saguenay Herald and the Canadian Heraldic Authority; Micheal O'Comain, Consulting Herald,

Office of the Chief Herald of Ireland; Fergus Gillespie, Deputy Chief Herald of Ireland; Elisabeth Roads, Lyon Clerk and the staff of the Court of Lord Lyon, Edinburgh; Andrew Martin Garvey; Jennifer Marin, Curator, The Jewish Museum, London; Dr Adrian Ailes; Mrs Marian Miles OBE; Distributed Technology Ltd, Robin Lumsden, Dame Stephanie Shirley DBE, and the staff of the Prior's Court Foundation; Adjutant Luc Binet and

the staff of the Service Historique de l'Armee de Terre, Vincennes; Dr. Jan Erik Schulte, Kultur/Kreismuseum, Buren; Bruce Purvis; Martin Davies; David Phillips; Dr Malcolm Golin; The staff of the Haermuseet, Oslo; Lt. Colonel Nick Bird OBE, RA (Retd) and staff of the Royal School of Artillery; Kevin Fielding; Per Nordenval, Riddarhuset, Stockholm; Anna Lilliehöök, KMO.

And finally, to all bonacons, wherever they may be.

PICTURE ACKNOWLEDGEMENTS

While every attempt has been made by the publishers to credit sources correctly, any further information would be welcome. **AKG London**: pp40bl, Erich Lessing; 44t; 46b, British Library, from Rothschild Bequest; 54bl, Erich Lessing, Warsaw Museum; 58tr, Erich Lessing; 62br, Dominige Museo Nazionale del Bargello, Florence, Italy; 108tr, British Library; 110b, British Library, Froissart's Chronicle; 132; 147t; 151b; 153tr; 197t; 208t; 221t&br; 233. **Ancient Art & Architecture Collection**: pp15br, 17tl, R. Sheridan; 111br; 152t; 207t. **Anness Publishing Ltd**, courtesy Daniel de Bruin, photography Jos Janssen: pp42t&bl; 77b; 84tr&bl; 92tl; 115tr; 128 all; 129; 130 all; 131; 149b. **Anness Publishing Ltd/Stephen Slater**, photography Mark Wood: pp14b; 25b; 26t; 36t; 36bl, King René's Tourney Book; 42t; 53t; 57t; 62t&bl; 64bl,bm&br; 65bl&t; 66ml; 68t; 70&89tl; 74tr; 88bl; 90ml; 91tl; 92tr; 102t&bl; 112tr; 113 all; 114bl; 115ml; 120b; 121br; 138b; 139; 140; 143b; 144bl; 146bl&bm; 157t; 162tl,tm&tr; 163tr,mr&br; 164t; 165t&bl; 168m&tl; 170bl; 171mr; 172b; 196t&b; 206br; 214bl&br; 215t; 218 all; 219ml; 221bl; 224b; 232br; 234 all; 239tr. Anness Publishing Ltd/unattributable: pp56tr&br; 57m; 59bl. Archive of Stato di Massa, Ministero peri Beni le Attivita Culturali, photograph Progra Immagini, Massa: p91br. **Art Archive**: pp7&17tr, Manesse Codex, University Library Heidelberg/ Dagli Orti; 8&24t British Library; 20t, Musée des Art Décoratifs, Paris/Dagli Orti; 23b, engraving by Hogenberg, Dagli Orti; 24t, British Library, from Roman de Petit Jean de Saintre; 26b, Musée de Versailles/ Dagli Orti, copy of anonymous painting at Hampton Court, Friedrich Bouterwick; 28bl, British Library; 43t, Bibliothèque Nationale, Paris; 44br, College of Arms/John Webb, designed by Maximilian Colt, the King's Carver; 141t; 156t; 157b; 158b; 188t; 204br. **Associated Press**:: p235t. **Bridgeman Art Library**: pp19t, British Library, Froissart's Chronicle; 22t, British Library; 22b, British Library, Book of Hours; 38br, William Henry Pyne, Herald, from Costume of Great Britain, William Miller, 1805; 43b, Victoria & Albert Museum, T. Rowlandson and A. C.

Pugin; 45b, Bibliothèque Nationale, Paris, Chronicle of Charles VII of France; 158t; 160b; 173t, courtesy St Bride's Church; 174tr. **British Association of Urological Surgeons, London**: pp154, 179tl. **Camera Press**: p142 all. **Collections**: pp178t, 189br, Oliver Benn. **The College of Arms, London**: p38bl. **Corbis**: pp41t; 161b.**Sylvia Cordaiy**: p166tl. **DERA**, Boscombe Down: p169br. **Ede & Ravenscroft Ltd**: p143t. **Edifice**: p217tl, Sarah Jackson. **Edimedia**: pp16t, Chronicle of William of Tyr; 16b, British Library; 18b; 24b; 56tl. **Eglinton County Park/North Ayrshire Council**: p27t&b. **Tim Graham**: p159b. **Sonia Halliday Photography**: pp19bl, Church of St Chad, Prees, England, Laura Lushington; 98t, Laura Lushington; 150t; 205t, F.H.C. Birch. **Hulton/Getty**: pp63tr; 212t; 239br, Stone. **Irish Heraldic and Genealogical Office, Dublin**: pp193; 194 all. **The Jewish Museum, London**: p223b. **Willem Jörg**: pp34; 48bm. **A.F. Kersting**: p25, Temple Church, London. **Leixlip Town Clerk**: p195t. **Gordon Lockie**: p187b. **Lothian & Borders Police photographic unit**: p171tl. **Maltese Tourist Board**: p153b. **Maryland Office of Tourism**: p223b. **Det Nationalhis-toriske Museum på Frederiksborg**: p224t. **Peter Newark's Pictures**: pp20m; 55tr, Codex Balduineus; 136br, from Froissart manuscript; 148t; 166tr; 198t; 223t. **Northern Territories of Australia Government**: p67tr. **Novosti** (London): pp40br; 214t; 215m; 216tl; 217tr. **Orlogsmuseet/ Copenhagen**: p166b. **University of Padua**: p176bl&br. **Press Association**: pp141b; 160t. **Resianische Militara-kademie, Wiener Neustadt**, Austria: p210t. **Photo RMN**, Paris, France: p197b, Arnaudet. **Royal Armouries**: p20bl, IV600.**Royal Palace of Stockholm**/Alexis Daflos: p225b. **Salisbury and South Wiltshire Museum**: p28tr. **Scala**: p17b; p20br; 23t; 32t; 103tl; 180bl; 200 all; 202tr; 207bl; 210bl. **Scottish Viewpoint**: pp184b; 186b. **Mick Sharp**: p189t. **Stephen Slater**: pp10; 13b; 14tr; 28br; 29b, Priory Church, Abergavenny, Wales; 30br; 41bl,bm&bmr; 45tl, Brunswick Cathedral, Germany; 45tr; 46t, Harefield Church, Middx, England; 47t&b, cour-

tesy of the Earl of Rothes and Clan Leslie; 48t, Bruges, Belgium; 48bl, Boyton Church, Wilts, England; 52 all; 56bl, Salisbury Cathedral, England; 59tl; 64t, Trowbridge Church, Wilts, England; 66tl&br; 68bl; 73bm; 87bl, Salisbury Cathedral, England; 90bl; 91bl, Abbey of St Denis, Paris; 94tm; 99m&bl; 109tl; 112bl, 112br, West Lavington Church; 114tm; 115tl&bl; 116tr; 116bl, Harefield Church, Middx, England; 117ml; Westbury Church, Wilts, England; 117bl; 121bl; 123tl; 124tr; 125tl; 126tl; 127tl,tr, ml&bl; 134; 136t; 137bl; 144t&br; 145; 146r; 147b; 148b; 149t; 151tl; 162b; 164bl,bm&br; 167bl&bm; 170tr&br; 171tr&br; 172t; 173b; 174bl&br; 175 all; 176t; 177tl&tr; 178b; 179br; 180br; 181br; 182&230tr; 184tr; 185tr,mr,br; 186t; 188b; 190bl&bm; 195b; 202bl; 203b; 205b; 206bl; 207br; 208b; 209 all; 211 all; 219tl,tr&br; 225tl; 229 br; 235bl&br; 239tl&bl; 242 all; 241tl,tr,mr; 242 all; 243 mr,bl&br. **Stockczech**: p87bm, Karla Koruna. **Swiss National Museum**, Zurich: p153b. **Victoria & Albert Museum**: pp40t, Daniel McGrath; 65br, Zeiner, Josef: p86br. **Private Collections**: pp213tr & 249t, Daniel de Bruin; 204t, Mr Jim Constant; 177br, Eton College; 89bl, Marco Foppoli; 249b, Stephen Friar; 246t, Peter Gwynn - Jones; 66tr, Lord Hanson; 117t, 226t, 227bl & 247br, Robert Harrison; 59tr, Jan Van Helmont Publishing Company, Belgium/a European Noble Gentleman; 109bl & 248 Denis E. Ivall; 189bl, Tony Jones; 229tr, Mike Mailes; 121bm, 168b,

169t&bl, 244 all, 245 all, Baz Manning; 187t, William Naesmyth of Posso; 225tr, Mr Naumberg; 29tl, Collection of the Duke of Northumberland; 181br, Les Pearson; 118, private collection; 215br, Risto Pyykko; 206t, 241b, Tony Ryan; 220t, Malina Scziesskowska; 106br, Carl Stiernspetz; 179br, Peter Taylor; 74bl, Derek Walkden.

Unattributable: pp12tr&b; 13tl, from John of Worcester's Chronicle; 13r; p15t&rml; 18t&rm; p21b; 29tr; 30t&bl; 31tl; 31b; 32br&bl; 32m, Matthew Paris, Chronicle Majora; 33t, Sir Thomas Wriothesley's Book of Standards; 37 all; 38t, Thomas Jenyns' Ordinary; 40ml; 42br; 44br; 48br; 53b; 54t,bm&br; 58bl; 60t; 60b, Biblioteca Trivulziana; 61bl; 63bl; 67br; 69bl; 73br; 79bl&br; 86tr, Zurich Roll; 86bl; 88tl, Ripon Cathedral, Yorks, England; 92bl; 93tl&tr; 95br; 96bl; 102br, Buckland Abbey, Devon, England; 104tr; 106bl; 111tr; 112m; 123tm; 124bl&br; 125tr,ml&bl; 126b; 127br; 136ml&bl; 138t; 150bl; 159t; 161tl; 166bl; 171bl; 179m; 185bl; 190t; 192bl&bm; 201bl; 204bl; 210br; 212bl; 213m&bl; 220b; 230 all; 231t&b; 232t&bl; 238t; 241tm&m.

Artworks: Antony Duke: p192tr,m&rmr. Dan Escott: pp236, 247br. David Hubber: p238b. Marco Foppoli: pp31tr; 33b; 50 & 69tl; 69tr&br; 79tl; 85 all; 87tl&br; 93br; 100&109tr; 103tr; 105t; 137tl, tm,tr&rm; 152bl&br; 153tl; 198b all; 199 all; 201tm,tr&br; 202tl; 203t; 215mr; 216b; 222 all; 246bl,bm&br. Roland Symons: p39 all. Alfred Znamierowski: pp12tr; 19br; 33m; 36br; 49 all; 55tl; 57b & box; 58br; 61m&t; 63tl; 64ml; 66bl; 67tl&bl; 68bm&br; 72 all; 73t&rm; 75 all; 76 all; 77t; 78; 80 all; 81 all; 82 all; 83 all; 88tl&m; 88bm&br; 89tr,mr&br; 90tr&br; 91tr; 92mr&br; 94tl,tr,bl,bm &br; 95ml,bl,tr&tm; 96tl, tr&br; 97 all; 98bl,bm&br; 99tl,tm,tr &br; 102mr; 103bl&br; 104br; 105b; 106t; 107 all; 108ml,bl&bm; 111tr&bl; 114tr&bm; 117br; 119; 120t; 121t; 122 all; 123 bl,bm,br; 151tr; 156bl&bm; 163tl; 167tm&tr; 181tl; 191 all; 212tr & br; 217b; 226b; 227t,m&br; 228 all; 229tl&mr; 231mr; 247ml&mb.

INDEX

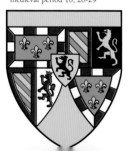

NOTES

NOTES

NOTES

NOTES

NOTES

NOTES